Mircea Eliade
AND THE
Dialectic of the Sacred

MIRCEA ELIADE
and the
Dialectic of the Sacred

by

THOMAS J. J. ALTIZER

THE WESTMINSTER PRESS
Philadelphia

PUBLISHED BY THE WESTMINSTER PRESS ®

PHILADELPHIA 7, PENNSYLVANIA

PRINTED IN THE UNITED STATES OF AMERICA

For Gayle

Contents

Acknowledgments   9

Abbreviations for Works of Mircea Eliade   11

Introduction   13

1 UNDERSTANDING THE SACRED   23
    I Modern Man and the Sacred   23
    II Knowledge and the Sacred   27
    III The Language of the Sacred   34
    IV Theology and the Sacred   37

2 ARCHAIC RELIGION   41
    I The Archaic Ontology   41
    II Shamanism   48
    III Repetition and Regeneration 52

3 CHRISTIANITY AND ARCHAIC RELIGION   59
    I The Problem of Christianity   59
    II The Doctrine of the Incarnation 66
    III Kierkegaard   73

4 THE COINCIDENCE OF THE OPPOSITES   81
    I Dialectic and the Sacred   81
    II Creation, the Fall, and the Orgy 83

   III Death and Yoga   92
   IV Androgyny and Alchemy   99

5 TIME AND THE SACRED   105
   I Modern Man and Time   105
   II Dostoevsky   107
   III Proust   115

6 SPACE AND THE SACRED   125
   I Modern Man and Space   125
   II Sartre   130
   III Teilhard de Chardin   139

7 THE UNCONSCIOUS AND THE SACRED   150
   I Eliade and the Unconscious   150
   II Freud   153
   III Marcuse and Brown   162

8 THE SACRED AND THE PROFANE   176
   I Yes-Saying and the Body   176
   II Eternal Recurrence   180
   III Christ and Dionysus   189

Notes   201

Index   217

Acknowledgments

Grateful acknowledgment is expressed to the following for permission to use material from their publications:

Basic Books, Publishers, for *The Interpretation of Dreams*, by Sigmund Freud, translated and edited by James Strachey.

Beacon Press, Inc., for *Eros and Civilization*, by Herbert Marcuse. Copyright © 1955 The Beacon Press.

Bollingen Foundation, Inc., for *The Myth of the Eternal Return* and *Yoga*, by Mircea Eliade, published by Pantheon Books, Inc.

Harper & Row, Publishers, Inc., for *Myths, Dreams and Mysteries*, by Mircea Eliade; for *The Divine Milieu*, by Pierre Teilhard de Chardin, and for *The Phenomenon of Man*, by Pierre Teilhard de Chardin.

Hutchinson Publishing Group, The, for *The Forge and the Crucible*, by Mircea Eliade, 1961.

New Directions, for *Nausea*, by Jean-Paul Sartre, translated by Lloyd Alexander. All rights reserved.

Penguin Books, Inc., for *The Bacchae*, by Euripides, translated by Philip Vellacott.

Philosophical Library, Inc., for *Being and Nothingness*, by Jean-Paul Sartre, translated by Hazel E. Barnes.

Random House, Inc., for *The Possessed*, by Dostoevsky.

Sheed & Ward, Inc., for *Patterns in Comparative Religion*, by Mircea Eliade, © 1958 Sheed & Ward, Inc., New York; and for *Images and Symbols*, by Mircea Eliade, published by Sheed & Ward, Inc., and © Harvill Press, 1961.

Viking Press, Inc., The, for *The Portable Nietzsche*, selected and translated by Walter Kaufmann. Copyright 1954 by The Viking Press, Inc.

Wesleyan University Press, for *Life Against Death*, by Norman O. Brown. Copyright 1959 by Wesleyan University.

Abbreviations for
Works of Mircea Eliade

BR *Birth and Rebirth,* tr. by Willard Trask (Harper & Row, Publishers, Inc., 1958).

C *Le Chamanisme et les techniques archaïques* (Payot, Paris, 1951); English translation in preparation.

FC *Forgerons et alchimistes* (Flammarion, Paris, 1956); *The Forge and the Crucible,* tr. by Stephen Corrin (The Hutchinson Publishing Group, London, 1961; Harper & Row, Publishers, Inc., 1962).

IS *Images et symboles* (Librairie Gallimard, Paris, 1952); *Images and Symbols,* tr. by Philip Mairet (Sheed & Ward, Inc., 1961).

MA *Méphistophélès et l'androgyne* (Librairie Gallimard, Paris, 1962).

MDM *Mythes, rêves, et mystères* (Librairie Gallimard, Paris, 1957); *Myths, Dreams and Mysteries,* tr. by Philip Mairet (Harper & Row, Publishers, Inc., 1960).

MER *Le Mythe de l'éternel retour: archétypes et répétition* (Librairie Gallimard, Paris, 1949); *The Myth of the Eternal Return,* tr. by Willard R. Trask (Bollingen Series XLVI, Pantheon Books, Inc., 1954).

PCR *Traité d'historie des religions* (Payot, Paris, 1949); *Patterns in Comparative Religion,* tr. by Rosemary Sheed (Sheed & Ward, Inc., 1958).

SP *Das Heilige und das Profane* (Rowohlt Deutsche Enzyklopädie, Hamburg, Germany, 1957); *The Sacred and the Profane,* tr. by Willard R. Trask (Harcourt, Brace & Co., 1959). The notes refer to the Harper Torchbook edition published in 1961.

Y   *Le Yoga: Immortalité et Liberté* (Payot, Paris, 1954);
Yoga: Immortality and Freedom, tr. by Willard R.
Trask (Bollingen Series LVI, Pantheon Books, Inc.,
1958).

Introduction

A T A TIME when intellectual inquiry has seemingly met an impasse, when all traditional meaning and value have been profoundly challenged, and when theology is moving in circles, it would seem all too obvious that the moment has arrived to engage in a radical quest for a new mode of religious understanding. The first requirement of such a quest is a forthright confession of the death of the God of Christendom, a full acknowledgment that the era of Christian civilization has come to an end, with the result that all cognitive meaning and all moral values that were once historically associated with the Christian God have collapsed. Furthermore, we must recognize that the death of God is a historical event: God has died in *our* time, in *our* history, in *our* existence. Insofar as we live in our destiny, we can know neither a trace of God's presence nor an image of his reality. We must acknowledge, therefore, that if God has died in our history, then insofar as the church has become Christendom, insofar as the church has entered history, it has become a corpse—as Kierkegaard knew so deeply; and *all* traditional theological meaning, *all* our inherited religious meaning, is in process either of dissolution or of transformation. The traditional form of the Christian faith can now be upheld—as, for example, in Barth's theology of the Word of God—only by preserving it inviolate from contact with the brute reality of history. In this situation, Christianity is increasingly becoming yet another Gnostic way of retreat from history: indeed, one can detect the presence of a contemporary form of Gnosticism at precisely those points at which the greatest emphasis is given to the traditional forms of faith!

One of the most fascinating developments of the twentieth-century rebirth of theology has been the contemporary theologian's insistence that the Christian faith transcends religion. Faith is now conceived of as being directed against "religion," against piety, against the interior religious life of the church itself. While this doctrine has its roots in the ancient prophet's protest against the priestly religion of Israel, it goes beyond this protest insofar as it challenges the *religious* meaning of faith. But we must ask why it is that the theologian in our time is forced to dissociate faith and religion. Surely one answer lies in the gradual evaporation of the religious life of the historic church. Is it accidental that Kierkegaard was the last great Protestant writer whose works were directed to the task of religious edification? Must we not confess that when a contemporary theologian, whether a Barth or a Bultmann, conceives of faith as lying beyond religion, he is thereby giving witness to the existence of a yawning void in even the most powerful expressions of *contemporary* religious life? A reader with some sense of the holy must be dismayed at the profane form of most recent theology: nor can he escape the suspicion that the "modern" theologian is himself unaware of his own alienation from the sacred. Consequently, we might well suspect that one of the most subtle yet devastating effects of the death of God has been that theology has lost all real contact with the sacred. Once granted that the Faustian spirit of modern man has poisoned all those wells of the Spirit associated with the West, then the study of non-Christian religions can be conceived of as a mode of reentry into the world of the holy. Of course, we can know these alien manifestations of the sacred only through a modern Western mode of understanding—which means a way of knowing that is itself a product of the death of God; yet fortunately we have not ourselves been immersed in the historical process of secularizing these religious forms, and thus they can speak to us most forcefully when they are most alien to our own interior lives.

Today, in Mircea Eliade, Christian theology is confronted by a great religious scholar and thinker whose vision of the sacred is incompatible with the established forms and traditions of Christianity. Can theology meet this challenge? I believe that it must: first, because Christianity will die if it continues to be so firmly bound to a history and a civilization that is already passing away; and, secondly, because theology itself will perish if it cannot absorb a form of the sacred that is not dead but *alive*. Mircea Eliade is well qualified to initiate contemporary theology into the mystery and reality of the world of the sacred; yet perhaps his chief qualification lies in the paradoxical fact that while both by training and tradition his religious roots lie in the East, he has nevertheless chosen to immerse himself in the most radical forms of the contemporary Western sensibility. Born in Bucharest, Romania, in 1907, he was nourished in Eastern Christianity; after studying at the University of Bucharest, he spent the years 1928 to 1931 in predoctoral studies at the University of Calcutta, and in studies in the techniques of Yoga at Rishikesh, India; from 1933 to 1939 he taught at the University of Bucharest, where he founded and edited *Zalmoxis: Revue des études religieuses* (Paris and Bucharest, 1938–1942). During the war, he served as cultural attaché in the Romanian legation in London and Lisbon; and after the war he settled in Paris, where he lectured in the history of religions at the École des Hautes-Études (Sorbonne), and began publishing those volumes which have since made him world-famous. Eliade has always chosen as his special field of study those manifestations of the sacred which are both most exotic and most profound, approaching them not simply as a historian but as a modern Western scholar and a *homo religiosus,* an artist, and a human being. The author of numerous novels and short stories (written in Romanian—a few of them have been translated into French and German, but none into English), Eliade has participated in the literary creativity of our time, thereby sharing, as no other modern religious thinker has done, in the world of the artist. Since 1950 he has lectured at all the Eranos congresses, thus becoming a regular participant in the Jungian circle. And since 1956 he has been professor and chairman of the department of the history of religions at the University of Chicago. He is now joint editor, with Ernst Junger, of *Antaios;* and in 1961 he founded *History of Religions,* "An International Journal for Comparative Historical Studies," published by The University of Chicago Press.

Among present-day religious scholars, Mircea Eliade is rivaled only by Rudolf Bultmann; but unlike Bultmann, he has established himself as the leading master of an arena of the sacred that has either remained little known in the West or has never been effectively encountered by Christian theology. Surely it is no exaggeration to claim that Eliade is the greatest living interpreter of the whole world of primitive and archaic religion, of alchemy in both East and West, and of the various forms of Indian Yoga. Furthermore, he is a true historian of religions, being able to write with authority and understanding of the whole vast realm of the sacred: where he has not himself been able to make original contributions to scholarship, he has thoroughly absorbed the scholarly contributions of others. Yet, perhaps most important of all, Eliade has been able to transform every manifestation of the sacred that he has touched into a new and living form, a form that is religiously powerful, philosophically meaningful, and strangely relevant to the contemporary sensibility. When reading Eliade, one immediately becomes aware of a power of the holy that would appear to be no longer present in Christianity. Now it is precisely for this reason that his work has such great importance for contemporary theology. Indeed, it is Eliade's dearest hope that Christianity will undergo a new and radical rebirth, a rebirth making possible its absorption and transformation of the universal sacred, and also a rebirth making possible the advent of a new man.

Eliade spurns the titles of prophet, seer, and shaman; yet it is almost impossible to refrain from identifying him with these roles. He himself says that he has chosen the task of saving the unknown past of archaic man, of revealing the treasure in myth: this is his vocation, and he has chosen to do it "scientifically." Accordingly, he insists that his is only a hermeneutical project. He simply describes myths, he does not make theological judgments. Nevertheless, Eliade freely confesses that he uses the "tools of the doomed West" to seek a way to freedom. His deepest interest lies in establishing a dialogue between East and West: a dialogue not simply between two distinct cultural spheres, but rather between "archaic man" and "modern man." Ultimately such a dialogue revolves about an encounter between the sacred and the profane; and it is Eliade's hope that modern man will be reborn through contact with the archaic sacred. Thus, despite the fact that Eliade has immersed himself in modern Western historical thinking, he is finally searching for a transhistorical meaning: paradoxically, he seeks a way to the sacred *in* and *through* those very forces which most deeply bind modern man to the profane. Thus it is not accidental that Eliade's favorite mythical symbol is the *coincidentia oppositorum*. Later on we shall attempt to show that Eliade has an almost inevitable tendency to understand this symbol in its Hindu, and specifically its Hindu Tantric, form; that is to say, as pointing to a pretemporal and precosmic Totality. Nevertheless, the vocation that Eliade has chosen must inevitably impel him to emphasize the paradoxical meaning of the *coincidentia oppositorum:* and surely this must mean an ultimate coincidence of the radical sacred and the radical profane.

Theology can learn from Eliade that paradoxically the very choice of a profane language can be an authentic path to the sacred in our time. Ours is a time in which all the traditional theological categories have become meaningless. However, if theology will open itself to a truly paradoxical language, it must be prepared for the possibility that the most radical expression of profane existence will coincide with the highest expressions of the sacred. Precisely at this point lies a new destiny for Christian theology: for with the death of the "Christian God" a wholly new meaning of Creation and Incarnation has dawned! No longer can the Christian believe that his existence here and now is a kind of prologue to his future life in a transcendent Kingdom of God. Nor can he believe that his life in "this world" derives its meaning and reality from an "other world" in the Beyond. Agonizing as this situation may be, the very collapse of the classical theological distinction between "this world" and "that world" has made possible a new epiphany of Christ: a Christ who has not descended from "above," but who is *wholly* and *fully* incarnate in our midst. Finally, only the Christian can greet the radical profane with faith: for only the Christian believes in both Creation and Incarnation, only the Christian believes in a Christ who is in some sense Creator and Redeemer at once. Let the Christian rejoice that only Christendom has given birth to a radically profane consciousness: for the "dark night" of profane existence is our way to Christ; the Christ who is Alpha and Omega, Beginning and End, Darkness and Light—the Christ who is Darkness and Light at once!

The preceding statements should make it obvious that I am employing Eliade as a route to a new form of theology. Let the reader be warned that this book is not a scholarly interpretation of Eliade's work. It is true that the first half of the book attempts to elucidate Eliade's understanding of the sacred, and in doing so, it explores various philosophical and theological implications of his thought about which he himself has chosen to be silent. Hopefully, this section of the book will present a meaning of the sacred that is real to our time, real because Eliade posits a sacred that is the opposite of the profane: it is this very dialectical opposition of the sacred and profane that makes the sacred meaningful to the profane consciousness.

Another goal of this book is to arrive at a theological understanding of Eliade's vision, an understanding that will unveil the profound relevance of Eliade's work to the problems of contemporary theology, and that will point the way to a new conception of the relation of Christianity both to the world of the sacred and to the world of the profane. At this point, the most important problem of Eliade's work arises: the meaning of the *coincidentia oppositorum*. Eliade himself has chosen the great task, as yet unfulfilled, of exploring the meaning of the *coincidentia oppositorum* throughout the whole vast range of the history of religions with the goal of arriving at the meaning of the universal sacred. Thereby he hopes to establish the meaning and reality of the dialectic of the sacred, revealing the nature of the movement of the sacred between its various manifestations, and looking forward to an ultimate dialectical synthesis of all the expressions of the sacred. The major goal of this book is the far more modest one of employing Eliade to raise the question of the possibility of a Christian dialectic between the sacred and the profane in the context of our present situation.

While the book as a whole is concerned with establishing a dialectical understanding of the sacred, the explicit problem of the meaning of a contemporary Christian understanding of the "coincidence of the opposites" is not approached until the second half of the book. A natural break in the book occurs at this point, for although the second half of the book rests upon the first, it is almost an independent unit in itself, inasmuch as it largely puts Eliade aside and deals directly with our major project. Here, an attempt is made to arrive at a theological understanding of the radical profane. If Eliade is only indirectly employed in this quest, it is because he has for the most part simply set aside the problem of the positive religious meaning of the profane; and, more deeply, because this section is devoted to a search for a Christian dialectical method, whereas Eliade seldom employs Christian theological categories in his work. It is my conviction that the first requirement of a contemporary theological method is a full acknowledgment of the death of God. This means that all traditional theological thinking is now irrelevant. In this situation, the task of the theologian becomes the paradoxical one of unveiling religious meaning in a world that is bathed in the darkness of God's absence. Paradoxically, he must search for light in precisely those corners which are most filled with darkness: thus our quest has seized upon those expressions of the profane consciousness which are most estranged from the world of the sacred.

A book such as this calls for precision of understanding, and for that reason it contains extensive citation from the materials examined.

I followed the policy of using single inverted commas (e.g., 'nature') when I was calling attention to a special meaning of a word that is not associated with any particular thinker, and double inverted commas (e.g., "cosmos") when the intended meaning does refer to a particular thinker. In the Nietzsche chapter, I wrote the term eternal recurrence when referring to its 'metaphysical' meaning, and Eternal Recurrence when referring to its 'existential' meaning. This distinction is crucial to the chapter as a whole, which contains an analysis of the problem posed by these two meanings. Sometimes the quotations in the book seem to contain many italicized words, but all the quotations are simply given verbatim.

Any apologetic motive was far from my mind and whatever theological understanding it contains was only reached at the end and not at the beginning of the book. Let me also confess that this book is in part a further development of the problems examined in my first book, *Oriental Mysticism and Biblical Eschatology,* problems that revolved about the relation between existence in faith and existence in the profane.

Unfortunately I was never a student of Professor Eliade's, but I nevertheless profess to be in large measure his disciple. Nor can I forgo the pleasure of expressing my profound sense of gratitude to Professor Eliade for the encouragement, the criticism, and the inspiration that he so freely gave me while I was writing this book. Needless to say, I alone am responsible for the book's inadequacies. Moreover, it is of vital importance to insist that Professor Eliade is in no way to be identified with the opinions expressed in this book, nor is it to be assumed that my interpretations of his work meet with his approval.

Among many friends and colleagues who rendered assistance during various stages of the preparation of the book, three are due a special debt of gratitude: John Cobb, Erich Heller, and Gregor Sebba. Acknowledgment must also be given to Nathan Scott, who asked me to write an article on Eliade for *The Christian Scholar,* an article that became the nucleus of this book. I am grateful for a grant received from the Research Committee of Emory University which made possible a trip to Chicago to consult with Professor Eliade; and I am also grateful to Miss Barbara Harkins, who so competently typed the manuscript of the book. Finally, many of the ideas in the book were inspired by my students and my wife, who led me to more clarity than I could reach by myself and who also made possible a courage that I know is beyond my own powers.

I

Understanding the Sacred

I. Modern Man and the Sacred

STRANGELY ENOUGH, Eliade, at least in his published work, has ignored Nietzsche's proclamation of the death of God. Yet perhaps no theologian has had so deep a sense of God's death in the modern world—of the eclipse of the transcendent realm—as has Mircea Eliade. Indeed, he has gone so far as to define "modern man" as the man who has negated the sacred: "Modern man's originality, his newness in comparison with traditional societies, lies precisely in his determination to re-gard himself as a purely historical being, in his wish to live in a basically desacralized cosmos."[1] Now by purely "historical" being Eliade means a radically profane mode of existence, a mode of existence that has withdrawn itself from an awareness of the transcendent, and immersed itself in the immediate tem-poral moment. This meaning of 'historical' is intimately re-lated to the modern idea of 'historicity': for, in this perspective, 'historicity' means a total immersion in historical time, an immersion that is totally isolated from any meaning or reality that might lie beyond it. So likewise "desacralized" cosmos means profane world, and Eliade's meaning is that modern man wills to live in a profane world, wills to know the world as profane. But, as Heidegger has shown, the world appears as 'world,' as "Worldhood" (*Weltlichkeit*), as a result of an ex-istential mode of man's being-in-the-world.[2] Insofar as modern

23

man is himself, insofar as he has "chosen" (Sartre's term) to live in a profane world, he is closed to the realm of the sacred. Or, as Nietzsche would have it, modern man can only be himself, can only truly be man, by being the murderer of God.

Noting that modern science has restored a principle that was endangered by the nineteenth century: 'It is the scale that makes the phenomenon,' Eliade has adopted a dialectical approach to the meaning of the sacred; for he has also noted (following Roger Caillois)[3] that all the modern definitions of the religious phenomenon have one thing in common: "each has its own way of showing that the sacred and the religious life are the opposite of the profane and the secular life."[4] Thus Rudolf Otto's famous analysis of the holy as the Wholly Other (deriving from what Otto termed the *mysterium tremendum* component of the numinous)[5] was in part the product of a uniquely modern historical and existential situation: it is modern man who can only know the holy as the Wholly Other. Having banished the transcendent from his horizon, modern man has chosen a wholly immanent mode of being, and thus can view the sacred only as the Other. Consequently, modern man can only know the sacred dialectically; now the sacred can appear only through a negative dialectic, insofar as modern man has chosen to be a profane being. At bottom, for Eliade, the sacred and the profane are two modes of being in the world, "two existential situations assumed by man in the course of his history."[6] Already we have arrived at an essential foundation of Eliade's understanding of the sacred: the sacred and the profane are human phenomena, they are created by man's existential choice.

In his study of alchemy, Eliade arrived at a remarkable analogy to illustrate modern man's alienation from the sacred: "We have only to imagine a communion, no longer limited to the eucharistic elements of bread or wine, but extending to every kind of 'substance,' in order to measure the distance separating a primitive religious experience from the modern experience of 'natural phenomena.' "[7] The world appears as

'nature'—perhaps Heidegger's *Seiendes,* 'existing beings' or
'entities' is relevant here—only through the eclipse of the
sacred, only when the religiousness of the cosmos becomes lost.
What modern man knows as "objective" knowledge, as "true"
or naked reality, has been created by a Faustian turning away
from the sacred and the transcendent. But, as Eliade has
learned from Indian philosophy, the fate of "secular" thought
is to be thought by objects.[8] In truly knowing the world, man
becomes bound to it: not only has the transcendent meaning
of the cosmos become opaque to modern nonreligious man, but
when man fully knows the world as time, and no longer knows
the world in relation to eternity, then "time" comes to constitute man's deepest existential situation. Accordingly, the problems that absorb contemporary man are created by his bondage
to time:

> It is the *human condition,* and above all the temporality of
> the human being, that constitute the object of the most recent
> Western philosophy. It is this temporality that makes all the
> other "conditionings" possible and that, in the last analysis,
> makes man a "conditioned being," an indefinite and evanescent
> series of "conditions."[9]

Above all, it is the genuinely modern—and uniquely modern—
experience of "historicity" that is the source of modern man's
anxiety and dread; for if dread (*Angst*) is the result of an encounter with the Nothing (as Kierkegaard and Heidegger
teach), it is a product of the dissolution of all that which the
religious consciousness knows as Being.

"Historical man," the man who *is* insofar as he *makes himself, within history,*[10] is forced to identify himself with the
historical moment, with "historicity," and therein becomes
bound to a destiny that he can only know as tragic, and an
existence that he can only know as absurd. By choosing a
profane mode of existence—i.e., by willing to abolish the
transcendent—modern man has made an existential choice;
he has "chosen" a tragic mode of existence, for he has "chosen"

an absolute autonomy which finally encloses him within the concrete moment itself. Therefore modern man's "choice" can be realized only through the abolition of the sacred:

> Modern nonreligious man assumes a new existential situation; he regards himself solely as the subject and agent of history, and he refuses all appeal to transcendence. In other words, he accepts no model for humanity outside the human condition as it can be seen in the various historical situations. Man *makes himself,* and he only makes himself completely in proportion as he desacralizes himself and the world. The sacred is the prime obstacle to freedom. He will become himself only when he is totally demysticized. He will not be truly free until he has killed the last god.[11]

Yet insofar as a dialectical relationship exists between the sacred and the profane, which is to say that neither can fully become itself apart from a total negation of the other, it is precisely the profane that is negated by the sacred. Thus the same 'reality' assumes a totally different meaning and value in accordance with man's existential "choice."[12] From the point of view of Indian philosophy, which Eliade regards as the fullest conceptual expression of the meaning of the sacred, the *profane reality* is quite simply existence in time:

> What modern Western philosophy terms "being situated," "being constituted by temporality and historicity," has its counterpart, in Indian philosophy, in "existence in *maya.*" If we can homologize the two philosophical horizons—Indian and Western—everything that India has thought on the subject of *maya* has a certain timeliness for us today. This becomes apparent if, for example, we read the *Bhagavad Gita.* Its analysis of human existence is conducted in a language that is familiar to us; *maya* is not only cosmic illusion but also, and above all, historicity; not only existence in the eternal cosmic becoming but above all existence in time and history.[13]

Just as the profane existence of modern man is created by an abolition of the sacred, the deepest expressions of religious experience must culminate in an abolition of the profane. Finally

Indian thought annihilates the profane reality itself: "Existence *in* Time is ontologically nonexistence, unreality."[14]

Eliade does not hesitate to speak of modern man's existential choice as a "fall" into profane existence: "from the Christian point of view, it could also be said that nonreligion is equivalent to a new 'fall' of man—in other words, that nonreligious man has lost the capacity to live religion consciously, and hence to understand and assume it."[15] After the second "fall" the religious sense has fallen even farther than after the first, for it has fallen into the depths of the unconscious; it has been "forgotten." Yet a dialectical relationship exists between that which man has become as a historical being, as a being who makes himself in time, and that which he has abandoned or forgotten: the *sacred reality* itself. In becoming a fully developed human consciousness (Heidegger's *Dasein* and Sartre's *pour soi*), a being who exists in "time," modern man has not simply bound himself to time and history, modern man has created himself as an absolutely *profane* being. But insofar as he exists as a profane being, modern man can only know the sacred as the Nothing. Moreover, the modern scholar can only discover the sacred as a reality that wholly inverts everything that modern man 'knows' to be real: the sacred can only appear to us as the Other, an Other whose very epiphany would dissolve our being in time.

II. Knowledge and the Sacred

In the preface to his phenomenology or morphology of religion (*Traité d'historie des religions,* 1949, translated as *Patterns in Comparative Religion*), Eliade remarks that there are no *purely* religious phenomena; "no phenomenon can be solely and exclusively religious."[16] That is to say, man has never been manifest historically as a purely religious being; but by employing his own kind of phenomenological *epoche,* Eliade has chosen to apprehend man in a purely religious moment, as a being who knows only—and is himself constituted by—the sacred. Unfortunately, Eliade has never fully presented the method of his phenomenological approach to the *Religions-wissenschaft* or the history of religions, although he has made numerous casual remarks about the 'metahistorical,'[17] the logic of the symbol, a transconscious logic,[18] and a 'metapsycho-analysis,' a study of man as a living symbol.[19] First let it be noted that Eliade, as a historian of religions, is related, if only tenuously, to the phenomenological approach to the study of religion initiated by Max Scheler, Gerardus van de Leeuw, and Joachim Wach.[20] Perhaps two principles decisively characterize the phenomenological method: "intentionality" and "bracket-ing." As defined by the founder of phenomenology, Edmund Husserl, intentionality is the unique peculiarity of experiences "to be the consciousness *of* something";[21] whereas bracketing, the phenomenological method of reduction or *epoche,* occurs when

> *We put out of action the general thesis which belongs to the natural standpoint,* we place in brackets whatever it includes respecting the nature of Being: this *entire natural world therefore* which is continually "there for us," "present to our hands," and will ever remain there, is a "fact-world" of which we continue to be conscious, even though it pleases us to put it in brackets.
>
> If I do this, . . . I use the "phenomenological" *epoche,* which *completely bars me from using any judgement that concerns spatio-temporal existence (Dasein).*[22]

Thus the phenomenological method demands not only the suspension of all ontological judgment but also the setting aside of all sciences that relate to the world, and therewith of all propositions relating to the spatiotemporal realm. As Husserl says: "The whole world as placed within the nature-setting and presented in experience as real, taken completely 'free from all theory,' just as it is in reality experienced, and made clearly manifest in and through the linking of our experiences, has now no validity for us, it must be set in brackets, untested indeed but also uncontested."[23] Furthermore, the phenome-nological reduction likewise suspends the inquirer's own em-

pirical existence,[24] allowing to remain over as the "phenomenological residuum" the pure experience (*Erlebnis*) or pure
consciousness of the "pure Ego."[25] Consequently, Husserl defines phenomenology as "a *pure descriptive* discipline which
studies the whole field of pure transcendental consciousness in
the light of *pure intuition;*"[26] and it is a primary rule of Husserl's that phenomenology can *"claim nothing that we cannot
make essentially transparent to ourselves by reference to Consciousness and on purely immanental lines."*[27]

Husserl himself remarks that the "principle of all principles"
is that complete clearness is the measure of all truth,[28] a principle that is obviously grounded in radical immanence, taking
as the most primordial experience "the living *now.*"[29] Accordingly, Husserl's phenomenological method is directed to an
intuitive description of the intentions of pure consciousness.
However, to every region of consciousness, and to all categories
of would-be objects of consciousness, there corresponds "phenomenologically not only a *basic kind of meaning or position,
but also a basic kind of primordial dator-consciousness* of such
meaning, and, pertaining to it, a *basic type of primordial self-
evidence.*"[30] In other words, every area of consciousness has *a
priori* contents that can be judged and understood only in
their own terms. Heidegger, at the very time when he was
breaking with Husserl, conceived of phenomenology as a
return to the things themselves, and maintained that the
formal meaning of phenomenology was "to let that which
shows itself be seen from itself in the very way in which it
shows itself from itself."[31] Proceeding by this means, Heidegger
discovered phenomenologically that *"knowing is a kind of
Being which belongs to Being-in-the-world."*[32] Thus, he re-
jected what he regarded as the idealistic and subjectivistic
grounds of Husserl's phenomenology and maintained that the
intentionality of consciousness is grounded in *Dasein*'s being-
in-the-world.

If we could imagine Eliade taking sides in this dispute, he
would certainly align himself with Heidegger, for Eliade re-

gards both modern knowledge and modern consciousness (as a radically immanent consciousness) as inevitable products of an existential choice of the profane. Nevertheless, Eliade does employ his own kind of phenomenological method, a method directed to "seeing" just what things are religious in nature and what those things reveal.[33] As the previous section should lead us to see, his phenomenological method is dialectical in nature, always leading to a negation of the meaning of the contents of consciousness. While embarking upon the first phenomenological investigation of religion, Max Scheler insisted that the phenomenological method was basically none other than that of 'negative theology.'[34] The phenomenological scrutiny of the essence is reached by a negative method of successively peeling away the correlates and contraries of a phenomenon, until its indefinable and inconceivable essence is revealed (for 'to conceive' means to reduce the object of a concept in terms of other concepts).[35] Scheler's method leads to this primary result:

> This is therefore the *first sure truth* of all religious phenomenology: on whatever level of his *religious development* he may be, the human being is *invariably* looking into a realm of being and value which is in basis and origin utterly different from the whole remaining empirical world; it is not inferred from that other world, neither won from it by idealization, and access to it is possible solely in the religious act.
>
> This is the proposition of the *originality and nonderivation of religious experience.*[36]

With this basic proposition, Eliade would wholly agree, but he carries it to far more radical results. For Eliade's phenomenological *epoche* is not only grounded in a bracketing of the sacred realm from the realm of the profane (which for Eliade, as will be shown, is also the spatiotemporal realm) but more deeply in a negative dialectic that posits the sacred by a process of negating the profane.[37] Thus Eliade's phenomenological method has genuinely mystical roots: the *via negativa* of classical mystical theology, a dialectical way that can know the sacred only by engaging in an absolute negation of the profane.

In one of his more recent essays, Eliade quoted with approval these words of one of his fellow historians of religions, Raffaele Pettazzoni:

> Phenomenology and history complement each other. Phenomenology cannot do without ethnology, philology, and other historical disciplines. Phenomenology, on the other hand, gives the historical disciplines that sense of the religious which they are not able to capture. So conceived, religious phenomenology is the religious understanding (*Verständnis*) of history; it is history in its religious dimension. Religious phenomenology and history are not two sciences but are two complementary aspects of the integral science of religion, and the science of religion as such has a well-defined character given to it by its unique and proper subject matter.[38]

Eliade often speaks of the study of religion as though it were an intellectual discipline like any other, implying that the history of religions, as he conceives it, is quite literally a 'history' or 'science' of religion. Yet this cannot be his real meaning. Indeed, it would be difficult to name a thinker who has a greater hostility both to historical thinking and to the historical realm itself. He can speak of all history as a fall,[39] of all cultures as being a fall into history,[40] of historiography as a sign of death,[41] of the historical consciousness as the source of the tragedy of existence,[42] and can align himself with Indian thought in insisting that "the state of ignorance and illusion is not that of *living* in History, but of *believing* in its ontological reality."[43]

> Above all it is historicism that has tried to innovate by postulating that man is no longer constituted by his origins alone, but also by his own history and by the entire history of mankind. It is historicism that definitely secularizes Time, by refusing to admit the distinction between a fabulous Time of the *beginnings,* and the time that has succeeded it. . . . Before God, all historical events are equal. Or, if one no longer believes in God—before History.
>
> One cannot be unmoved by this grandiose asceticism that

the European mind has thus imposed upon itself; by this fright-
ful humiliation, self-inflicted, as if in atonement for its innumerable sins of pride.[44]

As these statements indicate, Eliade has been deeply affected
by modern historical thinking, he has profoundly sensed the
power and threat of historicism as unveiled by Dilthey and
Troeltsch,[45] he has recognized that historicism is a product of
the decomposition of Christianity,[46] and thereby has seen that
the historical consciousness itself is a product of modern man's
choice of the profane, and thus of the death of God (one notes
with interest that the young Nietzsche was one of the first
thinkers to attack historical thinking as an expression of modern decadence,[47] and the mature Nietzsche spent himself upon
seemingly pointless polemics against David Friedrich Strauss).
Yet Eliade cannot deny that history is the arena of the sacred:

> There is no such thing as a "pure" religious datum, outside of
> history. For there is no such thing as a human datum that is
> not at the same time a historical datum. Every religious ex-
> perience is expressed and transmitted in a particular historical
> context. But admitting the historicity of religious experience
> does not imply that they are reducible to nonreligious forms
> of behavior. . . . We must never lose sight of one of the funda-
> mental principles of modern science: *the scale creates the
> phenomenon.*[48]

It is this last principle which delivers the sacred from the threat
of the historical consciousness; thus Eliade can say that the
sacred is always manifest historically but it is not always re-
ducible to history,[49] accordingly, an "original" religious phenomenon (such as shamanic ecstasy) is not to be identified with
its various historical expressions.[50] Finally, he can say that, in
the last analysis, the religious life is nonhistorical (*l'anhistori-
cité*); for all of history is a limitation and dimunition of the
sacred, in short, a "fall" of the sacred.[51]

In an essay on Hölderlin, Heidegger remarked that only
where 'world' predominates, is there history,[52] and with this
judgment Eliade would fully concur. Historical thinking did

not arise in a vacuum, it has a long 'spiritual' history, ultimately being rooted in an alienation of man from a transcendent ground. Indeed, the *cogito* of Western man, as Kierkegaard and Nietzsche have taught us, is grounded in a distinction between being and thinking, a distinction in which
Heidegger discerns the fundamental position of the Western
spirit, and against which his central attack is directed.[53] Eliade,
too, is deeply occupied with this dichotomy between being and
thinking, but unlike Heidegger he has not sought to unravel it
by returning to the origins of Western thought; he has chosen
the path of establishing a dialogue with the East. Thus, in
Indian philosophy, he has discovered an "absolute knowledge"
in which being and knowing are no longer separated. An
Indian text, quoted by Eliade, illuminates the meaning of such
a "knowledge":

> *Citta* [thought] becomes *nirvitarka* [nonargumentative] after
> the memory ceases to function, that is, after verbal or logical
> associations cease; at the moment when the object is empty
> of name and meaning; when thought reflects itself directly,
> by adopting the form of the object and shining solely with
> the object in itself.

Eliade comments upon this text as follows:

> In this meditation, thought is freed from the presence of the
> "I," for the cognitive act ("I know this object" or "This
> object is mine") is no longer produced; it is thought that
> *is* (becomes) the given object. The object is no longer known
> through associations—that is to say, included in the series of
> previous representations, localized by extrinsic relations (name,
> dimensions, use, class), and, so to speak, improvised by the
> habitual process of abstraction characteristic of secular thought—
> it is grasped directly, in its existential nakedness, as a concrete
> and irreducible datum.[54]

At this point it will be sufficient to note that Eliade is seeking
a form of knowledge in which cognition, as the Western
thinker understands it, will have disappeared. Rebelling

against the "secular" thought which has now overwhelmed the West, he seeks an authentic mode of understanding the sacred which will allow the sacred to be itself. Yet at the same time he is in quest of a meaning of the sacred that will be relevant to modern Western man. The remaining chapters of this book will be devoted to ascertaining his success in this endeavor.

III. The Language of the Sacred

When Nicolas Berdyaev speaks of history as "noumenal,"[55] and of the "meta-history" beyond history,[56] he speaks from a horizon that is also Eliade's, for it is ultimately the horizon of the sacred. However, it is no longer possible to imagine such a "meta-history" as existing in continuity with the "history" that we know; for our history is rooted in absolute autonomy, it is enclosed within itself, wholly isolated from a transcendent ground, it is simply the product of human and natural powers. So likewise the language of our history is a language created by a profane consciousness, it has abandoned a sacred or transcendent ground, having been created by an immanent consciousness that is wholly absorbed in the immediate here and now of profane existence. Consequently, the language of the sacred can be no more than a meaningless cipher to the language of the profane; and, for Eliade, the language of the sacred can have only a dialectical relation to the language of the profane: the sacred can become manifest only through a negation of the language of the profane.

Quite simply the language of the sacred is myth, but what we moderns understand as myth only appears when the sacred has disappeared from our horizon. Eliade, along with other modern scholars, has taught us that myth dissolves the world of concrete time and space: "myth makes man once more exist in a timeless period, which is in effect an *illud tempus,* a time of dawn and of 'paradise,' outside history."

> We moderns would say that myth (and with it all other religious experiences) abolishes "history." But note that the majority of myths, simply because they record what took place *"in illo tempore,"* themselves constitute an *exemplar history*

for the human society in which they have been preserved, and
for the world that society lives in. Even the cosmogenic myth
is history, for it recounts all that took place *ab origine;* but we
must, I need hardly say, remember that it is not "history" in
our sense of the word—things that took place once and will
never take place again—but exemplar history which can be
repeated (regularly or otherwise), and whose meaning and value
lie in that very repetition.[57]

Furthermore, inasmuch as myth describes the eruption of the
sacred into the world,[58] it appears with the dawn of a profane
consciousness, following a primal rupture between the sacred
and the profane.[59]

The sacred "speaks" or "reveals itself" through symbols, but
symbols do not reflect what we know as 'world,' they are wholly
other than signs, and cannot be translated into either the
"objective" or "subjective" language of modern man. In his
most important essay on symbolism,[60] Eliade has enumerated
six different aspects of the meaning of religious symbols: (1)
they are capable of revealing a modality of the real or a structure of the world that is not evident on the level of immediate
experience; (2) they always point to something real, for, in the
symbolic world of religious man, the *real* is equivalent to the
sacred; (3) they are multivalent, expressing simultaneously a
number of meanings whose continuity is not evident on the
plane of immediate experience; (4) thus the religious symbol
allows man to discover a certain unity of the world and, at the
same time, to disclose to himself his proper destiny as an in-
tegrating part of the world; (5) accordingly, religious symbolism can express paradoxical situations, or, certain structures
of ultimate reality, otherwise quite inexpressible, become expressed in religious symbols in such a way as to provide the
material for later philosophical speculations; and (6) religious
symbols are always "existential" inasmuch as they aim at a
reality or a situation in which human existence is engaged. At
bottom, religious symbols express a state, or a primal mode of
being in the world, in which man exists in continuity with
the world and the sacred. This state is one of nonalienation,

man is alienated neither from the world nor from the sacred; hence his 'existence' is wholly other than the 'existence' of modern man.

All these points will be taken up at later stages of this book; here it will suffice simply to note the chasm that separates the language of the sacred from the language of the profane. Again and again Eliade insists that myths tell "true" stories, they concern themselves with "realities"; but here 'truth' and 'reality' bear a meaning that is wholly other than their modern one. Modern man cannot think as a modern man and think of myth in its sacred form or meaning: therefore if myth is to be understood in its own terms, it cannot be given a modern definition.

> The myth defines itself by its own mode of being. It can only be grasped, as a myth, insofar as it *reveals* something as having been *fully manifested,* and this manifestation is at the same time *creative* and *exemplary,* since it is the foundation of a structure of reality as well as of a kind of human behaviour. A myth always narrates something as having *really* happened, as an event that took place, in the plain sense of the term—whether it deals with the creation of the World, or of the most insignificant animal or vegetable species, or of an institution. The very fact of *saying* what happened reveals *how* the thing in question was realised (and this *how* stands equally for *why*). For the act of coming to be is, at the same time, the emergence of a reality and the disclosure of its fundamental structures.[61]

All myths describe the eruption of the sacred into the world; therefore all mythology is ontophany, the plenary manifestation of Being. The man who speaks, and truly speaks, in the symbols of myth reflects in his own being the presence of the sacred; apart from that presence myth must remain an opaque language, or, at least, a language that he can never speak. As Eliade notes, the very recitation of myth in its true form is a hierophany, a manifestation of the sacred. What meaning can myth have when God is dead?

IV. Theology and the Sacred

There can be little doubt to any sensitive reader that Eliade's work has an immense theological significance; yet, from the beginning, Eliade has virtually ignored theology in his chosen task of elucidating the meaning of the sacred. Why? First, we must take account of Eliade's roots in Eastern Christendom; although it is never stated explicitly, one can sense in Eliade the Eastern Christian's hostility to the rational spirit of Western 'theo-logy.' We must remember that Dostoevsky traced the origins of Western atheism to the absorption of pagan philosophy by the Roman Church. Furthermore, Eliade shares the deeply mystical ground of the Eastern Church, and with it the mystic's opposition to any conceptual approach to the meaning of the sacred. One finds notably few references to God in Eliade's work, or, at least, to the theological category of God. While deeply concerning himself with Indian philosophy (a philosophy which, unlike the West's, has subordinated itself to the reality of the sacred), he has virtually ignored the whole tradition of Western philosophy and theology. Could it be that Eliade has detected in Christian theology itself a turning away from the meaning and reality of the sacred?

If so, we must turn to the one contemporary thinker who has detected a deep antipathy between 'faith' and 'theology,' Martin Heidegger. Heidegger believes that we are now living in a "new time":

> It is the time of the gods that have fled and of the god that is coming. It is the time of *need*, because it lies under a double lack and a double Not: the No-more of the gods that have fled and the Not-yet of the god that is coming.[62]

Adopting a word from a poem of Hölderlin, he speaks of "God's fail,"[63] of God's withholding his presence from man, despite the fact that, somehow, he is there. About his presence, we may *know* nothing, for theology has lost all contact with the holy. In 1927, Heidegger could write:

> *Theology* is seeking a more primordial interpretation of man's
> Being towards God, prescribed by the meaning of faith itself
> and remaining within it. It is slowly beginning to understand
> once more Luther's insight that the 'foundation' on which its
> system of dogma rests has not arisen from a system of inquiry
> in which faith is primary, and that conceptually this 'founda-
> tion' not only is inadequate for the problematic of theology,
> but conceals and distorts it.[64]

Despite the fact that he has since been baptized by numerous
German theologians, there is no reason today to think that
Heidegger would acknowledge that theology has recovered its
foundation. Instead, he has continued to attack theology, and
with much greater vehemence, for its adoption of the categories
of Greek philosophy. Thus, in 1949, after having quoted Paul's
words, "Has not God made foolish the wisdom of the world?"
(I Cor. 1:20), he asks: "Will Christian theology make up its
mind one day to take seriously the word of the apostle and
thus also the conception of philosophy as foolishness?"[65] By
1953, he could speak with even greater force:

> A "Christian philosophy" is a round square and a misunder-
> standing. There is, to be sure, a thinking and questioning
> elaboration of the world of Christian experience, i.e., of faith.
> That is theology. Only epochs which no longer fully believe in
> the true greatness of the task of theology arrive at the disas-
> trous notion that philosophy can help to provide a refurbished
> theology if not a substitute for theology, which will satisfy the
> needs and tastes of the time. For the original Christian faith
> philosophy is foolishness.[66]

Paradoxically, for Heidegger, the great fall of theology occurred in its creation, when it chose to express itself in the categories of Greek ontology. Yet Western metaphysics was itself
transformed when it was taken up by Christianity, and transformed in such a way as to lead to disaster.[67]

> Christianity reinterprets the being of the essent [*das Seiende*]
> as created being. Thought and knowledge come to be differ-
> entiated from faith (*fides*). This does not impede the rise of

rationalism and irrationalism but rather prepares the way for it and intensifies it.[68]

Patristic theology evolved a doctrine of creation wherein the world, i.e., existing being, (das Seiende), was held to have been created by God. Hand in hand with this doctrine of creation went a Logos theology that radically reinterpreted the logos of the Fourth Gospel so as to make it mean reason or ratio; and Heidegger (although saying little of the Logos theology) rightly says that the classical doctrine of creation understands the creation as having been rationally preconceived.

> Hence as soon as the creature's relationship to the creator is relaxed and, concomitantly, as man's reason makes itself predominant and even sets itself up as absolute, the being of the essent [das Seiende] inevitably becomes thinkable in terms of pure mathematical thought. This calculable and calculated being makes the essent into what can be mastered by modern, mathematically structured technology, which is something essentially different from every other hitherto known use of tools.[69]

When the world is understood as creation in this sense it is wholly isolated from faith, for it is granted its own rational autonomy, and thence becomes religiously meaningless.[70] Far more significant is the consequence that a theology which is so conceived isolates itself from the reality of faith. Now it can embark upon an understanding of the world, but in so doing it becomes little more than an appendix to Western philosophy.

No doubt Heidegger would trace the death of God to Western philosophy and theology, thereby joining hands with Kierkegaard and Dostoevsky. Nevertheless he has not succeeded in clearly identifying the nature of theology's fall. It is precisely at this point that Eliade's understanding of the sacred becomes pertinent, for, as has been shown, it is his cardinal principle that the sacred is the opposite of the profane. In choosing to understand the world as creation in a rational sense, theology transformed faith's understanding of the world as profane, so as to make of the world a religiously neutral being. Thereby the world ceased to be profane; but the necessary consequence of this transformation was that the sacred could no longer be related to the world, or, rather, the sacred could be related to the world only by the creation of a rational idea of God, an idea of God (borrowed from Greek philosophy) which at bottom was the projection of man's *understanding* of the world.[71] Theology fell in its creation of a rational idea of God, a creation grounded in the abolition of the profane, which means (according to Eliade's cardinal principle) an abolition of the sacred. Once an awareness of the profane is banished, therewith will vanish an awareness of the sacred: for if the sacred is the *opposite* of the profane it can no longer be manifest when the profane has disappeared. Consequently, the essence of theology is not grounded in faith, 'theo-logy' cannot witness to the presence of the sacred, the project of theology is turned away from the reality of the holy.

2

Archaic Religion

I. The Archaic Ontology

ONLY AN EXAMINATION of Eliade's actual work in the history of religions can unveil his mode of understanding the sacred. Note should immediately be taken, however, of the highly significant fact that he has chosen the world of primitive religious man as the arena in which the sacred is most fully manifest (even Eliade's book on Yoga interprets Yoga as a rebirth of the "primordial religion"). Indeed, Eliade has become the Frazer of our generation; yet, unlike Frazer, he has identified himself with primitive religious man, and taken up once more the romantic project of the recovery of primordial time, the *Urzeit,* the *illud tempus,* the "time" of the beginning. At this point no one could agree more fully with the Proustian statement that the only true paradise is always the paradise that we have lost. One can only stand in awe of Eliade's immense erudition in the whole field of primitive religions, for he has mastered a vast body of scholarship dealing with the world of primitive religious man. In truth, he has made a 'cosmos' of this world, and done so by means of a phenomenological *epoche* whose roots are ultimately mystical rather than scientific. This is why his work is apt to provoke a negative response in the American "scientific" anthropologist—despite the fact that it has been so highly praised by European anthropologists. For it is not primitive man himself who is the object of

41

Eliade's vision, but rather the *sacred reality* that occupies the center of primitive man's religious vision: it is the scale that creates the phenomena.

In *The Myth of the Eternal Return* (whose original title was "Cosmos and History"), Eliade has attempted to construct an archaic ontology: an elucidation of the conceptual meaning of being and reality that can be read from the behavior of the man—or, rather, the "religious" man—of the premodern societies. Premodern or "traditional" societies include both the world of primitive man and the ancient cultures of Asia, Europe, and America; already we encounter a nonhistorical method, for not only is no effort made to distinguish between the almost innumerable primitive groups, but the beliefs of these groups are not distinguished from those embodied in the higher cultures of the ancient world, nor are these various higher cultures distinguished from one another. Instead we have the unstated assumption, an assumption that betrays Eliade's romantic roots, that all these people shared at bottom a common world of belief, a world of belief that has no distinguishable historical origin, and that remained essentially the same throughout its various historical expressions. The truly remarkable fact is that Eliade can produce such an enormous body of evidence to buttress this romantic assumption; yet it is not genuine 'historical' evidence, for, like Frazer, Eliade has stripped his evidence of its historical particularity, and classified it according to its morphological continuity.

Another methodological problem derives from the fact that in attempting to construct an archaic ontology, Eliade is forced to write in the language of abstract theoretical concepts whereas archaic man spoke only in symbols, myths, and rites (for even ancient religious texts are nontheoretical, insofar as the symbolical world predominates, and "reason" has not yet become manifest). This problem was solved by adopting the categories of mystical theology, particularly those of Neoplatonism, categories that were themselves derived both from the archaic tradition and from a dialectical inversion of the conceptual categories evolved by man's profane life in the world. But this is in accordance with Eliade's basic dialectical position: the sacred is the opposite of the profane, and the sacred can become meaningful only by a process of negating the profane. Through a phenomenological *epoche* that brackets the sacred from the profane, Eliade can relive the symbolic world of archaic man, thus making possible a translation of archaic symbols into modern language. By this means, he discovers that:

> If we observe the general behavior of archaic man, we are struck by the following fact: neither the objects of the external world nor human acts, properly speaking, have any autonomous intrinsic value. Objects or acts acquire a value, and in so doing become real, because they participate, after one fashion or another, in a reality that transcends them. Among countless stones, one stone becomes sacred—and hence instantly becomes saturated with being—because it constitutes a hierophany, or possesses mana, or again because it commemorates a mythical act, and so on. The object appears as the receptacle of an exterior force that differentiates it from its milieu and gives it meaning and value. This force may reside in the substance of the object or in its form; a rock reveals itself to be sacred because its very existence is a hierophany: incompressible, invulnerable, it is that which man is not. It resists time; its reality is coupled with perenniality.[1]

Consequently archaic man has no historical memory; he revolts against personal events that, taken together, constitute history.[2] Moreover, the archaic world knows nothing of "profane" activities: every act that has a definite meaning in some way participates in the sacred.[3]

Now these judgments are not finally the product of a modern 'historical' analysis. It is true that they are set in the context of a modern historical perspective, for they have reference to a wide variety of peoples living in various historical times; yet the judgments themselves are arrived at by an intuitive process of identification with the religious consciousness of archaic man. By reproducing or reliving (Dilthey's *das Nachbilden oder Nacherleben*) the mythical and ritual world of archaic man, Eliade can "know" the sacred in its archaic manifestation. A knowing process of this kind differs from a modern imaginative and historical reconstruction insofar as it does not attempt to reproduce the lived experience (Dilthey's *das Erlebnis*) of a particular archaic man, but rather intends to allow the sacred to speak for itself and in its own terms. Ultimately such a mode of understanding demands a religious ground, hence its mystical roots. It is not human 'experience' in its modern sense that is the object of Eliade's vision, it is rather a human mode of participation in the sacred; and this participation is real, it is not created by the projection of a profane experience, it is reality itself.

Note that the judgments just quoted negate the classical and dominant Western ontologies: neither the "objects of the external world" nor "human acts" have any autonomous intrinsic value or reality. Archaic ontology is neither objective nor subjective in the modern sense, it transcends this dichotomy; or rather it lies beyond it in the sense that the archaic ontology was the horizon upon which the Western ontologies were created. Eliade illustrates these judgments in his analysis of the role and meaning of myth and symbol in archaic life. As has already been seen, the reality known to archaic man is one that "speaks" or "reveals itself" through symbols; and archaic symbols are always religious (i.e., they are capable of revealing a meaning that is not evident on the level of immediate experience) because they point to something *real*: "For on the archaic levels of culture, the *real*—that is, the powerful, the living—is equivalent to the *sacred*."[4] Insofar as symbols reveal the sacred, they point beyond concrete time to the mythical Time of the beginning, for it is essential to Eliade's vision to insist that the sacred negates the "actual" time and the "personal" experience of profane existence. Archaic man believes himself—in his deepest being—to be a product of mythical history, thus he makes himself by shaping his life in accord-

ance with a series of archetypal models believed to have been
established at the beginning of Time by the gods or by his
ancestors.

> This "sacred history"—mythology—is exemplary, paradig-
> matic: not only does it relate how things came to be; it also
> lays the foundations for all human behavior and all social
> and cultural institutions. From the fact that man was created
> and civilized by Supernatural Beings; it follows that the sum
> of his behavior and activities belongs to sacred history; and this
> history must be carefully preserved and transmitted intact to
> succeeding generations. Basically, man is what he is because, at
> the dawn of Time, certain things happened to him, the things
> narrated by myths.[5]

Once again the meaning of the sacred is reached by inverting
the reality created by modern man's profane choice:

> Just as modern man proclaims himself a historical being, consti-
> tuted by the whole history of humanity, so the man of archaic
> societies considers himself the end product of a mythical
> history, that is of a series of events that took place *in illo
> tempore*, at the beginning of Time. But whereas modern
> man sees in the history that precedes him a purely human
> work, more especially, believes that he has the power to con-
> tinue and perfect it indefinitely, for the man of traditional
> societies everything significant—that is, everything creative and
> powerful—that has ever happened took place *in the beginning*,
> in the Time of the myths.[6]

Eliade asks, What does living mean for a man who belongs
to an archaic culture? And, he answers: "Above all, it means
living in accordance with extrahuman models, in conformity
with archetypes."[7] It means living at the heart of the *real*
since, for archaic man, there is nothing truly real except the
archetype. Archaic man must refuse history, the contingent
events of actual time, must set himself in opposition to a series
of events that are irreversible, unforeseeable, possessed of autonomous value.[8] He acquires reality solely by participation in

the archetypes; everything that lacks an exemplary model is "meaningless," it lacks reality.

> Men would thus have a tendency to become archetypal and paradigmatic. This tendency may well appear paradoxical, in the sense that the man of a traditional culture sees himself as real only to the extent that he ceases to be himself (for a modern observer) and is satisfied with imitating and repeating the gestures of another. In other words, he sees himself as real, i.e., as "truly himself," only, and precisely, insofar as he ceases to be so.[9]

At this point the truly mystical form of the archaic ontology becomes fully apparent, and Eliade, like most Western mystics, does not hesitate to claim Plato as the mystical thinker, *par excellence:* "Hence it could be said that this 'primitive' ontology has a Platonic structure; and in that case Plato could be regarded as the outstanding philosopher of 'primitive mentality,' that is, as the thinker who succeeded in giving philosophic currency and validity to the modes of life and behavior of archaic humanity."[10]

A very serious charge that might be brought against archaic man's thirst for "being" is that this "being" is at bottom the "lost innocence" of a prehistoric state of animality. Quoting Hegel's dictum that "only the animal is truly innocent," Eliade attempts to face this charge by first noting that primitives did not always feel innocent; rather, they tried to return to the state of innocence by periodically confessing their sins.

> Can we see, in this tendency toward purification, a nostalgia for the lost paradise of animality? Or, in the primitive's desire to have no "memory," not to record time, and to content himself with tolerating it simply as a dimension of his existence, but without "interiorizing" it, without transforming it into consciousness, should we rather see his thirst for the "ontic," his will to be, to *be* after the fashion of the archetypal beings whose gestures he constantly repeats?[11]

Yet this is no true defense, for it simply assumes that "being" and animality cannot be identical. Once more taking up the charge, at a later point in the book, Eliade is on much firmer ground, for now he takes the offensive. Here, he says: "Modern man would be justified in seeing not only the primitive's amazement at their own first spontaneous and creative free gestures and their veneration, repeated *ad infinitum,* but also a feeling of guilt on the part of man hardly emerged from the paradise of animality (i.e., from nature), a feeling that urges him to reidentify with nature's eternal repetition the few primordial, creative, and spontaneous gestures that had signalized the appearance of freedom."[12] Can Eliade be speaking here to the typical modern idea of guilt, for example, the idea of Nietzsche and Freud that guilt is the result of the repression of a primordial, unconscious, instinctual desire? If so, he is speaking dialectically. Modern man must judge the archetypal behavior of primitive man to be guilty because it is a flight from autonomous existence, a flight from 'freedom,' from 'personality,' and from 'history.'

Thus the charge that archaic "being" is simply the prehistoric state of animality is perfectly true, according to the perspective of "modern man." Eliade can say:

> In the last analysis, modern man, who accepts history or claims to accept it, can reproach archaic man, imprisoned within the mythical horizon of archetypes and repetition, with his creative impotence, or, what amounts to the same thing, his inability to accept the risks entailed by every creative act. For the modern man can be creative only insofar as he is historical; in other words, all creation is forbidden him except that which has its source in his own freedom; and, consequently, everything is denied him except the freedom to make history by making himself.[13]

Contrariwise, everything that modern man knows as 'truth,' 'reality,' 'consciousness,' 'freedom,' etc., is, from the perspective of archaic man, quite simply equivalent to the *profane;* it is absolute unreality, for it is the ultimate barrier to the sacred.

II. Shamanism

While Eliade is quite capable of describing archaic religion as though it were a single and universal phenomenon, he is also capable of examining it as a series of diverse and scattered expressions, even though he seldom detects any fundamental breaks between these expressions. Of these expressions, the one that has most excited his attention has been shamanism.[14] Methodologically, Eliade is opposed to the evolutionary approach to the history of religions,[15] he refuses to admit that it is possible to reconstruct a historical series of increasingly complex hierophanies; and, at this point, he reflects a common view of the twentieth-century, as opposed to the nineteenth-century, historian of religions. Yet he has nevertheless seized upon shamanism as the religious phenomenon that lies closest to the primordial religion (if, indeed, it is proper to speak of a primordial "religion"). Shamanism is the first chapter in the history of religions as it is in the history of mysticism, and it continues to lie as the substratum in all the "higher" expressions of religion. By studying the manifestations of shamanism in Central Asia, Southern Asia, Southeast Asia and Oceania, North and South America, among the Indo-Europeans (including ancient Greece and India), and in China and Tibet, Eliade has concluded that the essential core of shamanism is an "original phenomenon," somehow embedded in the human condition itself, and consequently it is known to all archaic peoples.[16]

What is shamanism? Eliade believes that the specific element of shamanism is not the incorporation of "spirits" by the shaman, but the ecstasy provoked by the shaman's ascension to heaven or descent to hell;[17] it is this ecstasy which attracts Eliade's greatest interest, and he finds in its techniques the prototypes of all the higher forms of mysticism. Shamans are primitive "specialists in the sacred," men able to "see" the spirits, to go up into the sky and meet the gods, to descend to the netherworld and fight the demons, sickness, and death. Set apart from the community by special traits or powers, they may sometimes give the appearance of being psychopaths (which they may well have been, but those who had previously been ill have become shamans just because they succeeded in getting well);[18] nevertheless they have mastered the art of employing ecstasy for the benefit of the community. The shaman is the archetypal *homo religiosus,* for unlike the rest of the community, he undergoes a "concrete experience" of the sacred, he is believed to ascend to heaven and to descend to the netherworld, and he communicates with the gods, the spirits of the dead, the birds, and the animals.

Shamanism, like all religions, is a response to a primordial "fall" of man from the sacred; the shaman in his ecstasy reproduces a primordial "situation," he recovers the human condition before the "fall."[19] All the shamanic myths and rites that Eliade uncovers are dominated by a common idea: the primordial communication between heaven and earth is now realizable, the sacred time of the primordial *Urzeit* (*in illo tempore*) can be renewed in the shaman's initiation, an initiation that often follows a profound crisis bordering on madness, but an initiation that is nevertheless governed by strict rules.[20] Every initiation includes a period of isolation and a certain number of trials and ordeals forcing the novice to undergo an "initiatory illness," an illness revolving about an experience of mystical death and resurrection.

Very often, the syndrome of the "illness"—that is, as we have just seen, of the psychopathology exhibited by the future shaman—closely follows the classic ritual of initiation. The sufferings of the "elect" are in every way similar to the tortures of initiation; just as the candidate was slain by the demons— "masters of the initiation"—so the future shaman sees himself being cut to pieces by the "demons of the illness." The specific rites of shamanic initiation include a symbolic ascent to Heaven by means of a tree or a post; the sick man "chosen" by the gods or the demons sees himself, in a dream or in a series of dreams, upon his celestial journey right to the foot of

the Tree of the World. The ritual death, without which no
initiation is possible, is passed through by the "patient" in the
form of a descent into Hell. He is present, in a dream, at his
own dismemberment, sees the demons cut off his head, tear
out his eyes, etc.[21]

This symbolic experience of death produces a psychic "chaos"
that reproduces the "pre-cosmogenic chaos," the amorphous
and indescribable state that precedes the creation. For archaic
man, the symbolic return to chaos is indispensable to any new
creation: "Now, the same symbolism is discernible in the
'madness' of the future shamans, in their 'psychic chaos'; it is
a sign that the profane man is on the way to dissolution, and
that a new personality is about to be born."[22]

Shamanism is integrally related to the myth of paradise that is
found in various mythologies throughout the world; this myth
recounts a time when heaven and earth were not separated,
when an easy communication existed between them, and when
man could communicate with nature (e.g., he knew the language of the animals). Eliade enumerates the specific marks
of the men of the paradisiac epoch as follows:

> These marks are immortality, spontaneity, freedom; the possi-
> bility of ascension into Heaven and *easily meeting* with the
> gods; friendship with the animals, and knowledge of their
> language. These freedoms and abilities have been lost, as the
> result of a primordial event—the "fall" of man, expressed as
> an ontological mutation of his own condition, as well as a
> cosmic schism.[23]

Since the "fall," the sacred and the profane have become alienated from one another, and this rupture can be healed only
by an ecstasy that reverses man's profane condition and transforms him momentarily into his prefallen and paradisical state.
Thus, the shaman, during his trance, seeks to abolish the
human condition that is known in time—the condition that
is a consequence of the "fall"—and to enter once again the
primordial condition of man as described in the myths of
paradise: "The ecstasy re-actualizes, for a time, what was the

initial state of mankind as a whole—except that the shaman no longer mounts up to Heaven in flesh and blood as the primordial man used to do, but only in the *spirit,* in the state of ecstasy."[24]

A shamanic session generally consists of the following items: (1) an appeal to the auxiliary spirits (usually those of animals) and a dialogue with them in a secret language; (2) drum-playing and a dance, preparatory to the mystic journey; and (3) the trance during which the shaman's soul is believed to have left his body. While in the state of trance, the shaman can fly through the air or descend into hell, thereby fulfilling his mission of curing sickness and shepherding souls into the realm of the dead. Now in preparing for the trance, the shaman makes use of various ecstatic techniques (e.g., the imitation of bird songs), techniques intended to effect a transition from a profane to a sacred state, from concrete time and space to sacred time and space. Eliade believes that the essential core of the shamanic technique consists in a passage or voyage from one cosmic region to another: from earth to heaven, or from earth to hell.[25] Therein shamanism created a cosmic mythology, revolving about the three cosmic regions (heaven, earth, and hell), rooted in a central axis, the symbolic Center of the world[26]—which might be present in a sacred tree, mountain, or pillar, thus making possible an ascension from earth to heaven. These essentially shamanic symbols provided a mythical language for all of the later religions. Hence the great importance of shamanism: for Eliade maintains that although every religion is the product of a long interior transformation, and is possessed of its own autonomous structure, that nevertheless it is not entirely new, no religious message has entirely abolished the past, it is rather the renewal, the "revalorization," of an immemorial religious tradition.[27] Or, as Eliade insists in another context, "I should like simply to declare that almost all the religious attitudes man has, he has had from the most primitive times."[28]

If shamanism was created by a primordial rupture between the sacred and the profane, a rupture symbolized by the myth of the "fall," then its goal is an ecstatic trance that bridges this rupture and once more brings man the paradisical powers of his primordial state. By means of the trance, the shaman returns to paradise:

> He re-establishes the *communications* that used to exist *in illo tempore* between Heaven and Earth: for him, the cosmic Mountain or Tree becomes again a concrete means of access to Heaven, just as they were before the Fall. . . . In other words, the ecstasy reactualizes, provisionally and for a limited number of persons—the mystics—what was the original state of all mankind. In this respect, the mystical experience of primitives is equivalent to a *journey back to the origins,* a regression into the mythical time of the Paradise lost. For the shaman in ecstasy, this present world, our fallen world—which, according to modern terminology, is under the laws of Time and History—is done away with.[29]

Therefore it is possible in shamanism to encounter a concrete expression of the archaic ontology: the essence of shamanism is an ecstatic voyage to the sacred from the profane, a quest for the lost time of paradise, a journey that culminates in the recovery in ecstatic form of man's primordial powers. Yet the shamanic voyage is possible only by means of a reversal of the profane, and concrete time and space must be abolished so as to make possible an epiphany of the primal Beginning and the cosmic Center, the man who lives in "time" must dissolve himself in chaos so as to be reborn through ecstasy in his primal state. The shaman's ecstasy reveals another world: "the world in which *everything seems possible;* where the dead return to life and the living die only to live again; where one can disappear and reappear instantaneously; where the 'laws of Nature' are abolished; and where a certain superhuman 'freedom' is exemplified and made dazzlingly *present.*"[30]

III. Repetition and Regeneration

Hopefully the preceding analysis of Eliade's interpretation of shamanism has cast some light upon his understanding of

the archaic ontology. While it is true that the archaic religion
—or religions—extend considerably beyond shamanism, at no
point do they make an essential break with the world of the
shaman. Two of the most essential categories of the archaic
ontology, however, cannot be fully exemplified in shamanism,
or, at least, Eliade has not chosen to do so: these are "repetition" and "regeneration." Eliade defines archaic repetition as
an imitation of a primordial archetype, this imitation forming
the core of all ritual acts, and through such imitation man is
projected into the mythical epochs in which the archetypes
were first revealed[31] (for example, every sacrifice not only exactly reproduces the original sacrifice but also takes place in
the same primordial mythical moment).[32] Yet archaic repetition can take place only through an abolition of profane time
or "history"; thus ritual always projects concrete time into
mythical time, *in illo tempore* when the foundation of the
world occurred.[33] It might be well to think of repetition in
this context not as an 'imitation' (with its Platonic overtones
of 'participation,' although considering his background in
Eastern Orthodoxy, this may well be Eliade's meaning), but
rather as a 're-calling' or 're-presenting,' as in the meaning
of the Greek word *anamnesis* in the early Christian eucharist—
"Do this in *anamnesis* of me" (I Cor. 11:25). Dom Gregory
Dix has done much to uncover the early Christian meaning of
this word:

> Yet the whole pre-Nicene church was obviously not just
> denying the evidence of its senses about the bread and wine
> in pursuit of a phrase when it spoke of the eucharist as being
> in very fact that Body and Blood of Christ which was born and
> crucified for us. The explanation of its almost crudely 'real-
> istic' language lies, it seems to me, in two things. First, we have
> to take account of the clear understanding then general in a
> largely Greek-speaking church of the word *anamnesis* as mean-
> ing a 're-calling' or 're-presenting' of a thing in such a way that
> it is not so much regarded as being 'absent,' as itself *presently
> operative* by its effects. This is a sense which the Latin *memoria*

and its cognates do not adequately translate, and which the
English words 'recall' and 'represent' will hardly bear without
explanation, still less such words as 'memorial' or 'remembrance.'
Secondly, and perhaps chiefly, the explanation lies in the universal concentration of pre-Nicene ideas about the eucharist
upon the whole rite of the eucharist as a single action, rather
than upon the matter of the sacrament in itself, as modern
Westerns tend to do.[34]

If archaic repetition were so interpreted, this would mean that
the archaic rite 're-presents' the primordial mythical moment,
makes present once more the sacred time and space of the unfallen beginning.

Thus Eliade maintains that in all religion the periodic
recurrence of anything signifies primarily that a mythical time
is made present once more: "every ritual has the character of
happening *now*, at this very moment."[35] Contemporaneity with
the great moments of myth is an indispensable condition for
any form of religion; and Eliade goes so far as to insist that
Kierkegaard's understanding of the Christian faith as contemporaneity with Christ is simply a reformulation of an attitude common to archaic man.[36] Indeed, one of Kierkegaard's
most baffling concepts, that of "repetition" itself, is illuminated
by Eliade's analysis of the archaic ontology. In attempting to
define repetition, Kierkegaard characterized it as transcendent,
as a religious movement by virtue of the absurd, noting that
"eternity is the true repetition."[37]

> The dialectic of repetition is easy; for what is repeated has
> been, otherwise it could not be repeated, but precisely the fact
> that it has been gives to repetition the character of novelty.
> When the Greeks said that all knowledge is recollection they
> affirmed that all that is has been; when one says that life is a
> repetition one affirms that existence which has been now be-
> comes. When one does not possess the categories of recollection
> or of repetition the whole of life is resolved into a void and
> empty noise. Recollection is the pagan life-view, repetition is the
> modern life-view; repetition is the *interest* of metaphysics, and

at the same time the interest upon which metaphysics founders: repetition is the solution contained in every ethical view, repetition is a *conditio sine qua non* of every dogmatic problem.[38]

Moreover, repetition and recollection are the same movement, only in opposite directions; "for what is recollected has been, is repeated backwards, whereas repetition properly so called is recollected forwards."[39]

Now, if eternity is the true repetition, and repetition is recollected forward, then repetition must be an *anamnesis,* a re-presenting or concrete renewal of the sacred reality, of "eternity." These abstract statements of Kierkegaard become concrete in Eliade's analysis of the symbolic meaning of water:

> Principle of what is formless and potential, basis of every cosmic manifestation, container of all seeds, water symbolizes the primal substance from which all forms come and to which they will return either by their own regression or in a cataclysm. It existed at the beginning and returns at the end of every cosmic or historic cycle; it will always exist, though never alone, for water is always germinative, containing the potentiality of all forms in their unbroken unity. In cosmogony, in myth, ritual and iconography, water fills the same function in whatever type of cultural pattern we find it; it *precedes* all forms and *upholds* all creation. Immersion in water symbolizes a return to the pre-formal, a total regeneration, a new birth, for immersion means a dissolution of forms, a re-integration into the formlessness of pre-existence; and emerging from the water is a repetition of the act of creation in which form was first expressed.[40]

Here, we see that repetition is also regeneration, cosmic regeneration (a conclusion that Kierkegaard, living during the collapse of Christendom, could never have known). A true rite is always cosmic, for archaic man, it is always a renewal of the creation, it dissolves the world (of concrete time and space) only to renew it once more. All archaic ritual revolves about repetition and regeneration, the sacred time and space of the beginning is re-called or re-presented, but through this ritual action "history" is destroyed: "Differing in their formulas, all these instruments of regeneration tend toward the same end: to annul past time, to abolish history by a continuous return *in illo tempore,* by the repetition of the cosmogenic act."[41]

One of Eliade's dearest principles is that archaic religion is not mystical or Gnostic in a "spiritual" sense, but is, rather, "cosmic"; for he believes that "the world becomes apprehensible as world, as cosmos, in the measure in which it reveals itself as a sacred world"[42]—thus revealing the crucial role that the category of regeneration plays in his thought. Yet in no sense is Eliade's understanding of "cosmos" to be identified with the *kosmos* of Greek thought or the "nature" of modern science, Eliade's "cosmos" is cosmic sacrality, the world becomes a hierophany.[43] In this sense, the "cosmos" is sacred time and space, the time at the beginning, and the sacred space at the Center of the world; and this is the only world that archaic man can "know," for he can live only in a sacred world, only here does he have real existence.

> Religious man thirsts for *being.* His terror of the chaos that surrounds his inhabited world corresponds to his terror of nothingness. The unknown space that extends beyond his world —an uncosmicized because unconsecrated space, a mere amorphous extent into which no orientation has yet been projected, and hence in which no structure has yet arisen—for religious man, this profane space represents absolute nonbeing. If, by some evil chance, he strays into it, he feels emptied of his ontic substance, as if he were dissolving in Chaos, and he finally dies.[44]

Hence archaic man only exists, only lives in *being,* by a continual process of negating concrete time and space; however this negation goes hand in hand with affirmation, archaic man continually reconstitutes his world, his "cosmos," by a dialectic of regeneration whereby his existence is re-created in the image of its archetypal model.

Consequently, archaic man does not accept himself as a historical or a personal being, as a being living in concrete duration. His deepest will is directed to the destruction of concrete

time and space, and his behavior as a "symbolic being" revolves about a periodic abolition of that profane existence
which modern man knows as consciousness and history:

> Basically, if viewed in its proper perspective, the life of archaic
> man (a life reduced to the repetition of archetypal acts, that is,
> to categories and not to events, to the unceasing rehearsal of
> the same primordial myths), although it takes place in time, does
> not bear the burden of time, does not record time's irreversi-
> bility; in other words, completely ignores what is especially
> characteristic and decisive in a consciousness of time. Like
> the mystic, like the religious man in general, the primitive lives
> in a continual present.[45]

But the burden of time is removed not by simple negation,
nor even by indifference, but rather by the continual regeneration of time, whether by the annual New Year rites of agri-
cultural societies, or the simpler rites of the pastoral societies,
rites that have the effect of re-creating time, of annulling its
irreversibility. Such cosmic regeneration has the effect of con-
ferring a cyclic direction upon time:

> Everything begins over again at its commencement every instant.
> The past is but a prefiguration of the future. No event is ir-
> reversible and no transformation is final. In a certain sense, it
> is even possible to say that nothing new happens in the world,
> for everything is but the repetition of the same primordial arche-
> types; this repetition, by actualizing the mythical moment when
> the archetypal gesture was revealed, constantly maintains the
> world in the same auroral instant of the beginnings.[46]

Eliade finds that the Greek myth of eternal repetition, as
reinterpreted by Greek speculation,[47] captures the full meaning of the archaic religion's cosmic regeneration of time, for
the myth is a supreme attempt toward the "staticization" of
becoming, toward annulling the irreversibility of time.

> If all moments and all situations of the cosmos are repeated
> *ad infinitum*, their evanescence is, in the last analysis, patent;
> *sub specie infinitatis*, all moments and all situations remain

stationary and thus acquire the ontological order of the archetype. Hence, among all the forms of becoming, historical becoming too is saturated with being. From the point of view of
eternal repetition, historical events are transformed into categories and thus regain the ontological order they possessed in
the horizon of archaic spirituality.[48]

Furthermore, Eliade notes that the Greek theory of eternal
return is the final variant undergone by the myth of the
repetition of an archetypal gesture, just as the Platonic doctrine of the Ideas was the final version of the archetype
concept.[49]

Thus it is clear that for Eliade *archaic* man and *modern*
man are 'ideal types,' existing in a dialectical relationship
to each other; most deeply, modern man exists in the "time"
of the immediate moment, whereas archaic man exists in the
"time" of the primordial beginning. Moreover, this relationship is fully dialectical insofar as each moment of time can
only be itself by an absolute negation of the other. If modern
man must become the murderer of God, archaic man can only
be himself by abolishing the profane:

> It matters little if the formulas and images through which
> the primitive expresses "reality" seem childish and even absurd
> to us. It is the profound meaning of primitive behavior that is
> revelatory; this behavior is governed by belief in an absolute
> reality opposed to the profane world of "unrealities"; in the
> last analysis, the latter does not constitute a "world," properly
> speaking; it is the "unreal" *par excellence,* the uncreated, the
> nonexistent: the void.[50]

Just as modern man created a whole new 'world' by his abolition of the sacred, archaic man creates his 'world' by the
abolition of the profane; the regeneration of the "new world"
arises only out of the ashes of the "old," archaic man lives in a
"continual present"—creates a continual present—only by
negating the concrete past and the concrete future, only by
annulling the order of the time of duration.

3

Christianity and Archaic Religion

I. The Problem of Christianity

THE MOST DEEPLY ambivalent issue in Eliade's thought is the relation of Christianity to archaic religion. Believing that all manifestations of the sacred are equivalent as such, he believes that there is no essential discontinuity in the religious life of mankind; nevertheless, the supreme theophany is the Incarnation.

> The great mystery consists in *the very fact that the sacred is made manifest;* for . . . in making itself manifest the sacred *limits* and "historicises" itself. We realize how greatly the sacred limits itself by taking the form of a stone; but we are prone to forget that God himself was accepting limitation and histori-cisation by incarnating in Jesus Christ. This, let us repeat it, is the great mystery, the *mysterium tremendum:* the fact that the sacred accepted self-limitation. Jesus Christ spoke Aramaic; he did not speak Sanskrit or Chinese. He had accepted limitation by life and by history. Although he continued to be God, he was no longer the all-powerful—just as, upon another plane, when the sacred manifests in a rock or a tree, it gives up being Everything and limits itself. There are, of course, great differences between the innumerable hierophanies; but one should never lose sight of the fact that their structure and dialectic are always the same.[1]

One does well to remember that Eliade's background lies in Eastern Christendom, when he thinks of Christianity he thinks of the Incarnation, and he conceives of the Christian life as the regeneration of time, the divinization of the cosmos itself.

As has been seen, Eliade understands archaic religion as revolving about a repetition of eternal archetypes, a repetition that transforms profane time into mythical time; this repetition annuls the irreversibility of time, all "moments" of time acquire the ontological order of the archetype, for historical events are transformed into categories and thus regain the *being* of primordial "Time." Yet the monotheism that appeared among the Jewish prophets represents a new religious attitude toward time. For the first time, the prophets placed a value on "history," and thereby succeeded in transcending the traditional vision of the cycle by discovering a "one-way time."[2] This revolutionary transformation of the archaic religion was grounded in a new theophany, a new manifestation of the sacred as a personal God who ceaselessly intervenes in history, who reveals his will through events.

> Historical facts thus become "situations" of man in respect to God, and as such they acquire a religious value that nothing had previously been able to confer on them. It may, then, be said with truth that the Hebrews were the first to discover the meaning of history as the epiphany of God, and this conception, as we should expect, was taken up and amplified by Christianity.[3]

Stated succinctly, Eliade says that the originality of the Old Testament lies in the fact that its God transcends "cosmic sacrality."[4]

Underlying this new theophany is a new dimension in religious experience: "faith." While faith does not produce a basic modification of traditional conceptions, it does rest upon an "interiorization" of the archaic religion; the religious goals of the archaic religion now become open to individual instead of communal experience, the ritual acts of the religious community are transformed into modes of experience in the individual believer. Like Paul and Kierkegaard, Eliade associates the advent of faith with Abraham: "Abraham's religious act inaugurates a new religious dimension: God reveals himself as personal, as a 'totally distinct' existence that ordains, bestows, demands, without any rational (i.e., general and foreseeable) justification, and for which all is possible."[5] Basing his analysis upon Mark 11:22-24, the faith that can move mountains (for God all is possible), Eliade insists that faith means absolute emancipation from any kind of natural "law" and hence the highest freedom that man can imagine: "freedom to intervene even in the ontological construction of the universe"[6]—although, as we have already seen, Eliade discovers such a superhuman "freedom" in the shaman. Thus faith has a special relevance to modern man, for only faith in this radical sense can defend modern man from the terror of "history," only faith can liberate contemporary man from the despair of his autonomous "freedom" (one has only to think of the heroes of Dostoevsky and Kafka). Consequently, Christianity proves to be the religion of "fallen man": "and this to the extent to which modern man is irremediably identified with history and progress, and to which history and progress are a fall, both implying the final abandonment of the paradise of archetypes and repetition."[7]

However, it is precisely at this point that a disastrous contradiction exists in Eliade's thought, a contradiction deriving from the ambiguity of his treatment of "time." This contradiction is illustrated in the following statements:

> Christianity goes even further in valorizing *historical time.* Since God was *incarnated,* that is, since he took on *a historically conditioned human existence,* history acquires the possibility of being sanctified. The *illud tempus* evoked by the Gospels is a clearly defined historical time—the time in which Pontius Pilate was Governor of Judea—but it was *sanctified by the presence of Christ.* When a Christian of our day participates in liturgical time, he recovers the *illud tempus* in which Christ lived, suffered, and rose again—but it is no longer a mythical time, it is the time when Pontius Pilate governed Judea.[8]

Here, it would seem that Eliade is saying that the Incarnation valorizes historical time in the sense that historical time is sanctified, while nevertheless remaining concrete historical time ("the time when Pontius Pilate governed Judea"). But this is not Eliade's real meaning at all. He continues the preceding statement by affirming that time begins anew with the birth of Christ, for the Incarnation establishes a new situation of man in the cosmos.

> This is as much as to say that history reveals itself to be a new dimension of the presence of God in the world. History becomes *sacred history* once more—as it was conceived, but in a mythical perspective, in primitive and archaic religions.[9]

In other words, history is sanctified by becoming *sacred history;* the concrete, actual moments of *profane time* are transformed into the *illud tempus* of sacred "Time." Yet this is exactly the pattern of archaic religion; profane time is transformed into sacred time, history is regenerated by being abolished. The coincidence of Christianity with the archaic religion can be seen in the following more careful statement of Eliade's:

> In Christianity, on the other hand, the evangelical tradition itself implies that the Kingdom of God is already present "among" those who believe, and that hence the *illud tempus* is eternally of the present and accessible to anyone, at any moment, through *metanoia*. Since what is involved is a religious experience wholly different from the traditional experience, since what is involved is faith, Christianity translates the periodic regeneration of the world into a regeneration of the human individual. But for him who shares in this eternal *nunc* of the reign of God, history ceases as totally as it does for the man of the archaic cultures, who abolishes it periodically. Consequently, for the Christian too, history can be regenerated, by and through each individual believer, even before the Saviour's second coming, when it will utterly cease for all Creation.[10]

Therefore, and despite his numerous statements to the contrary, it would seem that Eliade has no real ground for drawing a radical distinction between Christianity and archaic religion, that he is incapable of formulating a doctrine that a Western Christian would recognize as a doctrine of the Incarnation, and that he can relate faith to modern man only by demanding that modern man cease to exist as a being in "time."

Eliade's dilemma derives from the fact that he has given two contrary meanings to "time"; first, "time" is the concrete, actual, immediate moment, a time that modern man knows as "historicity," a time which at bottom is simply equivalent to *profane time;* and, second, "Time" is the new time of the Jewish prophets, a "one-way time" that is redeemed by the actions of a personal God who transforms *profane time* into *sacred history;* but insofar as this "time" is *sacred time* it exists in a dichotomous relationship to the *profane time* that modern man knows as "time" and "history," and which modern man—in creating himself as modern man—has willed as *being* itself. At bottom the "time" that modern man knows in his deepest existence is a "time" created by the death of God, by the transformation of absolute transcendence (which is known in faith) into absolute immanence (which is known in man's immediate existence in the "here" and "now"). Therefore the "time" and "history" which is known by modern man is *profane time:* it is dialectically opposed to the *sacred time* which is known in faith. Moreover, the Incarnation can have no meaning whatsoever to the man who is immersed in *profane time,* for the "time" and "history" created by the Incarnation can bear only a negative relationship to the "time" and "history" known by modern man. If the death of God created a wholly negative relationship between the *sacred* and the *profane,* then modern man—and the modern Christian—can know the *sacred* only through a negative dialectic, a dialectic that negates all that he knows as "time" and "history."

Although he has never so formulated his position, it might be said that the real distinction in Eliade's thought between faith and archaic religion is that faith engages in a yet more radical negation of the profane. For example, in writing of Messianism, which he regards as a consistent development of the prophetic faith, Eliade says that the Hebrew tolerates "history" because he hopes that it will finally come to an end.

Here, history is tolerated because it has an eschatological function; in Messianism, "resistance to history appears as still more determined than in the traditional horizons of archetypes and repetitions."

> History is thus abolished, not through consciousness of living an eternal present (coincidence with the atemporal instant of the revelation of archetypes), nor by means of a periodically repeated ritual (for example, the rites for the beginning of the year)—it is abolished in the future. Periodic regeneration of the Creation is replaced by a single regeneration that will take place in an *in illo tempore* to come. But the will to put a final and definitive end to history is itself still an antihistorical attitude, exactly as are the other traditional conceptions.[11]

Thus the salvation of "time" is fundamentally an abolition of *profane time;* and faith is a new religious attitude insofar as it arises from a far more radical opposition to the profane.

Eliade's fullest discussion of Christianity is in an essay entitled "Symbolism and History," which was published as the concluding chapter of *Images and Symbols* (1952). Writing in the context of an argument that the Christian idea of salvation does no more than repeat and complete the ideas of perpetual renovation and cosmic regeneration of the archaic religion,[12] Eliade maintains that Christianity is the supreme hierophany because it transfigures a "historical event" (Jesus of Nazareth) into a total theophany. The uniqueness of Christianity derives from its redemption of time and history; renouncing the reversibility of cyclic time, it posits a time that is irreversible: for Christ has lived, died, and been resurrected only *once.* "Hence a complete fulfilment of the momentary: Time itself is ontologized; Time is made to *be*, which means that it ceases to become, it transforms itself into eternity."[13] In other words, time is redeemed by being abolished, by becoming eternity. Yet it is not *any* moment that opens out into eternity, but only the moment that is transfigured by the incarnation of the divine Word. This moment is saved by a theophany endowing it with the maximum of "being"; thus Christianity differs from modern historicism—which is a product of the decomposition of Christianity—in that it does not value a historical event for its own sake.

As might be expected in such a discussion, Eliade is guilty once again of his basic inconsistency: "Christianity strives to *save* history; first, because it accords a value to historic time; and also because, for the Christian, the historical event, while remaining just what it is, becomes capable of transmitting a trans-historical message."[14] Or, he can say that for the Christian, "even the most commonplace historical event, while continuing to be *real* (that is, historically conditioned) may conceal some new intervention of God in history."[15] Now by his own principles, the sacred and the profane are related by a negative dialectic, a single moment cannot be sacred and profane at once. At this point Eliade has not gone beyond Kierkegaard's category of the "knight of faith" (it is to be remembered that Kierkegaard abandoned this category in his mature work). Furthermore, Eliade's own thought carries him beyond this position:

> And yet it must not be lost sight of, that Christianity entered into History in order to abolish it: the greatest hope of the Christian is the second coming of Christ, which is to put an end to all History. From a certain point of view, for every Christian individually, this end, and the eternity to follow it—the paradise regained—may be attained *from this moment. The time to come* announced by the Christ is already accessible, and for him who has regained it, history ceases to be. The transformation of Time into Eternity commenced with the first believers. But this paradoxical transformation of Time into Eternity is not the exclusive property of Christianity. We have met with the same conception and the same symbolism in India.[16]

But Eliade has no sooner said this than he reverses himself and insists that the Christian must become the contemporary of Christ: "and this implies a concrete existence in history, as well as contemporaneity with the preaching, the agony and the resurrection of the Christ.[17] Finally, all Eliade's theological difficulties derive from an inadequate theological language. He is forced to speak in the language of traditional theological conceptions although his own thought has taken him far beyond the province of the theological tradition. This is particularly true in his discussions of the Incarnation, for he has not found a theological language by which to establish a positive relationship between the sacred and the profane.

II. The Doctrine of the Incarnation

Christian theologians and historians of religions are in large measure agreed that the one doctrine which decisively distinguishes Christianity from the other religions of the world is the doctrine of the Incarnation, a doctrine that was constructed and fully elaborated by the Greek fathers of the patristic church, following the teaching in the Gospel of John that the Logos was made flesh (sarx). Little attempt was made in succeeding centuries to pass beyond the patristic formulations, but in our own day the patristic conception has become fraught with danger, as can be seen in the following statement of Archbishop William Temple:

> It may safely be said that one ground for the hope of Christianity that it may make good its claim to be the true faith lies in the fact that it is the most avowedly materialistic of all the great religions. It affords an expectation that it may be able to control the material, precisely because it does not ignore it or deny it, but roundly asserts alike the reality of matter and its subordination. Its most central saying is: "The Word was made flesh," where the last term was, no doubt, chosen because of its specially materialistic associations.[18]

Despite a long tradition that has associated the Incarnation with the flesh (the very word 'incarnation' is derived from the late Latin incarnātus, past participle of incarnāre, to invest with flesh), it can now be seen that the idea that the Logos became flesh (John 1:14) represents a radical transformation both of primitive Christianity and of Jesus' own message.

Modern critical historical study has revealed that the doctrine of the Incarnation which appeared in the Fourth Gospel, and was gradually established as orthodox by the second-century fathers, is in radical discontinuity with the primitive Christian understanding of the Incarnation. So much is this the case that innumerable New Testament scholars assert that the orthodox Christological formulae were established only by means of a transformation of the original message of Jesus.[19] In his early book on Jesus, Rudolf Bultmann had decisively formulated the problem posed by the transformation of Jesus' message in the patristic understanding of the Incarnation:

> Also neither in his sayings nor in the records of the primitive church is there any mention of his metaphysical nature. The primitive community did indeed believe him to be the Messiah, but it did not ascribe to him a particular metaphysical nature which gave his words authority. On the contrary, it was on the ground of the authority of his words that the church confessed that God had made him Lord of the church. Greek Christianity soon represented Jesus as Son of God in the sense of ascribing a divine "nature" to him, and thus introduced a view of his person as far removed as possible from his own.[20]

Bultmann's words were written in the context of the modern historical discovery of the original meaning of the message and ministry of Jesus—a message and ministry deeply grounded in an eschatological expectation of the immediate end of the world. Twentieth-century New Testament scholarship has so securely established the original eschatological form of the gospel that there are now scarcely any critical objections at this point; yet it is equally true that the patristic development of Christian dogma virtually discarded the original eschatological foundation of the gospel.[21] It was the realization of this chasm between Christian orthodoxy and the original proclamation of Jesus that led Albert Schweitzer to formulate his now classical thesis that the whole of Christianity depends on the delay of the *parousia*.

The immense and seemingly unbridgeable differences that exist between the fully developed Catholic Church of the third and fourth centuries and the primitive church (as we know it in the New Testament) are too well known to require comment. Suffice it to note the discrepancy between the primitive eschatological conception of Jesus as the Messiah-Son of Man whose decisive redemptive role lay in the future and the mystical-sacramental conception of Jesus as the cosmic Logos whose incarnation has mediated salvation to the present, the one deriving from the categories of Jewish eschatological religion, and the other from the categories of Hellenistic mystical religion. And no path seems to lie from one to the other! Or, rather, the later conception can by no means be conceived as a "consistent" and "organic" development—in Newman's sense—of the early and primitive conception. On the contrary, the only historical relation that can clearly be seen between the two is one of pure negation: Christianity assumes its orthodox and Catholic form by a process of de-eschatologizing its original faith and proclamation. This is the thesis of Schweitzer; and thus far more recent scholarship has not succeeded in challenging its most basic position.

Unquestionably the most powerful presentation of Schweitzer's thesis is in his book *The Mysticism of Paul the Apostle.* Here, he creates the category of "eschatological mysticism" to describe the religious world of Paul's thought. Schweitzer emphasizes that Paul is the only Christian thinker who knows only Christ-mysticism, unaccompanied by God-mysticism; and thus Paul alone has been able to preserve both the ethical and the eschatological foundations of the original message of Jesus.

> In Paul there is no God-mysticism; only a Christ-mysticism by means of which man comes into relation to God. The fundamental thought of Pauline mysticism runs thus: I am in Christ; in Him I know myself as a being who is raised above this sensuous, sinful, and transient world and already belongs to the transcendent; in Him I am assured of resurrection; in Him I am a Child of God.

To this, Schweitzer adds: "Another distinctive characteristic of this mysticism is that being in Christ is conceived as a having died and risen again with Him, in consequence of which the participant has been freed from sin and from the Law, possesses the spirit of Christ, and is assured of resurrection."[22] Furthermore, the being-in-Christ is not conceived by Paul as a static participation in the 'spiritual' being of Christ, but rather as a real "co-experiencing" of Christ's dying and rising again. Paul knows only a "resurrection-mysticism" (a participation even now in the dawning Kingdom of God), and is completely free of the Hellenistic "rebirth-mysticism," the foundation of the Fourth Gospel and the patristic fathers. Pauline mysticism is genuinely eschatological insofar as it revolves about a participation "even now" in the sacred time of the End—an end whose realization has already been inaugurated by the triumphant resurrection of Jesus.

> In the death of Jesus begins the cessation of the natural world, and in His resurrection the dawning of the supernatural world. This cosmic event translates itself in the created being, man, as a dying and rising again.[23]

And it is precisely through this dying and rising with Christ that the Christian receives God's forgiveness and knows the new reality of the Kingdom of God.

At no point is Schweitzer's power, both as a scholar and as a disciple, more evident than in his treatment of ethics. He demonstrates that ethics is the necessary outward expression of the translation from the Old Aeon to the New Aeon that takes place in the being-in-Christ. Unlike Jesus and the primitive Christian community, ethics for Paul is no longer repentance. Paul's ethics derives instead from his conviction that the believer who has died and risen again with Christ already knows the power and the Spirit of the Kingdom of God, and therein knows a new life, a life only possible through liberation from the world.

> Paul's ethics is therefore nothing else than the mysticism of the being-in-Christ, conceived from the point of view of will. Its greatness lies in the fact that it is wholly supernatural, without thereby becoming unnatural. . . . The demands which

Paul's views of ethics set up presuppose not the natural man but the "new creation" endowed with the Spirit, who has come into existence in the dying and rising again with Christ.[24]

The believer wills his death to flesh and sin by continually opening himself to the new life that is his in the Spirit. But this new life is radically ethical, if only because of the liberation that it bestows upon the believer. Through suffering and dying with Christ, the Christian is freed from the world, and it is precisely this freedom from the world that makes possible—that demands—a new life of ethical obedience.

Therefore Paul's understanding of redemption is integrally associated with ethics. Yet it was so only because of its eschatological form; when the Christian understanding of redemption assumed a noneschatological form, it lost its immediate association with ethics. Schweitzer depicts this process as follows: "The Hellenization of Christianity by Ignatius and by the Asia Minor theology consists, therefore, in taking over the Pauline mysticism of 'being-in-Christ' as the proper formulation of the Christian doctrine of redemption, but giving it for content, not the eschatological conception of the dying and rising again with Christ, but the Hellenistic conception of the union of flesh and Spirit."[25] In this conception of the "union" of flesh and Spirit (*pneuma*) lies the origin of the traditional doctrine of the Incarnation. But to conceive of redemption as the union of flesh and Spirit is to nullify the radical opposition between the Old and New Aeons—or, in Eliade's language, between the *sacred* and the *profane*—and to sanction the structure of the natural order by making it the arena of sanctification. By this means, the eschatological foundations of faith are abandoned, and so likewise is surrendered every real hope of liberation from the world—which Schweitzer identifies as the one firm ground of Christian ethics.

With equal firmness Schweitzer shows that the Hellenistic extension of the believer's being-in-Christ to a being-in-God constitutes a radical transformation of genuine eschatological mysticism. The idea of rebirth (as present in the Fourth Gospel and the apostolic fathers) makes possible a "spiritual" redemption, a redemption taking place without any effect upon the world. Here, a noneschatological conception of Spirit makes belief in Jesus a means of attaining being-in-God. Union with Christ occurs independently of any regard for the actual condition of the creation. Therein is introduced a lack of "realism" (and thus a betrayal of Biblical faith), and a consequent dissociation of ethics and redemption. Precisely because, as now conceived, redemption has no effect upon the natural or actual condition of human existence, it can have no immediate and integral relation with ethics. Now redemption is understood to occur in *this* world, in *this* present life, in *this* body; and thus its occurrence is wholly independent of a new creation. As Schweitzer's disciple, Martin Werner, has said: "Redemption in this world had neither the aim nor the effect of changing or abolishing in any essential sense the natural and basic conditions of human existence."[26] The world—as world, as *profane*—remains intact, being neither destroyed nor replaced by the Kingdom of God. Nor was this new understanding of redemption of only incidental importance, it initiated a decisive process of transformation: "At first it was the transformation of the doctrine of redemption, but finally the whole corpus of dogma was transformed from the primitive eschatologically determined faith into a non-eschatological doctrine of the Catholic Church" (Werner).[27] Spirit is independent of nature, redemption has no real effect upon the world, and so radical a cleavage is made between Christ and the Kingdom of God that Christ can now be known independently of the Kingdom of God. Indeed, whereas Jesus himself proclaimed the Kingdom of God, the church now proclaimed Jesus as the Christ in such a way as to nullify Jesus' own proclamation. Thus the new idea of redemption necessitated a new idea of Christ: the Messiah–Son of Man, whom the early church had proclaimed, and whose coming marked the advent of the end of the world, now became the Logos Christ in whose image the world had been made. Redemption occurred in the present through union with the Logos Christ, and this meaning of redemption demanded a "redeemer" who was wholly detached from the eschatological message of Jesus.

Regardless of the historical validity of this interpretation, it has great relevance to Eliade's understanding of the sacred, and thus this excursion into Schweitzer's understanding of "consistent eschatology" has been deemed necessary. When Schweitzer says that the Incarnation must not be conceived as the union of flesh and Spirit in such a way as to allow the flesh to remain flesh, as to allow the world to remain the world, we may translate and say that the sacred is only truly manifest when it effects a decisive transformation of the profane. When redemption fails to effect either the annihilation of or delivery from the "flesh" (or, in Eliade's terms, the *profane*) its ethical ground is dissolved; for when redemption is no longer understood as the abolition of the "natural conditions" of existence in the world, it can supply no indicative that is susceptible of translation into a moral imperative. Thus Schweitzer insists that the absolute demand with which Jesus confronts the believer can never be real apart from a liberation of the believer from the world. Finally, it was the ancient church's acceptance of the world, of "time" and "history," that necessitated its transformation of the gospel. From this point of view, it becomes obvious that no religious position which rests upon a dialectical relationship between the sacred and the profane can uncritically accept the traditional Christian doctrine of the Incarnation. Can it be any wonder that Eliade has been unable to assimilate the doctrine of the Incarnation?

By this circuitous means we have arrived at a striking confirmation of Heidegger's well-known, although privately published, words: "If I were to write a theology, which I am sometimes tempted to do, the term 'being' would not be allowed to appear in it. . . . Faith does not need the thought of being, and if it needs it, it is no longer faith."[28] Not only is authentic faith compromised by an acceptance of the *reality* of the profane (of "being," of the world), but thereby it loses its immediate expression in ethics. Nor can faith treat 'flesh' as a neutral term: flesh is the Old Aeon, it is the power of sin, the form of existence that annihilates the presence of the sacred. Ancient Christianity's religious neutralization of the world, the flesh, and the profane, went hand in hand with an abandonment of the original eschatological form of the gospel, and with a corresponding syncretistic absorption both of classical culture and of alien religious forms. We need not doubt that such a transformation was necessary if Christianity was to become Christendom, but Christendom is now collapsing, and the time has come for a recovery of the original meaning and power of the gospel! Quite naturally Eliade's recovery of the sacred has taken him beyond the Christian tradition, he can find no means of making the sacred meaningful in terms of the traditional conceptions of the creation and the Incarnation, but thereby he is moving beyond the compromise of the ancient church, moving in the direction of the original gospel, and, perhaps, most significant of all, is evolving an understanding of the sacred that is genuinely universal, that draws all manifestations of the sacred into a unifying dialectical process.

III. Kierkegaard

Perhaps the supreme irony of modern faith is that the greatest religious thinker of the modern world, Søren Kierkegaard, should have been forced by the very nature of the development of his religious thought to renounce not only Christendom but the historic Christian church itself. A late parable of Kierkegaard's illustrates this situation:

> Imagine a fortress, absolutely impregnable, previsioned for an eternity.
> There comes a new commandant. He conceives that it might be a good idea to build bridges over the moats—so as to be able to attack the besiegers. *Charmant!* He transforms the fortress into a country-seat—and naturally the enemy takes it.
> So it is with Christianity. They changed the method—and naturally the world conquered.[29]

Kierkegaard's thought, like Pascal's and Dostoevsky's, is incompatible with life in the church; thus when Karl Barth took up his task of writing a church dogmatics, he was forced to abandon his earlier discipleship to Kierkegaard. Yet Kierkegaard created virtually all the categories through which faith has become meaningful to the modern world. To achieve "contemporaneity" (Tillich's term),[30] a theologian is forced to employ these categories—albeit much contemporary theology reads like a parody of Kierkegaard.

Already by the time he was twenty-two, Kierkegaard could write: "Philosophy and Christianity, however, can never be united";[31] and fourteen years later, a little more than a year after he had undergone his great "metamorphosis," he continued to maintain that modern philosophy is simply paganism, its real secret being: *cogito ergo sum, to think is to be.*" The Christian motto, on the contrary, is: "As thou believest, so art thou; to believe is to be."[32] Even if Kierkegaard never fully succeeded—at least in his theoretical writings—in casting off Hegel's philosophical mantle, he succeeded, nevertheless, in creating a theological Copernican revolution by discovering religious "subjectivity," a discovery, it is true, anticipated by Augustine, but a radical discovery nonetheless, insofar as Kierkegaard's subjectivity is fully dialectical—it becomes manifest only through a total negation of the reality which is *known* by modern man. In his early work, *Fear and Trembling,* the major theme of the "knight of faith"—a theme having its personal roots in Kierkegaard's futile desire to regain Regina—is threatened by the minor theme that "the individual is incommensurable with reality,"[33] that "subjectivity is incommensurable with reality."[34] The following year, in *The Concept of Dread,* Kierkegaard went beyond the Hegelian concept of eternity (which had blocked his progress in *Philosophical Fragments*) by uniting eternity and inwardness:

Inwardness, certitude, is seriousness. . . . If inwardness is lacking, the spirit is finitized. Inwardness is therefore eternity, or the determinant of the eternal in a man.[35]

Finally, in his *Concluding Unscientific Postscript* (1846), Kierkegaard's dialectic of subjectivity was virtually complete.

As is well known, in this work Kierkegaard evolved an "existential" solution to the unresolved problem of the *Fragments*, a problem that he now states as follows: "Is an historical point of departure possible for an eternal consciousness; how can such a point of departure have any other than a mere historical interest; is it possible to base an eternal happiness upon historical knowledge?"[36] Ironically, the answer is both yes and no; but the deeper answer—despite the established commentaries—is no. Kierkegaard quickly and decisively establishes his dialectical thesis that faith is in no sense the result of scientific inquiry or speculative reflection, nor does true Christianity lend itself to objective observation, "precisely because it proposes to intensify subjectivity to the utmost."[37] Instead, faith is in some sense the product of subjective thinking, a thinking that assimilates the "universal" in inwardness, becoming more and more subjectively isolated, by turning its attention inward to the subject, desiring in this intensification of inwardness to realize the "truth."[38] Thus, subjective thinking is "existential"; and "passion is the culmination of existence for an existing individual."[39]

> In an attempt to make clear the difference of way that exists between an objective and a subjective reflection, I shall now proceed to show how a subjective reflection makes its way inwardly in inwardness. Inwardness in an existing subject culminates in passion; corresponding to passion in the subject the truth becomes a paradox; and the fact that the truth becomes a paradox is rooted precisely in its having a relationship to an existing subject.[40]

Why must "subjective truth" be paradoxical? Because subjectivity and objectivity are antithetically related, subjectivity realizes itself only to the extent that it negates objectivity. Hence Kierkegaard defines subjective truth as follows: "An objective uncertainty held fast in an appropriation-process of the most passionate inwardness is the truth, the highest truth attainable for an existing individual."[41]

When subjectivity—or inwardness—is the truth, the truth becomes objectively a paradox: "Faith is precisely the contradiction between the infinite passion of the individual's inwardness and the objective uncertainty."[42] So important, for Kierkegaard, is the antithetical relationship between objectivity and subjectivity that he can insist—and is forced by his own position to so insist—that only the absurd can be the object of faith.[43] Following, but going beyond his romantic roots, he conceives the degree of subjectivity to be in accordance with its distance from, or, rather, inversion of, objectivity; accordingly, the deepest inwardness is produced by the most radical absurdity. And what is the truly absurd? "The absurd is—that the eternal truth has come into being in time, that God has come into being, has been born, has grown up, and so forth, precisely like any other individual human being, quite indistinguishable from other individuals."[44] Like Tertullian in his reaction to classical philosophy, Kierkegaard conceives the truth of Christianity to lie in its absurdity; and Christianity is absolutely true because it is the absolute paradox, it paradoxically unites the most extreme contraries of thought, bringing together the eternal and the temporal, the infinite and the particular, God and man.

Another paradox of this supreme ironist is that while Kierkegaard throughout his life played the role of defender of theological orthodoxy, he continually went beyond, and even inverted, the theological tradition in the creation of his own religious categories. At no point is this more true than in the doctrine of the Incarnation. First, note must be taken of a peculiar meaning of the Kierkegaardian category of "existence." For Kierkegaard: "God does not think, He creates; God does not exist, He is eternal. . . . Man thinks and exists, and existence separates thought and being, holding them apart from one another in succession."[45] Shortly after publishing the *Postscript*, Kierkegaard wrote in his journal:

Immanently (in the fantastic medium of abstraction) God does not *exist*, he only is—God only *exists* for an existing man, i.e., he can only exist in *faith*. . . . Faith is therefore the anticipation of the eternal which holds the factors together, the cleavages of existence. When an existing individual has not got faith God *is* not, neither does God *exist*, although understood from an eternal point of view God is eternally.[46]

Now, for Kierkegaard, God is a "subject," and therefore exists only for subjectivity in inwardness.[47] There can be no objective way to God; therefore there is no "objective truth" in Christianity.[48]

If the uniqueness of Christianity derives from the fact that it reaches the eternal by means of the historical, the problem nevertheless remains of what 'eternal' and 'historical' mean for Kierkegaard. In the *Fragments,* Kierkegaard introduced the category of the Moment, defining it as the realization of eternity in time.[49] The perfection of the eternal is that it has no history,[50] but in the paradox of the Incarnation the eternal becomes historical: "the Paradox unites the contradictories, and is the historical made eternal, and the eternal made historical."[51] Yet, at the same time that he was writing the *Fragments,* Kierkegaard employed the category of the "instant" in *The Concept of Dread,* saying that "the historical sphere and all the knowledge which reposes upon a historical presupposition has the category of the instant."[52] Only in the instant does "history" begin, yet the instant *is* only through the positing of the eternal; thus the instant occurs only in Christianity: "The concept around which everything turns in Christianity, the concept which makes all things new, is the fullness of time, is the instant as eternity."[53] Precisely because the instant is eternity in Christianity, "is the 'eternal fact' that God became man," it is a paradox incommensurable with the objective reality of time and history.

What then, from the point of view of faith, is time? Kierkegaard could say: "Time does not really exist without unrest; it does not exist for dumb animals who are absolutely without anxiety."[54] Existentially or subjectively considered, time is a product of sin, appearing only through *Angst,* through dread and anxiety, through the "qualitative leap" of sin:

> The instant sin is posited, the temporal is sin. We do not say that the temporal is sinfulness, any more than that the sensuous is sinfulness; but for the fact that sin is posited the temporal signifies sinfulness. Therefore that man sins who lives merely in the instant abstracted from the eternal.[55]

Since despair is possible only through the eternal, all existence apart from God is despair, therefore despair is sin.[56] Following the qualitative leap of sin, time becomes *Angst*—although, for Kierkegaard, dread is the presupposition for original sin. Time becomes isolated from eternity through the "fall": thereby human "existence" comes into being, *now* God can "exist" only in the faith of the existing individual. Only in a fallen mode of existence is reality the order of time. The "fall" creates the dichotomy between time and eternity, between objectivity and subjectivity, a fall that is transcended when eternity is actualized in time. Yet this transcendence occurs only in faith, and faith is merely "occasioned" by the historical[57]—for the instant and the Moment are existential categories, having no genuine objective meaning whatsoever. As James Brown rightly interprets Kierkegaard, "History, as such, is in the end irrelevant: faith is an event outside time."[58] Or, as Kierkegaard himself said in *Training in Christianity:*

> For in relation to the absolute there is only one tense: the present. For him who is not contemporary with the absolute— for him it has no existence. And as Christ is the absolute, it is easy to see that with respect to Him there is only one situation: that of contemporaneousness.[59]

Does Kierkegaard have a doctrine of the Incarnation? If we conceive the Incarnation as the entrance of God into time, or as the union of eternity and time, then the answer must be no. True, he continually says that the uniqueness of Christianity lies in its reaching eternity through time, that Christianity is the ultimate paradox because here eternity becomes time. But eternity, for Kierkegaard, is radical "inwardness," it is a "subjective" truth, having no objective meaning, or, rather, objectively, it is an absurdity. If the eternal appears in objective time and history only by means of the Paradox, then, the eternal, as such, does not appear, does not "exist," in the time and history that is known objectively. Here, there is no "union" of time and eternity. Only in faith does eternity become time; thus faith is the ultimate paradox, the ultimate "offense" to objectivity, the "passion" of absolute subjectivity. Yet where is faith to be found? In history? In Christendom? In the church? No! Only in inwardness, in subjectivity, in the passionately existing individual who by his passion has negated the reality of time and history. Consequently, Kierkegaard spent his final days in violently attacking the church:

> O Luther, thou hadst 95 theses—terrible! And yet, in a deeper sense, the more theses, the less terrible. This case is far more terrible: there is only one thesis.
> The Christianity of the New Testament simply does not exist. Here there is nothing to reform; what has to be done is to throw light upon a criminal offense against Christianity, prolonged through centuries, perpetuated by millions (more or less guilty), whereby they have cunningly, under the guise of perfecting Christianity, sought little by little to cheat God out of Christianity, and have succeeded in making Christianity exactly the opposite of what it is in the New Testament.[60]

Walter Lowrie wisely remarks that this attack was the consistent development of Kierkegaard's life and thought.[61] Thereby Kierkegaard found a Christian way of proclaiming the death of God, for the death of God is the death of faith: faith died by imagining that it existed in time and history, by building a bridge over the moat separating objectivity and subjectivity, by attempting too easily to 'unite' the sacred and the profane.

The greater part of the ambiguity and confusion in Kierkegaard's work derives from his desperate effort to speak in the language of theological orthodoxy, a language that he never quite succeeded in shattering—even though he recognized so deeply that the language itself was dead. Kierkegaard was not a dogmatic theologian, never was he able to speak fully within the confines of the dogmatic tradition. His great task was that of the recovery of faith—indeed, of the discovery of faith—the rescue of faith from the great compromise of Christendom. In spite of appearances to the contrary, Kierkegaard has had few true followers. Surely one of the greatest of these is Mircea Eliade, for it cannot be mere coincidence that Eliade's understanding of the archaic ontology has so many points of contact with Kierkegaard's understanding of faith—contemporaneity, repetition, the abolition of time and history. Nor is it accidental that the great problems for both Kierkegaard and Eliade are the uniqueness of Christianity, the meaning of the Incarnation from the point of view of faith, the Christian understanding of the relation between time and eternity, between the sacred and the profane. Kierkegaard believed that the immediate relationship to God is "paganism," and only after the "breach" has taken place can there be any question of a true God-relationship.[62]

> All paganism consists in this, that God is related to man directly, as the obviously extraordinary to the astonished observer. But the spiritual relationship to God in the truth, i.e., in inwardness, is conditioned by a prior eruption of inwardness, which corresponds to the divine elusiveness that God has absolutely nothing obvious about Him, that God is so far from being obvious that He is invisible. It cannot immediately occur to anyone that He exists, although His invisibility is again His omnipresence.[63]

If we translate Kierkegaard's paganism into Eliade's archaic religion, we could say that it is only through the advent of the fully profane—of time and history—that the "leap" of faith becomes possible. Faith is truly dialectical, it comes into existence only through the negation of the profane: hence a radical "breach" between the sacred and the profane is a necessary presupposition for the appearance of faith, for the existence of Christianity. Can it be that this is the path to the solution of the problems of Kierkegaard and Eliade?

4

The Coincidence of the Opposites

I. Dialectic and the Sacred

WHETHER WE TURN to India, to China, or to Greece, we find that the beginnings of philosophical thought, of pure thinking, are dialectical: knowing reveals itself by understanding the opposites, only through negation do 'truth' and 'being' become manifest. Dialectical thinking has always dominated the East, but in the West, a genuine dialectical method was surmounted by the dominance of *logos*, of pure reason. Perhaps we should follow Ernst Cassirer in tracing this victory of *logos* to Parmenides:

> It is his great achievement that for the first time in the history of thought he made the *logos* the measure of being, from which the final decision, the *krisis*, concerning being and nonbeing is expected. And for him the power of time and change become mere illusion. Only for myth is there a temporal origin, a "genesis" of being—for the *logos* the very question of an origin loses its meaning. . . . The power of time is broken, since time, seen from the standpoint of philosophical thought, negates itself dialectically, reveals its own inner contradiction. For religious feeling, particularly in India, time signifies above all the burden of *suffering;* but for philosophical thinking, here where it first appears in full consciousness, time is annihilated by the burden of contradiction.[1]

In a rather different manner, Heidegger says that the fundamental ontological basis of time has been ignored in the

81

Western philosophical tradition, and thus the being of *Dasein* has been "forgotten." Yet it is obvious that in the West pure dialectical thinking, while appearing briefly in Heraclitus, was overthrown by Plato's vision of Being, then moved underground into religious thinking—for dialectical thought has dominated religious thinking in the West from Augustine to Kierkegaard—only to be reborn in a radically profane form in the thought of Hegel, Marx, and Freud.

Genuine dialectical thought, in its various expressions, revolves about the crucial principle that ultimately negation is affirmation, that the opposites coincide, that the acts of radical negation and radical affirmation are finally two poles of *one* dialectical movement. This truth can clearly be seen in the great dialectical schools of the East, particularly in the Madhyamika and Zen schools of Mahayana Buddhism,[2] as well as in Chinese Taoism. Christianity must assume a fully dialectical form, both if it is to be a full expression of the sacred and if it is to relate itself to the modern expressions of the profane—hence the importance of the dialectical method of Kierkegaard's thought, as well as the dialectical implications of Schweitzer's understanding of eschatological mysticism. But the foundations of the Western dogmatic tradition are nondialectical— one finds here neither radical negation nor radical affirmation, neither the radical sacred nor the radical profane; here, faith and world enter into a nondialectical, nonopposing synthesis —therefore they must be transcended if Christianity is not to perish with Christendom.

It is precisely at this point that Eliade's thought has its deepest contemporary theological relevance. Again and again, Eliade refers to the ancient mythical symbol of the *coincidentia oppositorum*, finding in it the foundation of the dialectic of the sacred: "One of the most important discoveries of the human spirit was naïvely anticipated when, through certain religious symbols, man guessed that the polarities and the antimonies could be articulated as a unity."[3] Delighting in Cusanus' doctrine that the *coincidentia oppositorum* is the most appropriate definition of the nature of God, Eliade finds that the purer expressions of the sacred reveal a paradoxical mode of being which is at once both inside and outside of time,[4] in which the sacred and the profane no longer exist in a state of simple opposition. Indeed, the greatest problem that Eliade's work and method reveal is precisely the problem posed by the *positive* relationship between the sacred and the profane; in the sacred manifesting itself in the profane.

> In fact, this paradoxical coming-together of sacred and profane, being and non-being, absolute and relative, the eternal and the becoming, is what every hierophany, even the most elementary, reveals. . . . This coming-together of sacred and profane really produces a kind of breakthrough of the various levels of existence. It is implied in every hierophany whatever, for every hierophany shows, makes manifest, the coexistence of contradictory essences: sacred and profane, spirit and matter, eternal and non-eternal, and so on. That the dialectic of hierophanies, of the manifestation of the sacred in material things, should be an object for even such complex theology as that of the Middle Ages serves to prove that it remains *the* cardinal problem of any religion. One might say that all hierophanies are simply prefigurations of the miracle of the Incarnation, that every hierophany is an abortive attempt to reveal the mystery of the coming together of man and God.[5]

Thus the Incarnation is the final realization of the ancient symbol of the *coincidentia oppositorum*, it is prefigured in all hierophanies, paralleled in the highest expressions of Oriental religion, but is unique—is Christian—insofar as it is a dialectical coming-together of the most radical expressions of the sacred and the profane, a dialectical synthesis of the radical sacred and the radical profane.

II. Creation, the Fall, and the Orgy

In a recent statement, Eliade has said that the symbol of the *coincidentia oppositorum*—which he regards as a universal symbol—betrays a nostalgia for a lost paradise, a nostalgia for a paradoxical state in which contraries coexist without opposing one another and where all multiplicities compose aspects of a mysterious Unity. In the final analysis, it is the desire to recover this lost paradise which constrains man to conceive the opposites as complementary aspects of a unique reality.[6] Noting that that which is true in eternity is not necessarily true in the temporal realm, Eliade says: "The world has come into existence following a rupture in the primordial unity."[7] The existence of the world and man's existence in the world are particular situations: only here does existence presuppose the separation of the opposites, the distinction between good and evil, the disjunction between the sacred and the profane. Now a chasm exists between the transcendental and atemporal perspective, and the perspective of man's immediate experience. Man is separated from his pretemporal and atemporal state, and this separation is created by a rupture, a rupture existing both in himself and in the world. Eliade calls this rupture a "fall," not necessarily in the Judeo-Christian sense of the term, but a "fall" nevertheless, a fatal catastrophe that has transformed the human race and changed the ontological structure of the world.[8]

Eliade's position, which reflects a long mystical tradition, partially resembles Paul Tillich's doctrine of creation. Tillich believes that the doctrine of creation is not the story of an event that took place in time, but rather an ontological description of the relation between God and the world. Human existence is such that man asks the question of his finitude without receiving an answer: but the answer to this question is given in the classical Christian doctrine of *creatio ex nihilo*. If existence has its origin in nothingness as well as in God, then creatureliness implies nonbeing. The tragic character of existence is not rooted in God; hence it does not belong to the esssential nature of things. Accordingly, the dual source of reality in God and nothingness accounts for the ambivalence between human "existence" and human "essence." Yet this ambivalence is essential to the "divinely willed destiny" of human being. The heart of Tillich's position is contained in the first volume of his *Systematic Theology:*

> Man and the rest of reality are not only "inside" the process of the divine life but also "outside" it. Man is grounded in it, but he is not kept within the ground. Man has left the ground in order to "stand upon" himself, to actualize what he essentially is, in order to be finite freedom. This is the point at which the doctrine of creation and the doctrine of the fall join. . . . Fully developed creatureliness is fallen insofar as it is outside the divine ground of the divine life. . . . To be outside the divine life means to stand in actualized freedom, in an existence which is no longer united with essence. Seen from one side, this is the end of creation. Seen from the other side, it is the beginning of the fall.[9]

Thus the creature is destined to separate itself freely from the divine ground by effecting a break between "existence" and "essence": "Creaturely freedom is the point at which creation and the fall coincide."[10]

In the second volume of his *Systematic Theology,* Tillich answers the critics of his position by insisting that his doctrine of creation is intended to be an answer to the "ontological" estrangement of human existence. Opposing those who believe that history has evolved out of a primordial state of bliss, he maintains that there has never been a time when created goodness was actualized and had existence: "Actualized creation and estranged existence are identical."[11] Creation is good in its essential character; but, if actualized, "it falls into universal estrangement through freedom and destiny."[12] Hence Tillich's cardinal principle: existence cannot be derived from essence (or, as Eliade might say, time cannot be derived from eternity). For Tillich, the "leap" from essence to existence is the "original fact" about reality. The estrangement of human existence is grounded in the creation; man's alienation from the divine ground—and from his own essential being—is the divinely willed destiny of his freedom, of his fully developed creatureliness. Although the "leap" establishes human existence, it is not a historical fall; it is ontological, grounded in the very nature of created being itself, in the creature's dual source in God and nothingness. Consequently, it is essential to Tillich's position to maintain that creation and the fall coincide, that ontological estrangement is the destiny of created being.

Eliade's position is illuminated by comparing it with Tillich's, for, on the one hand, Tillich is willing in a way that Eliade is not to ground the "fall" in the power of the sacred, and thus to make a religious affirmation of the profane, whereas, on the other hand, Eliade insists upon the reality of man's prefallen state, and upon the possibility of recovering it in time, that makes possible for Eliade, in a way that is closed to Tillich, a radical affirmation of the sacred. At this point, although they complement each other, neither Tillich's nor Eliade's position is fully dialectical. Quite recently, in an Eranos lecture, "The Creator and His Shadow," Eliade has explored various myths recounting the Devil's role in creation; he is particularly interested in the cosmogenic myths of Romania and Southeastern Europe, myths that have never been fully absorbed by Christianity, and that have distinctive negative elements: the fatigue of God after having created the world, his profound sleep, and the decline of his intelligence. Hand in hand with these themes goes the mythical motif, which Eliade discovers in various places throughout the world, that God had need of the Devil in the creation, a Devil who was originally God's "shadow," his servant and companion. Only with the advent of religious dualism did God's "shadow" become his adversary. Such myths of the Devil's role in creation serve both to explain the origin of evil, and, in a Christian context, to point to God's withdrawal from man after the creation, thus explaining the pain and mystery of life in the world, but, at the same time, pointing to God's original unity with his "shadow," to the primordial *coincidentia oppositorum*.[13]

Such myths have an integral point of contact with the vast

number of myths of a primordial High God that are found in the most primitive societies, a creator god who has become a *deus otiosus*, following the creation or a primal sin, a god who is no longer worshiped since he is no longer *there*, having abandoned the creation to another god or to a demiurge.[14] Nowhere in primitive religion do these High Gods (or supreme beings of the sky) play a leading role, their place has been taken by "lower" religious forms—totemism, animism, devotion to the spirits of the dead and local deities, etc.—as man comes increasingly to direct his attention to the vitalities of "life."

> What is clear is that the supreme sky god everywhere gives place to other religious forms. The morphology of this substitution may vary; but its meaning is in each case partly the same: it is a movement away from the transcendence and passivity of sky beings towards more dynamic, active and easily accessible forms. One might say that we are observing a "progressive descent of the sacred into the concrete"; man's life and his immediate natural surroundings come more and more to have the value of sacred things.[15]

From one point of view, the advent of the common forms of primitive religion represents a new "fall" of man, a fall from the early, noncultic monotheism of the High Gods. But the dialectic of history is grounded in the "fall"; all culture is a "fall" into history[16]—and, to judge by modern Western culture, the higher the culture, the greater the "fall." Thus every "fall" is a fall into "life."

> This passage from "creator" to "fecundator," this slipping of the omnipotence, transcendence and impassiveness of the sky into the dynamism, intensity and drama of the new atmospheric, fertilizing, vegetation figures, is not without significance. It makes quite clear that one of the main factors in the lowering of people's conception of God, most obvious in agricultural societies, is the more and more all-embracing importance of vital values and of "Life" in the outlook of economic man.[17]

The whole drama of the "religious degeneracy" of humanity lies in man's discovery of the sacredness of life; man allows himself to be immersed in the immediate experiences of life, thus turning his attention away from the transcendent sacred: "The first 'fall' of man—which led to the fall into history that characterises modern man—was a fall into life: man was intoxicated by the discovery of the powers and the sacredness of life."[18]

That history is a "fall" is a crucial theme in Eliade's thought, a theme having its background in European romanticism, but its deeper roots in various religious traditions, such as the prophetic movement of ancient Israel,[19] and, perhaps most clearly, in Chinese Taoism. The *Tao Te Ching* calls men to return to a primal and harmonious prehistoric state in which virtue and knowledge had not yet come into existence. Knowledge and goodness come into existence only when the *Tao* (the "way") has receded from view.

> It was when the Great Way declined
> That human kindness and morality arose;
> It was when intelligence and knowledge appeared
> That the Great Artifice began. (XVIII)[20]

The *Tao* is a wordless doctrine, and therefore all formal teaching distracts the hearer from its reality. Only in stillness, in the suspension of sensory, intellectual, and moral experience and judgment can the *Tao* be known. In the cessation of all activity (*wu wei*), the Taoist makes possible the realization of an authentic spontaneity that carries him to the ground of things: he is in quest of the *Tao* both in himself and in the world. As Arthur Waley says: "In the individual it is the Uncarved Block, the consciousness on which no impression has been 'notched,' in the universe it is the Primal Unity underlying apparent multiplicity."[21] The Uncarved Block (*p'u*) is the Taoist symbol of man's primordial state, when his inborn power (*Te*) has not been dissipated and obscured by the artificialities and falsities of society and civilization.

Employing this Taoist theme, we can see that for Eliade the *coincidentia oppositorum* is the most important symbol of the primordial and prefallen state of man and the world—prehistoric because history and nature were not yet disjointed—symbolizing both the authentic meaning of existence and the actual nature of the sacred itself. Thus this primal symbol points both to the deepest meaning of the sacred, and to the path by which man *returns* (as in Taoism) to the sacred: "However, although this conception, in which all contraries are reconciled (or rather, transcended), constitutes what is, in fact, the most basic definition of divinity, and shows how utterly different it is from humanity, the *coincidentia oppositorum* becomes nevertheless an archetypal model for certain types of religious men, or for certain of the forms religious experience takes."[22] These forms are found at both the lowest and the highest levels of religion; at the most elementary level of religious life it appears in the orgy:

> So men lose their individuality in the orgy, combining into a single living unity. They effect thus a total fusion of emotions in which neither "form" nor "law" is observed. They try once more to enter the primal, pre-formal, chaotic state—a state that corresponds in the cosmological order to the chaotic formlessness before the creation. . . . And further, by bringing back the mythical chaos that existed before the creation, the orgy makes it possible for creation to be repeated. For a time man goes back to the amorphous, nocturnal state of chaos that he may be reborn, more vigorous than ever in his daylight self. Like immersion in water, the orgy destroys creation while at the same time regenerating it; man hopes, by identifying himself with formless, pre-cosmic existence, to return to himself restored and regenerated, in a word, "a new man."[23]

Unfortunately, Eliade has ignored Nietzsche in his elucidation of the meaning of the orgy, but one has only to recall that the young Nietzsche (following Schopenhauer) conceived of the Dionysian rapture as a shattering of the *principium individuationis;* and Nietzsche also saw that: "Not only does the bond between man and man come to be forged once more by the magic of the Dionysiac rite, but nature itself, long alienated or subjugated, rises again to celebrate the reconciliation with her prodigal son, man."[24] For Nietzsche, the Dionysian state is universal, but it received its fullest—and only aesthetic—expression in ancient Greece. The fullest statement of the meaning of the Dionysian ecstasy to be found in Greek literature is contained in an opening choral ode of *The Bacchae* of Euripides:

> O what delight is in the mountains!
> There the celebrant, wrapped in his sacred fawnskin,
> Flings himself on the ground surrendered,
> While the swift-footed company streams on;
> There he hunts for blood, and rapturously
> Eats the raw flesh of the slaughtered goat,
> Hurrying on to the Phrygian or Lydian mountain heights.
> Possessed, ecstatic, he leads their happy cries;
> The earth flows with milk, flows with wine,
> Flows with nectar of bees;
> The air is thick with a scent of Syrian myrrh.
> The celebrant runs entranced, whirling the torch
> That blazes red from the fennel-wand in his grasp,
> And with shouts he rouses the scattered bands,
> Sets their feet dancing,
> As he shakes his delicate locks to the wild wind.
> And amidst the frenzy of song he shouts like thunder:
> "On, on! Run, dance, delirious, possessed!
> You, the beauty and grace of golden Tmolus,
> Sing to the rattle of thunderous drums,
> Sing for joy,
> Praise Dionysus, god of joy!"[25]

In the wild ecstasy of the Dionysian orgy, man loses his historical existence, his differentiated and individual nature, and returns to the womb of nature: "While the transport of the Dionysiac state, with its suspension of all the ordinary barriers of existence, lasts, it carries with it a Lethean element in which everything that has been experienced by the individual is drowned."[26]

Clearly the *coincidentia oppositorum* is a religious goal bringing about a reintegration of man with the cosmos. But reintegration occurs only when all attributes disappear and all contraries are merged: this is the goal of the orgy, but so likewise is it the goal—although interiorly conceived—of the Oriental mystic.[27] The Indian and Chinese mystic strives to obliterate every sort of "extreme" from his consciousness, hoping to attain a state of perfect indifference and neutrality:

> This transcending of extremes through asceticism and contemplation also results in the "coincidence of opposites"; the consciousness of such a man knows no more conflict, and such pairs of opposites as pleasure and pain, desire and repulsion, cold and heat, the agreeable and the disagreeable are expunged from his awareness, while something is taking place within him which parallels the total realization of contraries within the divinity. . . . The neophyte begins by identifying all his experiences with the rhythms governing the universe (sun and moon), but once this "cosmisation" has been achieved, he turns all his efforts towards *unifying* the sun and moon, towards taking into himself the *cosmos as a whole;* he remakes in himself and for himself the primeval unity which was before the world was made; a unity which signifies not the chaos that existed before any forms were created, but the undifferentiated *being* in which all forms are merged.[28]

Although Eliade refuses to admit that there is a breach in continuity between archaic man and the mystic of the great historic religions,[29] it would appear that the mystical goal transcends the archaic goal insofar as it seeks not the precosmic chaos but the undifferentiated *being*—Nietzsche's "womb" of being—which paradoxically contains *all* reality within itself. Unlike archaic man, the mystic does not have the goal of repeating the creation, but rather of abolishing it, of radically and finally transcending it.[30] Eliade is ever in danger of identifying man's religious goal with his pristine and archaic state; but to do so is to dissolve the religious ground of the "fall" (which Tillich so clearly perceives), and to abandon a dialectical mode of understanding the sacred that is absolutely essential if the higher expressions of religion and the Incarnation itself are to become fully meaningful in their own terms.

III. Death and Yoga

As deeply as we may grant that the modern consciousness is grounded in the death of God, we cannot deny that this same consciousness, precisely in and through its grounding in the death of God, has given expression to profound religious vision. This paradox is nowhere more manifest than in the peculiarly modern experience of death, particularly as this experience has been articulated poetically by Rainer Maria Rilke, and philosophically—following Rilke—by Martin Heidegger. Nowhere, not even in Shakespeare, may one find a more profound vision of death than in Rilke's *Duino Elegies.* Writing to his Polish translator, Rilke said:

Affirmation of life-AND-death appears as one in the "Elegies." To grant one without the other is, so it is here learned and celebrated, a limitation which in the end shuts out all that is infinite. *Death* is the *side of life* averted from us, unshone upon by us: we must try to achieve the greatest consciousness of our existence which is at home in *both unbounded realms, inexhaustibly nourished from* both. . . . The true figure of life extends through *both* spheres, the blood of the mightiest circulation flows through *both: there is neither a here nor a beyond, but the great unity* . . . Transiency everywhere plunges into a deep being. And so all the configurations of the here and now are to be used not in a time-bound way only, but, as far as we are able, to be placed in those superior significances in which we have a share. But *not in the Christian sense* (from which I am more and more passionately moving away), but, in a purely earthly, deeply earthly, blissfully earthly consciousness, we must introduce what is *here* seen and touched into the wider, into the widest orbit. Not into a beyond whose shadow darkens the earth, but into a whole, into the *whole.*[31]

Here we find a radically modern coincidence of the opposites, following the mythical pattern it is true, but now that pattern is inverted, eternity becomes time, not time eternity, the beyond is drawn into the here and now, life and death are united by a total immersion in man's immediate existence (*Dasein*).[32]

The ecstatic celebration of Rilke's elegies are re-created in a conceptual form in Heidegger's understanding of authentic human existence as an "impassioned *freedom towards death.*"[33]

> The full existential-ontological conception of death may now be defined as follows: *death, as the end of Dasein, is Dasein's ownmost possibility—non-relational, certain and as such indefinite, not to be outstripped. Death* is, as *Dasein*'s end, in the Being of this entity *towards* its end. . . . But Being towards this possibility, as Being-towards-death, is so to comport ourselves towards *death* that in this Being, and for it, death reveals itself *as a possibility.* Our terminology for such Being towards this possibility is *"anticipation" of this possibility.*[34]

As always, Heidegger's thought straddles the borderline between the sacred and the profane, and despite Heidegger's nontheological intentions, his ideas are at least partially susceptible of translation into theological language. Thus the distinguished Catholic theologian, Karl Rahner, a former student of Heidegger's, has employed Heidegger in his elucidation of a contemporary Christian understanding of death:

> We have remarked before that it is in death, and in death alone, that man enters into an open, unrestricted relationship to the world as a whole. Only in death will man be integrated, as a constant and determining factor, into the world as a whole, through his own total reality achieved in his life and in his death. In other words, because death in some way opens to man the real-ontological relationship of his soul to the world as a whole, it is through his death that man in some way introduces as his contribution the result of his life into the basic, real oneness of the world.[35]

Applying this understanding of death to the doctrine of the atonement, Rahner can say that it is through Christ's death that his "spiritual reality," as enacted in his life and brought to consummation in his death, "becomes open to the whole world and is inserted into this world as a permanent destiny of

real-ontological kind"[36]—thus the death on the cross is fulfilled in Christ's descent into hell.

By raising the problem of the meaning of death in the
modern world, we have once again unveiled Eliade's deep roots
in the contemporary sensibility, but in such a way as to reveal
Eliade's deepest interest: the relation of modern man to the
whole horizon of the sacred. If every "fall" is a fall into "life,"
then a return to the sacred is effected by the reversal of life, by
an annihilation of the profane; in short, by an experience of
death. Eliade, throughout his career, has been fascinated by
the problem of ritual initiation, finding that a considerable
number of initiation rites and ordeals, which effect a transition
from the profane world to the sacred realm, force the novice to
undergo the experience of death: "Death prepares the new,
purely spiritual birth, access to a mode of being not subject
to the destroying action of Time."[37] Many of Eliade's most
profound insights revolve about death, perhaps nowhere else
is his religious genius so evident. But it is in his great book on
Yoga (1954) that Eliade brings together the theme of death
with the religious goal of the *coincidentia oppositorum*.

He connects the origins of Yoga with the protohistorical religion of India, maintaining that Yoga represents a living
fossil, "a modality of archaic spirituality that has survived
nowhere else";[38] and he finds the archaism of Yoga confirmed
by its initiatory structure:

> We have called attention to the yogic symbolism of death and
> rebirth—death to the profane human condition, rebirth to a
> transcendent modality. The yogin undertakes to "reverse" nor-
> mal behavior completely. He subjects himself to a petrified
> immobility of body, rhythmical breathing and arrest of breath,
> fixation of the psychomental flux, immobility of thought, the
> "arrest" and even the "return" of semen. On every level of
> human experience, he does the *opposite* of what life demands
> that he do. Now, the symbolism of the "opposite" indicates both
> the post-mortem condition and the condition of divinity. . . . The
> "reversal" of normal behavior sets the yogin outside of life. But

he does not stop halfway—death is followed by an initiatory
rebirth. The yogin makes for himself a "new body," just as the
neophyte in archaic societies is thought to obtain a new body
through initiation.[39]

Yoga continues the "immemorial symbolism" of initiation, in
other words, it finds its place in a universal religious tradition,
"the tradition that consists in anticipating death in order to
ensure rebirth in a sanctified life—that is, a life made *real* by
the incorporation of the sacred."[40] Nevertheless, Yoga is not to
be identified with archaic spirituality, as a comparison of Yoga
with shamanism makes clear. In their pursuit of the sacred,
both Yoga and shamanism abolish time and history, but the
shaman attains the sacred only momentarily in a state of
ecstasy, whereas the yogin has the goal of absolute freedom
(*samādhi*) where he "enjoys this nonconditioned situation con-
tinuously—that is, he has succeeded in definitively abolishing
time and history."[41]

Indian thought, from its very beginnings, was grounded in a
radical rejection of the "being" that is manifest in the world.
Indian texts, of all varieties, again and again repeat the thesis
that the cause of the soul's enslavement and consequently, "the
source of its endless sufferings lies in *man's solidarity with the
cosmos,* in his participation, active and passive, direct or in-
direct, in nature."[42] But here "cosmos" and "nature" mean a
desacralized world, a *profane* nature.

For Samkhya and Yoga, the world is *real* (not illusory— as it is,
for example, for Vedānta). Nevertheless, if the world *exists* and
endures, it is because of the "ignorance" of spirit; the innumerable forms of the cosmos, as well as their processes of manifestation and development, exist only in the measure to which the
Self (*purusa*) is ignorant of itself and, by reason of this metaphysical ignorance, suffers and is enslaved. At the precise moment when the last Self shall have found its freedom, the creation in its totality will be reabsorbed into the primordial
substance.[43]

Consequently, nature has no true ontological reality, and man's solidarity with the cosmos is the consequence of a progressive "desacralization" of human existence: hence the road toward freedom necessarily leads to a "desolidarization" from the profane life of a fallen cosmos.[44]

For Eliade, Yoga has the goal, not of an absolutely empty consciousness, but, on the contrary, of a state of consciousness that is emptied of all objects, thereby making possible a saturation with a direct and total intuition of "being."[45] By radically reversing the self that exists in the world, and by withdrawing to his own center by completely dissociating himself from the cosmos, the yogin gains real transcendence or absolute freedom, a state that he calls *samādhi*. And *samādhi* effects a coincidence of the opposites:

> It is true that, in this case, the coincidence is not merely symbolic, but concrete, experiential. Through *samādhi*, the yogin transcends the opposites and, in a unique experience, unites emptiness and superabundance, life and death, Being and nonbeing. Nor is this all. Like all paradoxical states, *samādhi* is equivalent to a reintegration of the different modalities of the real in a single modality—the undifferentiated completeness of precreation, the primordial Unity. The yogin who attains to *asamprajñāta samādhi* [the ecstasy induced by contemplation rather than meditation, where the differentiated consciousness vanishes] also realizes a dream that has obsessed the human spirit from the beginnings of its history—to coincide with the All, to recover Unity, to re-establish the initial nonduality, to abolish time and creation (i.e., the multiplicity and heterogeneity of the cosmos); in particular, to abolish the twofold division of the real into object-subject.[46]

However, the yogin, unlike archaic man, does not simply return to the *beginning;* he recovers the original situation enriched by the dimensions of "freedom" and "transconsciousness": "For, by liberating himself, man creates the spiritual dimension of freedom, and 'introduces' it into the cosmos and life—that is, into blind and tragically conditioned modes of existence."[47]

A favorite discipline of Indian mysticism is that of reliving one's past lives, and thus of traveling back through them to the primordial instant that launched the first existence. As Eliade says:

> One arrives at the beginning of time and finds nontime, the eternal present that preceded the temporal experience begun by the first fallen human life. In other words, one "touches" the nonconditioned state that preceded man's fall into time and the wheel of existence. This is as much as to say that, setting out from any moment of temporal duration, one can succeed in *exhausting* that duration by traveling through it in the reverse direction, and will finally reach nontime, eternity. But to do so was to transcend the human condition and enter *nirvana*.[48]

Nontime is the undiscriminated state of the original Totality, it is the "time" of the original undifferentiated state of all things, that primordial state which preceded the subject-object dichotomy, and which thus exists in a dialectically inverse relationship with the "time" of the cosmic process and of history. Yet Eliade is not satisfied with establishing a negative dialectical relationship between the two "times," but insists that in some sense the opposites must be united.

Consequently, he seizes upon Tantrism, and tantric yoga, as the religious form most fully exemplifying the union of the opposites (there can be little doubt of Eliade's deep attraction to Tantrism—an Indian religious way that Westerners have long looked upon as being no more than a sexual orgy—and, no doubt, this attraction is based in large measure upon the Tantric goal of reuniting man with the cosmos). The Tantric "void" (*sunya*) is not simply nonbeing; for Eliade, it is more like the *brahman* of the Vedānta.

> For tantric metaphysics, both Hindu and Buddhist, the absolute reality, the *Urgrund*, contains in itself all dualities and polarities, but reunited, reintegrated, in a state of absolute Unity (*advaya*). The creation, and the becoming that arose from it, represents the shattering of the primordial Unity and the separation of the two principles (Siva-Sakti, etc.); in consequence, man experiences a state of duality (object-subject, etc.)—and this is suffering,

illusion, "bondage." The purpose of tantric *sādhana* ["realization"] is the reunion of the two polar principles within the
disciple's own body.[49]

Tantrism strives to transcend the opposites, and it does so by
means of a reabsorption of the cosmos through inverting the
cosmic processes of "time." It has the goal of creating the coincidence of time and eternity, which on the purely "human"
plane is the reintegration of the primordial androgyny, "the
conjunction, in one's own being, of male and female—in a
word, the reconquest of the completeness that precedes all
creation."[50]

Eliade's book on Yoga is nothing less than a masterpiece of
modern scholarship and religious understanding, it is a book
that is unique of its kind, reflecting at once a long and deep
meditative immersion in the Yoga texts themselves, and an
incredible mastery of a wide range of scholarship dealing with
the various forms and expressions of this most basic of all
Indian religious ways. In this book, Eliade has done more than
repay his debt to his former Indian masters, he has portrayed
the world of the sacred—which Eliade believes received its
fullest expression in India—with a depth and power that is
without parallel in religious scholarship, and at the same time
has succeeded in making this world meaningful to the profane
mind of modern man. Throughout the book, one theme predominates: the recovery of the primordial Unity that preceded
the creation. While this theme is undoubtedly primary in
Yoga—at least in its Hindu forms—it is also paramount in
Eliade's lifework. Yet the highest expressions of Indian spirituality know other themes, particularly that of the Madhyamika
school's dialectical identification of *nirvana* (the radical sacred)
and *samsara* (the radical profane), which became the foundation of Mahayana Buddhism. Eliade has paid scant attention
to Madhyamika Buddhism, just as he has ignored the purely
mystical expressions of Taoism and the whole world of Zen
Buddhism. Can it be that Eliade is so bound to the Hindu
forms of spirituality that he is closed to the more radical

dialectical expressions of the sacred? If so, his own project of dialectically relating the sacred and the profane stands in danger of never being completed.

IV. Androgyny and Alchemy

Eliade believes that androgyny is the primary symbol of the primordial Totality.[51] Throughout the history of religions, in both its lower and its higher forms, androgyny has been a symbol of the prefallen state of man and the cosmos. On the archaic level of spirituality:

> Divine androgyny is simply a primitive formula for the divine bi-unity; mythological and religious thought, before expressing this concept of divine two-in-oneness in metaphysical terms (*esse* and *non esse*), or theological terms (the revealed and unrevealed), expressed it first in the biological terms of bisexuality. . . . And the divine androgyny which we find in so many myths and beliefs has its own theoretical significance. The real point of the formula is to express—in biological terms—the coexistence of contraries, of cosmological principles (male and female) within the heart of the divinity.[52]

Eliade has explored the symbol of androgyny in primitive religion, Hindu mythology, Tantrism, Christianity, and European romanticism (to say nothing of his early Romanian work, *Mitul Reintegraii,* which is unknown to this author).[53]

Paul's words in Gal. 3:28 are well known: "There is neither male nor female; for you are all one in Christ Jesus." Eliade also calls attention to an important text in the Gnostic Gospel of Thomas:

> Jesus said to them: "When you make the two one, and when you make the inner as the outer and the outer as the inner and the above as the below, and when you make the male and the female into a single one, so that the male will not be male and the female not be female, . . . then shall you enter the Kingdom." (Log. 22.)

Or, uniting this theme with one of Eliade's favorite New

Testament texts: "When you make the two one, you shall become sons of Man, and when you say: 'Mountain, be moved,' it will be moved" (log. 107).[54] Following Ernst Benz, Eliade shows that the primordial androgyny was a major motif in the mystical thought of Jacob Boehme, who conceived of the "fall" as a fall from androgyny, comparing the division of Adam's androgynous nature to the crucifixion of Christ.[55] This mystical theme appears once again in another Eastern Orthodox religious thinker, Nicolas Berdyaev:

> The great anthropological myth which alone can be the basis of anthropological metaphysic is the myth about the androgyne. . . . According to his Idea, to God's conception of him, man is a complete, masculinely feminine being, solar and teluric, logoic and cosmic at the same time. . . . Original sin is connected in the first instance with division into two sexes and the Fall of the androgyne, i.e., of man as a complete being.[56]

Nor should it be thought that the androgynous motif is limited to the religious sphere; one of the most gifted contemporary literary scholars, G. Wilson Knight, has concluded that: "the bisexual consciousness *is* the creative consciousness."[57]

From one point of view, it could be said that the symbol of androgyny is transsexual or even presexual, it gives witness to a primordial time when sex as we know it did not exist. Eliade himself has said that it is the idea of life which, projected on to the cosmos, sexualizes it.[58] But for Eliade, as we have seen, man knows "life" only through a "fall." Furthermore, androgynous symbols pervade alchemy, which has been one of the principal means by which man has attempted to reintegrate the cosmos with the sacred. Eliade has long been a student of alchemy, studying its expressions in Babylonia, China, India, and Europe, and finding, as might be expected, that its prehistory lies in primitive myth and ideology. With his goal of the transmutation of common metals into gold, the alchemist is collaborating in the work of nature, assisting it to give birth more rapidly by changing the modalities of matter. Thus Eliade conceives alchemy as follows:

The tendency of Nature is to perfection. But since gold is the bearer of a highly spiritual symbolism ("Gold is immortality," say the Indian texts repeatedly), it is obvious that a new idea is coming into being: the idea of the part assumed by the alchemist as the brotherly saviour of Nature. He assists Nature to fulfill her final goal, to attain her 'ideal', which is the perfection of its progeny—be it mineral, animal or human—to its supreme ripening, which is absolute immortality and liberty (gold being the symbol of sovereignty and autonomy).[59]

The great discovery of alchemy was that man could take upon himself the work of time, this idea is the basis and justification of the alchemical operation, the *opus alchymicum* that haunted the philosophic imagination for more than two thousand years: "the idea of the transmutation of man and the Cosmos by means of the Philosopher's Stone."[60]

While one of the primary sources of alchemy, according to Eliade, was the experience of primitive man engaged in mining, fusion, and smithcraft (men who were already embarking upon the 'conquest of matter'), and while the alchemical operation has its formal—and perhaps historical—antecedent in primitive initiation rites, nonetheless, alchemy represents a new situation of man in the cosmos, now man is the transformer of nature. Eliade says that the alchemists' innovation was that: "they projected on to Matter the initiatory function of suffering." "Thanks to the alchemical operations, corresponding to the tortures, death and resurrection of the initiate, the substance is transmuted, that is, attains a transcendental mode of being: it becomes gold."[61] Matter now acquires a spiritual dimension, but it does so, in Near Eastern and Western alchemy, because the alchemist treats his matter as the savior god was treated in the ancient mystery rites: "It is the mystical drama of the God—his passion, death and resurrection—which is projected on to matter in order to transmute it."[62] Western alchemists integrated their symbolism into Christian theology, thus the 'death' of matter was sanctified by the death of Christ who assured its redemption (in the alchemical operation, the metal must undergo an initiatory death by returning to its primal and precosmic state). Furthermore, the alchemical operation transforms the alchemist himself: "The Western alchemist by endeavoring to 'kill' the ingredients, to reduce them to the *materia prima,* provokes a *sympatheia* between the 'pathetic situations' of the substance and his innermost being."[63] One starts with the *materia prima* in order to arrive ultimately at the Philosopher's Stone.

Consequently, the intention of the Western alchemist was to effect a reconciliation of God with a fallen nature, to reintegrate the cosmos with the sacred.

> In the mind of many alchemists, the procuring of the Philosopher's Stone is equated with the perfect knowledge of God. This, moreover, is why the Stone makes possible the identification of opposites. According to Basil Valentine, "evil must become the same as good." Starkey describes the Stone as "the reconcilation of Contraries, a making of friendship between enemies." We are here face to face with the very old symbolism of the *coincidentia oppositorum,* universally widespread, well attested in primitive stages of culture, and which served more or less to define both the fundamental reality (the *Urgrund*), and the paradoxical state of the totality, the perfection and consequently the sacredness of God.[64]

The alchemist, in taking upon himself the responsibility of changing nature, puts himself in the place of time; but, for the alchemist, nature is a hierophany, it has a divine dimension, and it is thanks to this sacred quality that the freeing of nature from the laws of time went hand in hand with the deliverance of the alchemist himself. Eliade claims that the alchemists, in their desire to supersede time, "anticipated what is in fact the essence of the ideology of the modern world."[65] Modern man hopes to become nature's rival without being the slave of time; he takes upon himself the function of temporal duration; in other words, he takes on the role of time. Yet, the alchemist, unlike modern man, while putting himself in the place of time, took care not to assume its role: "He did not admit himself to be an essentially temporal being, he longed for the beatitude of paradise, aspired to eternity and pursued immortality, the *elixir vitae*."[66] The tragic grandeur of modern man lies in the fact that he took on the work of time not only in his relations with nature but also in respect to himself; modern man chose time, as opposed to eternity, he identified himself with time, thereby exercising a radically profane choice.

Eliade's major study of alchemy, published shortly after his books on shamanism and Yoga, brought him face to face with a problem that has obstructed his progress ever since: the positive religious significance of modern man's choice of the profane. Overwhelmed by the profoundly negative religious meaning of modern man's identification of himself with time—of his immersion in a wholly *profane reality*—Eliade cannot bring himself to face the full dialectical implications of a radical negation of the sacred. He refuses to conceive the possibility that an ultimate coincidence of the opposites could reconcile the radical sacred and the radical profane. Perhaps the closest that he comes to this possibility is with this statement: "But a reconciliation with temporality remains a possibility, given a more correct conception of Time."[67] Here lies the deepest religious problem facing contemporary man. Is a radically profane existence open to the sacred? Does the symbol of the *coincidentia oppositorum* finally promise a reconciliation of the sacred with the profane, an ultimate dialectical synthesis of man's two existential choices? Will the dichotomy of the sacred and the profane disappear in the deepest epiphany of the Real? Now this epiphany can never have appeared in the past—at least not in the historical past—if only because a radically profane mode of existence was created by modern man (as Nietzsche saw, the death of God is the most important event in history). If he is to meet this problem, perhaps Eliade will eventually be forced to arrive at a dialectical identification of the "nontime" before the creation with the full "time" of man's postsacred existence. Both "times" have an existential intensity and actuality that is present on no other plane of time, and, finally, to affirm the one and negate the other is to engage in either an ultimate negation of time and history or a final abolition of eternity. Can Eliade remain content with the idea that the goal of man's choice of the sacred is simply to arrive at a precosmic state?[68] If so, he will be forced to abandon both his dialectical method and his Christian ground. The remainder of this book will be devoted to exploring various approaches to the possibility of an ultimate dialectical reconciliation between the radical sacred and the radical profane.

5

Time and the Sacred

I. Modern Man and Time

WE NEED NOT hesitate to say that modern man is obsessed with time. Not only is time the horizon of his existence, but, as Eliade has taught us, modern man is unique insofar as he has identified himself with temporal duration, with the flow of concrete moments of time. In a remarkable passage in James Joyce's *Ulysses*, the young hero, Stephen Dedalus, expresses a theme that pervaded Joyce's work:

> —History, Stephen said, is a nightmare from which I am trying to awake.
> From the playfield the boys raised a shout. A whirring whistle: goal. What if that nightmare gave you a back kick?
> —The ways of the Creator are not our ways, Mr. Deasy said. All history moves towards one great goal, the manifestation of God.
> Stephen jerked his thumb towards the window, saying:
> —That is God.
> Hooray! Ay! Whrrwhee!
> —What? Mr. Deasy asked.
> —A shout in the street, Stephen answered, shrugging his shoulders.[1]

God, a shout in the street? What more apt image could be evoked to portray the meaning of a symbol of the Beyond immersed in a nightmare of time and history whose only witness

105

to eternity is the everlasting vacuity of its own nothingness?

Again, let us employ Heidegger's conceptual framework to elucidate the peculiar situation—the unique *Existenz*—of modern man:

> Although one can concern oneself with time in the manner which we have characterized—namely, by dating in terms of environmental events—this always happens basically within the horizon of that kind of concern with time which we know as astronomical and calendrical *time-reckoning*. Such reckoning does not occur by accident, but has its existential-ontological necessity in the basic state of *Dasein* as care. Because it is essential to *Dasein* that it exists fallingly as something thrown, it interprets its time concernfully by way of time-reckoning. *In this,* the 'real' *making-public* of time gets temporalized, so that we must say that *Dasein's thrownness is the reason why 'time is' time publicly.*[2]

This major thesis of *Being and Time* is carried forward in Heidegger's book on Kant, where time is linked with finitude. "More primordial than man is the finitude of the *Dasein* in him,"[3] and by virtue of the finitude of the *Dasein* in man, the comprehension of Being must be projected on time.[4] From the first, the struggle for Being has always taken place within the horizon of time, thus Being has always appeared through finitude:

> As a mode of Being, existence is in itself finitude and, as such, is only possible on the basis of the comprehension of Being. There is and must be such as Being only where finitude has become existent. The comprehension of Being which dominates human existence, although man is unaware of its breadth, constancy, and indeterminateness, is thus manifest as the innermost ground of human finitude.[5]

While this comprehension of Being is the innermost essence of finitude, it is nevertheless true that: "The finitude of *Dasein*—the comprehension of Being—lies in forgetfulness."[6] The ultimate *Seinsvergessenheit* (forgetfulness of Being) occurred in Nietzsche's nihilistic proclamation of the eternal recurrence of all things, but Nietzsche's proclamation was a prophetic vision of the deepest *being* of modern man: in renouncing the infinite, man has been swallowed up by finitude.

If we allow Heidegger to speak for the being that is manifest in our time, we could then say that genuinely contemporary human existence *is* finitude, that the nothingness which has been resurrected by the death of God is the source of the *Angst* that has identified being and time, that in the "night of the world" in which we live, transcendence can only appear as immanence, eternity can be present, if at all, only in time itself. But can a genuine epiphany of eternity in time take place in the context of such a mode of human existence? Is a radically profane mode of existence open to the presence of the sacred? Can eternity become manifest upon the plane of radical finitude? Such momentous issues as these cannot properly be formulated by means of abstract language, therefore one must turn to literature if one wishes to discover the record of the paradoxical pilgrimage of a radically finite mode of existence in quest of an unrealizable eternity. Indeed, this very pilgrimage was the primary motif of the work of two of our greatest novelists, Dostoevsky and Proust, whose novels— along with those of Kafka and Joyce—might almost be said to constitute a *Divina Commedia* of modern man.

II. Dostoevsky

Albert Camus interpreted Dostoevsky's novels as propounding a metaphysical problem, existence is illusory *or* it is eternal, and answering it: existence is illusory *and* it is eternal.[7] Granted that this interpretation oversimplifies Dostoevsky's work, it remains true that his novels do indeed revolve about some such paradox. No writer has simultaneously lived so deeply within the worlds of faith and unbelief. Immediately upon being released from prison, he wrote:

And yet God sometimes sends me moments of complete serenity. It is in such moments that I have composed in my mind a profession of faith, in which everything is clear and holy. This

profession of faith is very simple. This is what it is: to believe
that there is nothing finer, deeper, more lovable, more reason-
able, braver and more perfect than Christ; and, not only there
is nothing, but I tell myself with a jealous love, there cannot be
anything. More than that: if anyone had told me that Christ is
outside truth, and if it had really been established that truth
is outside Christ, I should have preferred to stay with Christ
rather than with truth.[8]

One suspects that already the young Dostoevsky knew that
Christ is outside truth, and although he never abandoned this
confession—it appears on the lips of Shatov in *The Possessed*—
his mature work witnesses to the death of God with a depth
and power that even Nietzsche could not surpass.

Dostoevsky dreamed of writing a comprehensive work, which
was originally to have been called *Atheism*, split up into five
novels, recounting "the life of a great sinner" and containing
"everything for which (he himself had) lived":

The chief problem, which will be propounded in all the different sections of the work, will be the one that has consciously
tortured me all my life: the problem of the existence of God.
In the course of his life the hero will be now an atheist, now a
believer, now a fanatic, now a heresiarch, and then an atheist
once more.[9]

Although this book was never written, it could be said that all
Dostoevsky's novels, as well as all his major characters, are
so many discordant parts of such a never-to-be-finished whole.
The title, *The Life of a Great Sinner*, is doubly significant, for
as Paul Evdokimoff has pointed out:

In Russian, the coupling of these words in itself brings out the
mystical character of the plan. The word *Jitie* (life) is the
Slavonic form of the word *jisn* (life), used only in hagiographic
language, for the life of a saint. This word denotes the essential
and complete orientation of a life towards God, life actually
in God. Sin is life outside God. In coupling these two notions,
Dostoyevsky wished to underline the paradoxical character of
human destiny.[10]

Thus it is that even the great atheists whom Dostoevsky created—Raskolnikov, Stavrogin, Kirillov, and Ivan Karamazov—
are simultaneously men of faith. The maddest of these is undoubtedly Kirillov (the young engineer who is writing a
treatise on suicide in *The Possessed*), yet he is Dostoevsky's
profoundest creation, and may be taken as embodying Dostoevsky's deepest religious vision.

"God has tormented me all my life," declares Kirillov,[11] the
God-obsessed atheist who has taken upon himself the project
of becoming God. Kirillov knows both that God is necessary
and so must exist and that he doesn't and can't exist.[12]

> "He does not exist, but He is. . . . God is the pain of the fear
> of death. He who will conquer pain and terror will become him-
> self a god. Then there will be a new life, a new man; everything
> will be new . . . then they will divide history into two parts:
> from the gorilla to the annihilation of God, and from the anni-
> hilation of God to . . . the transformation of the earth, and of
> man physically. Man will be God, and will be transformed
> physically, and the world will be transformed and things will
> be transformed and thoughts and all feelings."[13]

Everyone who wants the supreme freedom must dare to kill
himself; thereby he will discover the secret of the great decep-
tion of God, knowing that there is nothing beyond: "He who
dares kill himself is God."[14] Kirillov, whose favorite book is the
Apocalypse, and whose most cherished idea is the teaching of
the angel in the Apocalypse who declares that there will be no
more time, is an atheistic mystic who prays to everything, believes that all is good, and reverences Christ.

> "Listen to a great idea: there was a day on earth, and in the
> midst of the earth there stood three crosses. One on the Cross had
> such faith that he said to another, 'Today thou shalt be with
> me in Paradise.' The day ended; both died and passed away and
> found neither Paradise nor resurrection. His words did not come
> true. Listen: that Man was the loftiest of all on earth, He was
> that which gave meaning to life. The whole planet, with every-
> thing on it, is mere madness without that Man. There has never

been any like Him before or since, never, up to a miracle. For that is the miracle, that there never was nor never will be another like Him. And if that is so, if the laws of nature did not spare even Him, have not spared even their miracle and made even Him live in a lie and die for a lie, then all the planet is a lie and rests on a lie and on mockery. So then, the very laws of the planet are a lie and the vaudeville of devils. What is there to live for? Answer, if you are a man."[15]

Kirillov has no higher idea than disbelief in God, believing, furthermore, that he is the first one in history who would not invent God: "Man has done nothing but invent God so as to go on living, and not kill himself; that's the whole of universal history up till now."[16] Suffering from epilepsy, Kirillov has moments of eternal harmony, moments when time vanishes, and he is reconciled to existence in all its horror.

"There are seconds—they come five or six at a time—when you suddenly feel the presence of the eternal harmony perfectly attained. It's something not earthly—I don't mean in the sense that it's heavenly—but in that sense that man cannot endure it in his earthly aspect. He must be physically changed or die. This feeling is clear and unmistakable; it's as though you apprehend all nature and suddenly say, 'Yes, that's right.' God, when He created the world, said at the end of each day of creation, 'Yes, it's right, it's good.' It . . . it's not being deeply moved, but simply joy. You don't forgive anything because there is no more need of forgiveness. It's not that you don't love—oh, there's something in it higher than love—what's most awful is that it's terribly clear and such joy. If it lasted more than five seconds, the soul could not endure it and must perish. In those five seconds I live through a lifetime, and I'd give my whole life for them, because they are worth it. To endure ten seconds one must be physically changed."[17]

Not believing in a future eternal life, Kirillov believes in eternal life here and now, moments when time suddenly stands still and death no longer exists at all.[18] Kirillov longs for the supreme moment when time will become eternity, when by

killing himself—for in killing himself he kills the God who is
the pain of the fear of death—he will himself become God,
will become eternity.

In truth, Kirillov is enacting the role of Christ, is repeating
the crucifixion in a world in which God is dead. What a mar-
velous coincidence that Dostoevsky—who was ignorant of New
Testament scholarship—should have anticipated in his por-
trayal of Kirillov a radically modern understanding of Jesus
himself! Thus, Albert Schweitzer speaks of the historical Jesus
as follows:

> There is silence all around. The Baptist appears, and cries:
> "Repent, for the Kingdom of Heaven is at hand." Soon after
> that comes Jesus, and in the knowledge that He is the coming
> Son of Man lays hold of the wheel of the world to set it moving
> on that last revolution which is to bring all ordinary history to
> a close. It refuses to turn; and crushes Him. Instead of bringing
> in the eschatological conditions, He has destroyed them. The
> wheel rolls onward, and the mangled body of the one immeasur-
> ably great Man, who was strong enough to think of Himself as
> the spiritual ruler of mankind and to bend history to His pur-
> pose, is hanging upon it still. That is His victory and His reign.[19]

Kirillov, too, died an absurd death; he was crushed by the
wheel of history, by the laws of nature. Yet he died to liberate
mankind from the pain and terror of life, believing that his
death, because freely chosen—"the attribute of my godhead is
self-will"[20]—will create a new humanity, freed of all illusion,
for whom it will be the same whether to live or not to live.[21]

Having chosen total freedom, Kirillov must resist God because if God exists, "all is His will and from His will I cannot
escape." "If not, it's all my will and I am bound to show self-
will."[22] Such absolute freedom must manifest itself in an ultimate act of the will: suicide, a self-destruction abolishing
everything that threatens the sovereignty of the will. Dostoevsky associated the coming of Christ with the end of the
world—the end of time—thereby anticipating yet another
historical discovery of a later time; and this motif was deeply

embedded in Dostoevsky's conception of Kirillov, as the following dialogue between Kirillov and Stavrogin reveals:

"I am good."
"That I agree with, though," Stavrogin muttered, frowning.
"He who teaches that all are good will end the world."
"He who taught it was crucified."
"He will come, and his name will be the man-god."
"The god-man?"
"The man-god. That's the difference."[23]

Kirillov's independence, his new "terrible freedom," derives
from his realization of eternity, from his discovery of "man-
godhood." Russian Christianity had long known the ideal of
God-manhood, an ideal associated with a kenotic emptying of
human autonomy—hence the profound importance of the
'lacerations' theme of Dostoevsky's novels, particularly in *The
Brothers Karamazov*—and this ideal was later elaborated
philosophically by Dostoevsky's friend, Soloviëv. But Dostoevsky reversed this idea, almost in spite of himself, which is
certainly one reason why his atheists are so much more powerful than his saints. In the world that Dostoevsky created,
salvation and damnation are two sides of the same coin;
dialectical opposites that are united by a radically modern
coincidentia oppositorum. This explains Dostoevsky's deep
attraction to the Devil, his immersion in a demonic sensibility,
and his inability to portray a pure act of redemption.

How are we to look upon Kirillov theologically? First, there
can be little doubt that Dostoevsky intended Kirillov to be a
modern image of Christ; whether by way of parody, or saintly
imitation, or both, remains, of course, another matter. Second,
we can see that no character of Dostoevsky's is so deeply a
product of modern atheism as is Kirillov, whose whole life is
a continual proclamation of the death of God. Third, no other
character in Dostovesky—and certainly not Prince Myshkin in
The Idiot, whose character remains unresolved, both theologically and artistically—so fully realizes eternity. Fourth,
through no other character, and in no other novel, does Dosto-

evsky so clearly and so decisively present a gospel of redemption. Taken together, these points must mean that in Kirillov
we have Dostoevsky's fullest portrait of the "great sinner" who
is Christ and Antichrist at once, who undergoes a *descensus
ad inferos* that is paradoxically an ascent to heaven, thereby
reenacting—or repeating, re-presenting—Christ's redemptive
death on the cross in the context of an absolutely profane
world. All of Kirillov's acts embody Eliade's conception of
the sacred; yet each of them is wholly profane. Most deeply,
Kirillov's goal of "man-godhood" is not simply a blasphemous
reversal of God-manhood; it is a portrait of the only image of
redemption that could be meaningful in a world in which God
is dead. Finally, is it not possible to say that here Dostoevsky—
whatever may have been his conscious intention—was struggling to create a symbolical vision of a modern "coincidence
of the opposites"? If so, this would mean that in Kirillov we
have Dostoevsky's vision of a salvation reached through damnation, of an eternity realized through a total immersion in
time, of an imitation of Christ attained by way of Antichrist,
of the ultimate sacred known through the radically profane
way of "man-godhood."

At the very least Dostoevsky's novels demonstrate that a
Christian sensibility can be open to the profane—indeed, can
be immersed in the profane—while yet remaining indubitably
Christian. Moreover, Dostoevsky's vision of eternity (which
largely anticipated, as we shall see, Nietzsche's idea of Eternal
Recurrence) is sacred and profane at once; it remains deeply
rooted in the horizon of the sacred while being fully open to
the immediacy of the profane. Can it be denied that the overwhelming power of the world that Dostoevsky created derives
in large measure from its *simultaneous* participation in the
sacred and the profane? If not, then it follows that Dostoevsky
discovered a bridge between the sacred and the profane, a
bridge hitherto unknown, because prior to Dostoevsky's time
the death of God had not yet fully entered the consciousness
of Western man. Paradoxically, it was the deeply Christian

Dostoevsky who was the first to discover the creative power of the radically profane: like the shaman, Dostoevsky descended to the inferno of a demonic reality as a means of attaining the healing power of the sacred. Again, Dostoevsky, who realized so profoundly the chasm separating the sacred and the profane, nevertheless, in his greatest work, effected a reconciliation between the sacred and the profane, a reconciliation dissolving the boundaries between the saint and the sinner, faith and doubt, eternity and time. Consequently, Dostoevsky's vision is genuinely and radically dialectical; it points to that ultimate *coincidentia oppositorum* when the sacred will be identical with the profane, all things will be one, and God will be all in all.

Dostoevsky was the first Christian artist to give himself to a total affirmation of the profane. A comprehensive theological analysis of his novels would almost certainly reveal that his celebration of the demonic finally has its source in his faith itself, and this means in his faith in Christ. Through his novels we learn that the terrifying power of darkness is inseparable from the redemptive power of the sacred, that the deeper we are drawn into the *creative* depths of darkness the more real the actual presence of the sacred becomes. Thus it is by means of the very power of the demonic—of the profane—that an epiphany of the sacred occurs. Only a manifestation of the sacred that arises within the very heart of the profane could be meaningful or real to modern man, who is so deeply immersed in the profane. It is precisely his passionate affirmation of the profane that makes Dostoevsky's vision so real to modern man; and, dialectically, it is the power of the profane that makes possible a full epiphany of the sacred. Now the Incarnation has assumed a new meaning, a new dimension, a new epiphany: Dostoevsky's imitation of Christ—his repetition of the death on the cross and the descent into hell—has issued in a new resurrection. This supreme metamorphosis of modern faith has transformed the radical profane into the radical sacred; death has become life, time has become eternity. No longer does eternity lie in a beyond, it is *here* and *now*. Time is negated by being affirmed, and when time assumes its fullest reality, it gives witness to the deepest meaning of eternity.

III. Proust

Proust's novel *A la recherche du temps perdu* (literally translated, the 'search' or 'quest' for 'lost time') has often been considered the fullest stylistic expression of the art form of the novel; and, if the fullest, it is also the final, expression, for with Joyce the form of the novel is transcended, and thus dissolved. We must not consider Proust's work in isolation, it was the last flower of what Northrop Frye has called the ironic age of literature; and the ironic mode, for Frye, entails complete objectivity and the suppression of all explicit moral judgments, taking life exactly as it finds it.[24] The central theme of Proust's novel—which is accurately reflected in the title—is, according to Frye, the dominant theme of the ironic age:

> The poets who succeed the Romantics, the poets of French *symbolisme* for example, begin with the ironic gesture of turning away from the world of the market-place, with all its blurred sounds and imprecise meanings; they renounce rhetoric, moral judgement, and all other idols of the tribe, and devote their entire energy to the poet's literal function as a maker of poems. We said that the ironic fiction-writer is influenced by no considerations except craftsmanship, and the thematic poet in the ironic age thinks of himself more as a craftsman than as a creator or "unacknowledged legislator." That is, he makes the minimum claim for his personality and the maximum for his art—a contrast which underlies Yeats' theory of the poetic mask. At his best he is a dedicated spirit, a saint or anchorite of poetry. Flaubert, Rilke, Mallarmé, Proust, were all in their very different ways "pure" artists. Hence the central episodic theme is the theme of the pure but transient vision, the aesthetic or timeless moment, Rimbaud's *illumination,* Joyce's epiphany, the *Augenblick* of modern German thought, and the kind of non-didactic revelation implied in such terms as *symbolisme* and imagism.[25]

Let us grant, then, that the form of Proust's vision is not wholly unique. Yet in no other work of literature does the modern consciousness receive so full an expression, nowhere else may one find so many facets of that consciousness brought to light. In this novel, the 'inner self' of modern man is illuminated, but illuminated with such power that it breaks into a thousand fragments, and ultimately disappears.

Atheism was so deeply rooted in Proust's vision that he is perhaps the one major modern writer who never betrays the slightest anxiety in the presence of the sacred. All tension between the sacred and the profane has disappeared from Proust's sensibility; here we find the modern consciousness in its most profane form; so profane, indeed, that in losing its dialectical relationship to the sacred, it ceases, in a very real sense, to be 'profane.' Immediately, however, a paradox confronts us: lying at the center of this profane vision—and likewise at the center of the novel—is a genuinely mystical experience. As we shall see, the Proustian "ecstasy" (his own word)[26] preserves all the major forms of the classical mystical experience. Thus, a leading interpreter of Oriental mysticism, R. C. Zaehner, has discovered in Proust a nature or "pan-enhenic" mysticism, with a Buddhist form, in which, however, there is no merging into nature, but only a complete realization of self.[27] Zaehner employs the category of "profane mysticism" to describe the visions both of Proust and Rimbaud, and sees in these visions a peculiarly modern form of religious experience: thus providing a remarkable confirmation of Rudolf Otto's thesis that the religious faculty is universal, it is *a priori* and autonomous, operating even in the presence of the death of God.

Although *A la recherche du temps perdu* is frequently interpreted as a record of the decline and fall of the French aristocracy, it may more properly be considered an ecstatic yet fully orchestrated vision of the dissolution of the self of Western man. This accounts for the baffling fact that the novel, unconsciously as it were, reproduces the form of Buddhist mysticism, while yet remaining so fully open to the depths and powers of the Western psyche. Through the eyes of the narrator, we see the whole world collapsing about us, but this world is not another world, it is our own. As Proust says, "each reader reads only what is already within himself";[28] and his reader, like the Buddhist novice, is forced to undergo a collapse of his inner self. One by one the reader lives through a passing away of all those realities and moral values of the self which we so passionately cherish: love, friendship, human society, and all temporal pleasures whatsoever. Following the Buddhist pattern, the individual person dissolves into a maelstrom of a seemingly infinite number of disparate fragments, each one dying that the other may be born, thereby removing all genuine continuity between the fragments of a self in time. Samuel Beckett, in his book on Proust, has spoken of tragedy as the expiation of original sin;[29] from this point of view, Proust's novel might be looked upon as an expiation of the original sin of Western man, his choice of autonomous selfhood.

If it is possible to make moral judgments in the presence of Proust—and one cannot do so while remaining bound to his vision—then his novel is deeply immoral, perhaps the most immoral novel that has ever been written, and immoral because it destroys the grounds of moral judgment. Who but Proust could have written, "As soon as one is unhappy one becomes moral"?[30] Yet few writers have had such a profound sense of the creative value of suffering, and Proust could also say: "As for happiness, it has hardly more than one useful quality, namely to make unhappiness possible."[31] Sorrow pervades this novel, a sorrow that can be removed only by oblivion, and a sorrow that makes possible a realization of the vacuity of the self, an inner realization of the totally destructive power of time. Believing that the mind is everything, that is to say in the purely mental character of reality,[32] Proust believes that: "Only the subjective impression, however inferior the material may seem to be and however improbable the outline, is a criterion of truth and for that reason it alone merits being apprehended by the mind, for it alone is able, if the mind can extract this truth, to lead the mind to a greater perfection and impart to it a pure joy."[33] The "subjective impression" belongs to the province of art, for the artistic sense is submission to subjective reality, and "art is the most real of all things, the sternest school in life and truly the Last Judgment."[34] As always, Proust has ingenuously chosen his metaphor, for with Proust art becomes eschatological, it resurrects for us the reality from which we have become removed by the acts of the intellect, reversing what we know as "life," in order to make possible a "revelation," a "vision."[35]

Georges Poulet interprets *A la recherche du temps perdu* as a novel of redemption, opening with a self who has lost his "being" because memory and the past have been lost, and culminating in a "human eternity," where time is transcended by being regained.

> Proust's novel is the history of a search: that is to say a series of efforts to *find again* something that one has lost. It is the novel of an existence in search of its essence.
>
> .   .   .   .
>
> The human being, for Proust, therefore is a being who tries to find justification for his existence. Not knowing who he is, either he is like someone stricken with amnesia who goes from door to door asking people to tell him his name, or he feels himself to be what things indifferently become in him: a bundle of anonymous images that obliterate themselves and reform, like the iridescent spray from fountains of water. He is nothing or anything by turns, anything which is still nothing. Now this being who is nothing finds himself thrown into a moment lost in the midst of others, that is to say, a moment which resembles nothing and rests on nothing.[36]

This present instant, which is inevitably going to be annihilated by another, is too meaningless and too painful in its nakedness to be endured by the self which it encloses. Yet hope in the future is both absurd and impossible; therefore existence

in the present can be transcended only by recapturing the past.
Thus Poulet does not hesitate to say that memory plays the
same role in Proustian thought as grace in Christian thought.[37]
A memory no longer supernatural, but a "fallen" memory that
cannot by its own power restore us to that primordial state
which we seek; it occurs only by chance, but then it offers us
an invitation to transcendence.

As Poulet defines it, Proust's problem revolves about a
transformation of the present, a transformation allowing the
present to become past, an exterior perception to become
memory, thereby transmuting an exterior object into an interior and immaterial reality. This "spiritualization of the
object," according to Poulet, is an operation by which, *"in
miming within his own depths the exterior gesture of the
sensible object,* one *imagines,* one creates something which is
still the object of sense, but this time no longer outside: rather
it is on the inside, no longer strange and impenetrable, but
recognizable, identifiable: for this thing comes of us; it is us."[38]
Consequently, an "essential self" has been created—a self outside of time and contingency—by a "metaphoric" memory, a
memory uniting a regained sensation with a present sensation,
and by this means transmuting the present moment into time-
lessness. Poulet's interpretation of Proust places an enormous
burden upon the past, as he himself remarks: "In the Proustian
world, it is not God, it is simply the past which confers on the
present its authentic existence."[39] Now there is no doubt that
the past plays a central role in Proust's vision, one has only to
remember the famous Proustian statement that the only true
paradise is always the paradise that we have lost.[40] But Poulet's
analysis, brilliant as it is, fails to account for Proust's realization of eternity, it cannot explain how the recovery of lost
time can so radically transform the present, and this because
Poulet regards the Proustian past as "simply the past," thereby
disregarding its genuinely mystical qualities.

Proust presents a concrete analysis of his process of recovering the past in *The Past Recaptured,* the final volume of the

novel, which we now know was entirely conceived, if not entirely written, before any other portion of the work.[41] An un-
expected moment has just occurred, when the narrator, thoroughly disillusioned with life, is about to enter a reception at
the Princess de Guermantes. He has accidentally struck his
foot against a stone, and immediately all his discouragement
vanishes before an ecstatic feeling of happiness. Quickly he
discovers that the ecstasy was not induced by the action of
stumbling: "Each time that I merely repeated the action
physically, the effort was in vain; but if I forgot the Guermantes reception and succeeded in recapturing the sensation
I had felt the instant I placed my feet in that position, again
the dazzling, elusive vision brushed me with its wings, as if to
say, 'Seize me in my flight, if you have the power, and try to
solve the riddle of happiness which I propound to you.' "[42]

Despite his inclination to remain outside, the narrator enters
the house, and while waiting in a small library, hears a servant
accidentally strike a spoon against a plate, and immediately
the ecstatic sensation recurs, carrying him back to moments in
the past which now, for the first time, he can enjoy. Then,
within seconds, he wipes his mouth with a napkin, and the
sensation occurs once more.

> The impression was so vivid that the moment I was re-living
> fused with the real present. . . . I thought the servant had
> just opened the window toward the beach and everything called
> me to go down and stroll along the embankment at high tide;
> the napkin which I had taken to wipe my mouth had precisely
> the same sort of starchy stiffness as the towel with which I had
> so much trouble drying myself before the window the first day
> of my stay at Balbec, and now, in this library of the Guermantes
> mansion, it spread out in its various folds and creases, like a
> peacock's tail, the plumage of a green and blue ocean. And I
> drew enjoyment, not only from those colours, but from a whole
> moment of my life which had brought them into being and had
> no doubt been an aspiration toward them, but which perhaps
> some feeling of fatigue or sadness had prevented me from en-
> joying at Balbec and which now, pure and disembodied, freed

from all the imperfections of objective perception, filled me with
joy.[43]

He had known such experiences before, while a child at Com-
bray in tasting the little *madeleine,* and much later, when
standing upon two uneven flagstones in the baptistry of St.
Mark's at Venice; but never before had the experiences had
such intensity, and only now, at the end of the novel, does he
realize their meaning.

Proust brings light to this experience by means of his theory
that we can never enjoy the present moment because the
imagination, our sole organ of enjoyment, is not able to function in the present, by virtue of the "inexorable law" that
decrees that only that which is absent can be imagined. He
goes on to say that this harsh law was neutralized or suspended
by a "miraculous expedient" of nature by which a sensation
"was reflected both in the past (which made it possible for my
imagination to take pleasure in it) and in the present, the
physical stimulus of the sound or the contact with the stones
adding to the dreams of the imagination that which they
usually lack, the idea of existence—and this subterfuge made
it possible for the being within me to seize, isolate, immobilise
for the duration of a lightning flash what it never apprehends,
namely, a fragment of time in its pure state."[44] One might also
note that the form of the Proustian ecstasy coincides almost
exactly with the *satori* experience of Zen Buddhism, an accidental event provokes a transformation of consciousness in
which the mind is shattered and the primordial *Tao* is momentarily made incarnate. Proust himself, moreover, freely
confesses the mystical nature of his experience:

But let a sound already heard or an odour caught in bygone
years be sensed anew, simultaneously in the present and the past,
real without being of the present moment, ideal but not abstract,
and immediately the permanent essence of things, usually con-
cealed, is set free and our true self, which had long seemed dead
but was not dead in other ways, awakes, takes on fresh life as
it receives the celestial nourishment brought to it. A single

minute released from the chronological order of time has re-
created in us the human being similarly released, in order that
he may sense that minute. And one comprehends readily how
such a one can be confident in his joy; even though the mere
taste of a *madeleine* does not seem to contain logical justification
for this joy, it is easy to understand that the word 'death' should
have no meaning for him; situated outside the scope of time,
what could he fear from the future?[45]

Thus Proust can go so far as to employ the traditional language of the mystics, saying that the person who comes into
play in this experience is a "timeless person," existing entirely
outside of time.[46]

Undoubtedly the crux of the problem posed by the Proustian ecstasy is the fusion of past and present, a conjunction
that miraculously makes possible a momentary realization of
eternity. Following the classical pattern of the mystical experience, it is only when all immediate activity and enjoyment
is suspended that the "timeless person" becomes manifest; but
the uniquely Proustian dimension of the experience is provided by the "miracle" of a resemblance with things past
enabling the self to escape out of the present moment.[47] Furthermore, the past that the Proustian remembrance recovers
is a moment of time in its pure state, wholly isolated from
contact with the vacuity of the present:

The slightest word we have spoken or the most insignificant
gesture we have made at a certain moment in our life was sur-
rounded and illumined by things that logically had no relation
to it and were separated from it by our intelligence, which had
no need of them for reasoning purposes; and yet, in the midst
of these irrelevant objects . . . the most insignificant gesture,
the simplest act remained enclosed, as it were, in a thousand
sealed jars, each filled with things of an absolutely different
colour, odour and temperature. . . . Yes, if, thanks to our ability
to forget, a past recollection has been able to avoid any tie, any
link with the present moment, if it has remained in its own
place and time, if it has kept its distance, its isolation in the
depths of a valley or on the tip of a mountain peak, it suddenly

brings us a breath of fresh air—refreshing just because we have
breathed it once before—of that purer air which the poets have
vainly tried to establish in Paradise, whereas it could not con-
vey that profound sense of renewal if it had not already been
breathed, for the only true paradise is always the paradise we
have lost.[48]

In this, the best-known of all passages in Proust's work, we find
that it is our ability to *forget* which isolates a moment of past
time and thus makes possible its preservation in a pure state.
Only when we are released from all attachment to the present,
and in this detached state undergo an *accidental* experience
which coincides with a past moment of time that we have
preserved in its pure state, does the Proustian ecstasy occur.

What does the accidental sensation—the taste of the *madeleine,* the stumbling against the stone, etc.—supply to this
experience? Proust has told us that it brings the "idea of existence" to the dreams of the imagination, supplying them with
that which otherwise they would lack, *reality* itself. And it is
a moment of *real* time that has been preserved in a pure state,
a moment that is real because it once occurred in the present;
its subsequent isolation from the present made possible its
"spiritualization," but this pure moment can never become
eternity—can never be realized in ecstasy—until it is united
with the reality of the present moment, and in such a way as
to touch the *reality* of the present without in any way becoming involved with the viscissitudes of time. Thus the *reality*
of the present moment is absolutely essential to the Proustian
ecstasy: eternity occurs *here* and *now,* it is conceived neither
as a celestial beyond nor as a primordial moment of time.
Indeed, it is only when every shadow of a transcendent reality
has been obliterated that the Proustian eternity can dawn.

What are the primary theological conclusions that are to be
drawn from Proust's vision of eternity? First, a mystical experience and a mystical process of spiritualizing a state of
consciousness by isolating it from time, can occur in a radically
profane sensibility, and in the historical situation created by

the death of God. Second, a mystical experience of this profane type is in continuity with the classical form of the mystical experience, particularly insofar as it depends upon an isolation of consciousness from time, and upon an attitude of detachment from all forms of existence in time: thus Proust's vision of the dissolution of the self was an absolutely essential presupposition for his realization of eternity. Third, the Proustian ecstasy is in radical discontinuity with the traditional forms of mystical experience insofar as it revolves about the recovery of a pure moment of *concrete* time. Once again we are witnessing the birth of a uniquely modern *coincidentia oppositorum*. Time is regained by being negated, and when it is totally negated, it is regained as eternity. Not only does eternity occur *in* the present moment, it occurs *as* the present moment —and as the present moment alone—and in such a way as to identify existence in time with eternity itself. This realization of time as eternity is possible only through an absolute negation of time; but this negation must be dialectical, which means that ultimately it must be affirmation. Only in the horizon created by the death of God can human existence give itself to such a total affirmation of time. If time now becomes eternity, it does so only through the absence of faith; yet this wholly immanent eternity coincides with the highest expressions of faith.[49] Eternity has become *real,* and it has done so with such power as to at least momentarily transform time into eternity, exactly as it does in all of the higher expressions of religion; only here, in its profane form, eternity has become the concrete, present moment itself.

6

Space and the Sacred

I. Modern Man and Space

ONLY YESTERDAY, it would seem, reason was thought to be autonomous; and space and time to be universally identical, if not *a priori*, categories, operative everywhere, and everywhere providing human consciousness with a common framework. Today we know better. For we know, or think we know, that space and time can be judged to be universal categories in this sense only by a process of abstraction. In fact, space and time assume a different meaning—if not a different reality—in accordance with the way in which they are experienced (scientific, economic, aesthetic, etc.), to say nothing of the fact that differing historical situations create distinctly different ways of knowing time and space. One glance at a Chinese landscape painting should provide a sufficient corrective for anyone still naïve enough to believe that all men know and experience a common spatiotemporal world. Certainly the student of the history of religions knows full well that the space which is symbolized in myth and ritual differs profoundly from the space that is known by the modern consciousness. Our problem in this chapter will be to assess the relationship between sacred space and profane space, and, most particularly, to see if a dialectical relationship exists between these radically different forms of man's encounter with the world.

In his essay on Kafka, Erich Heller has spoken of "negative transcendence," in the context of his thesis that Kafka's world is an epiphany of the demonic sacred. Heller's analysis of *The Castle* does much to illuminate a peculiarly modern experience of space:

> In his personal confessions Kafka never, not once, utters the belief that the incessant striving of his spirit was directed towards God, or prompted by *amor Dei*. All the time his soul is preoccupied with the power of Evil; a power so great that God had to retreat before it into purest transcendence, for ever out of reach of life. Life itself is the incarnation of Evil: "Knowledge of the diabolical there can be, but no belief in it, for there is nothing more diabolical than what exists." And then again the reality of life, still identical with Evil, is denied completely: "There is only a spiritual world; what we call the physical world is the evil in the spiritual one. . . ." Thus the idea of final authority, merely by assuming the shape of physical reality in *The Castle*, falls, without the author either willing it or being able to help it, under the spell of Evil. It is the paradox of spiritual absolutism that the slightest touch of concreteness will poison the purest substance of the spirit, and one ray of darkness blot out a world of light.[1]

Heller admits, however, that Kafka is not a dogmatic follower of Gnosticism, and while no comfort can be found *within* this world, yet the power, not only to experience, but poetically to create, this world, must have its source *outside:* "Only a mind keeping alive in at least one of its recesses the memory of a place where the soul is truly at home, is able to contemplate with such creative vigour the struggles of a soul lost in a hostile land; and only an immensity of goodness can be so helplessly overcome by the vision of the worst of all possible worlds."[2]

Unquestionably Kafka's notes, stories, and novels supply one of our most important records of modern man's interior experience of space; and although an analysis of his work will not be attempted here, it is nevertheless essential to this argument to unveil the problem posed by the depth with which

Kafka could open himself to what Heller has so aptly called "negative transcendence." There is much to be said for Martin Buber's judgment that, despite everything, Kafka remained a Jew, and thus was ultimately unable to dissociate God from the creation. In accordance with his understanding of the "eclipse" of God from our time, Buber can say of Kafka:

> God is hiding Himself from the time in which he lives, and so from him, its most exposed son; but in the fact of God's being only hidden, which he knows, he is safe. . . . His unexpressed, ever-present theme is the remoteness of the judge, the remoteness of the lord of the castle, the hiddenness, the eclipse, the darkness; and therefore he observes: "He who believes can experience no miracles. During the day one does not see any stars."[3]

This interpretation of Kafka is somewhat strained, if only because of Kafka's deeply ambivalent relationship to Judaism; furthermore, it is difficult to imagine that Kafka's vision, which has had such an immense impact upon the contemporary sensibility, could be so specifically Jewish. Nevertheless, the paradox remains that Kafka's terrifying vision of the world, which surpasses even Gnostic mythology in its portrait of the evil of being, is somehow grounded in acceptance and affirmation.

Buber believes that the world of "I-It" has become dominant in our time, as the "eternal Thou" has receded into darkness. But he also believes that fate becomes more oppressive in each new historical age, and "turning" or faith more shattering. Thus he concludes *I and Thou* with these words:

> History is a mysterious approach. Every spiral of its way leads us both into profounder perversion and more fundamental turning. But the event that from the side of the world is called turning is called from God's side redemption.[4]

The very "turning" to which we are called must go hand in hand with "perversion"; for the truly contemporary believer is inevitably destined to share all the perversity of a world in which God is dead. At this point, Kafka's work can bring light to our Christian dilemma. Granting that Kafka's vision is pervaded by a negative transcendence, is it really possible that a negative transcendence can finally be detached from a positive transcendence? Or, employing Rudolf Otto's categories in a different context, can the numinous manifest itself as *mysterium tremendum* wholly apart from its parallel manifestation as *mysterium fascinosum?* Three aphorisms from Kafka's "Reflections on Sin, Suffering, Hope, and the True Way" illustrate Kafka's paradoxical acceptance of a demonic world:

> Beyond a certain point there is no return. This point has to be reached.
>
> . . . .
>
> If you were walking across a plain, had an honest intention of walking on, and yet kept regressing, then it would be a desperate matter; but since you are scrambling up a cliff, about as steep as you yourself are if seen from below, the regression can only be caused by the nature of the ground, and you must not despair.
>
> . . . .
>
> Expulsion from Paradise is in its main aspect eternal; that is to say, although expulsion from Paradise is final, and life in the world unavoidable, the eternity of the process (or, expressed in temporal terms, the eternal repetition of the process) nevertheless makes it possible not only that we might remain in Paradise permanently, but that we may in fact be there permanently, no matter whether we know it here or not.[5]

Thus, the same Kafka who could speak of this world as our going astray,[6] could speak—although ambivalently—of our existence here as Paradise. Our regression in the world is caused by the nature of the ground; yet we must reach the "point" from which there is no return.

Here, Kafka's symbolical language reproduces an ancient symbol of mythical language, the symbol of the "Center," a symbol that has long attracted the interest of Eliade. The mythical center is preeminently the zone of the sacred, the zone of absolute reality; with a history at least as old as shamanism, this center is associated with sacred trees, mountains, and cities, and is thought to be the meeting point of heaven, earth, and hell. As Eliade says:

> In archaic and traditional societies, the surrounding world is conceived as a microcosm. At the limits of this closed world begins the domain of the unknown, of the formless. On this side there is ordered—because inhabited and organised—space; on the other, outside this familiar space, there is the unknown and dangerous region of the demons, the ghosts, the dead and of foreigners—in a word, chaos or death or night.[7]

Every microcosm has a "Center," where the sacred manifests itself in all its totality; outside of this center there is only void and nothingness. Now Eliade believes that man can "live" only in a *sacred space*, only in the "Center." Man's longing for this mythical center betrays once again a nostalgia for Paradise: "By this we mean the desire to *find oneself always and without effort* in the Center of the World, at the heart of reality; and by a short cut and in a natural manner to transcend the human condition, and to recover the divine condition—as a Christian would say, the condition before the fall."[8]

Kafka abandons the "short cut" and the "natural manner," dissolves the line between sacred space and chaos, and, in rejecting what has now become a futile quest for a prefallen state, was able to open himself to *this* world, in all its horror and nothingness, as the "Center," the point from which there is no return. True, Kafka's image of the castle—as well as the numerous images of space that play so central a role in his work as a whole—is a symbolic portrait of the demonic sacred; yet Kafka finds a "Center" in this demonic nothingness, it is the heart of reality, and precisely for this reason Kafka can meet it with acceptance and affirmation, agonizing as this acceptance may be. Heller has said that Kafka presents us with the modern mind living in sin with the soul of Abraham.

Thus he knows two things at once, and both with equal as-
surance: that there *is* no God, and that there *must* be God.
It is the perspective of the curse: the intellect dreaming its
dream of absolute freedom, and the soul knowing of its terrible
bondage. The conviction of damnation is all that is left of faith,
standing out like a rock in a landscape the softer soil of which
has been eroded by the critical intellect. Kafka once said: "I
ought to welcome eternity, but to find it makes me sad."[9]

We must realize, however, that the sense of damnation is a
product of faith, that here faith is engaging in a confronta-
tion with the "curse" of a Godless world, and that simply to
meet the naked horror of this world with the stance of faith is
itself a manifestation of faith. If it is not a misnomer to speak
of 'modern faith,' then Kafka is surely a pilgrim of faith for
the modern world. Finally, the Christian too must follow
Kafka, and say with Buber: "That He hides Himself does not
diminish the immediacy; in the immediacy He remains the
Savior and the contradiction of existence becomes for us a
theophany."[10]

II. Sartre

In an article on the mysticism of Simone Weil, Susan Anima
Taubes speaks of an "atheistic mysticism," a mysticism created
in the context of the modern experience of the absence of God:

Atheism, which used to be a charge leveled against skeptics, un-
believers, or simply the indifferent, has come to mean a *religious*
experience of the death of God. The godlessness of the world in
all its strata and categories becomes, paradoxically and by a
dialectic of negation, the signature of God and yields a mystical
atheism, a theology of divine absence and nonbeing, of divine
impotence, divine nonintervention, and divine indifference.[11]

Surely no sensitive interpreter of literature could deny that a
genuine religious sensibility is present in the work of such
writers as Baudelaire, Rimbaud, Rilke, Camus, and Beckett;
yet neither can it be denied that this same sensibility is rooted
in a radical atheism. Let us follow Susan Anima Taubes in

speaking of such atheism as a *"religious* experience of the death of God." She has also seen that this atheism is produced by a dialectic of negation; the very denial of God, man's deepest rebellion against God, creates a religious response to his absence. Man inverts the relationship between the sacred and the profane, elevating the profane to the level of the sacred, and reducing the sacred to the level of the profane.

Allowing the word 'mystical' to be employed in referring to this unique religious experience of our time, it does not seem amiss to interpret the philosophical system of Jean-Paul Sartre as being grounded in atheistic mysticism. Indeed, Sartre has provided a mystical theology for the atheistic mystic, and, as will be seen, his most basic ontological categories are derived from the death of God. Already a mystical response, although a negative one, to the Godlessness of the world is present in Sartre's first and most important novel, *Nausea*. This novel revolves about a primal experience of nausea produced by man's naked encounter with the world, an experience of deep revulsion against the shear 'isness' of the world. Antoine Roquentin, the diarist who is the hero or the anti-hero of the novel (and who is at least an unconscious repetition of Dostoevsky's underground man), has a dread of touching objects, because they are not alive, they are only to be used, not lived among. His first real experience of nausea comes when he holds a stone, thus reversing archaic man's experience of the sacred stone:

> Now I see: I recall better what I felt the other day at the seashore when I held a pebble. It was a sort of sweetish sickness. How unpleasant it was! It came from the stone, I'm sure of it, it passed from the stone to my hand. Yes, that's it, that's just it —a sort of nausea in the hands.[12]

Nor is nausea produced only by natural objects:

> The Nausea is not inside me: I feel it *out there* in the wall, in the suspenders, everywhere around me. It makes itself one with the cafe, I am the one who is within *it*.[13]

When man opens himself to the naked *reality* of the world, its very 'isness' overwhelms and engulfs him.

In this novel, Sartre introduces one of his most important philosophical categories, *de trop* ('too much'), to characterize human existence in its relation to the world: "But my place is nowhere; I am unwanted, *de trop*."[14] Even suicide is denied Roquentin because:

> My death would have been *In the way* [*de trop*]. *In the way*, my corpse, my blood on these stones, between these plants, at the back of this smiling garden. And the decomposed flesh would have been *In the way* in the earth which would receive my bones, at last, cleaned, stripped, peeled, proper and clean as teeth, it would have been *In the way:* I was *In the way* for eternity.[15]

This experience brings Roquentin not the idea, but the actual feeling, of the absurdity of existence: "And without formulating anything clearly, I understood that I had found the key to Existence, the key to my Nauseas, to my own life."[16]

> This moment was extraordinary. I was there, motionless and icy, plunged in a horrible ecstasy. But something fresh had just appeared in the very heart of this ecstasy: I understood the Nausea, I possessed it. To tell the truth, I did not formulate my discoveries to myself. But I think it would be easy for me to put them in words now. The essential thing is contingency. I mean that one cannot define existence as necessity. To exist is simply *to be there* . . . . No necessary being can explain existence: contingency is not a delusion, a probability which can be dissipated; it is the absolute, consequently, the perfect free gift.[17]

Sartre tries but fails in this novel to create an acceptance of nausea—by Roquentin's ritual-like listening to a record of a Negro jazz singer (Billie Holiday?) singing "Some of These Days." Yet he succeeds marvelously in re-creating the actual experience of the radical contingency of existence, an experience made possible by nausea, by an interior contact with the brute reality of being.

The insights of his first novel lie at the core of Sartre's *magnum opus, Being and Nothingness* (where nausea becomes

the taste of the facticity of existence), for his philosophical
system revolves about the chasm between consciousness and
being. Abandoning the classical distinction between being and
appearance, Sartre introduces a "new" dualism, that between
the finite and the infinite, a dualism created by Sartre's primary
ontological categories of human consciousness (*pour-soi,* 'For-
itself') and being (*en-soi,* 'In-itself'). It is clearly apparent that
Sartre's deepest concern throughout his work is the preservation of human freedom; but so great is the threat of the sheer
reality of the world that ontologically this can be accomplished
only by drawing an absolute distinction between man and
being. Sartre's goal is to make consciousness the sole cause of
its own existence, but to do so he must identify consciousness
as pure appearance: "But it is precisely because consciousness
is pure appearance, because it is total emptiness (since the
entire world is outside it)—it is because of this identity of
appearance and existence within it that it can be considered
as the absolute."[18] Only by engaging in a radical negation of
being can consciousness come into existence. Thus Sartre defines consciousness as follows:

> The human being is not only the being by whom *négatités* are
> disclosed in the world; he is also the one who can take negative
> attitudes with respect to himself. In our Introduction we defined
> consciousness as "a being such that in its being, its being is in
> question in so far as this being implies a being other than itself."
> But now that we have examined the meaning of "the question,"
> we can at present also write the formula thus: "Consciousness is
> a being, the nature of which is to be conscious of the nothingness
> of its being."[19]

Nothingness is the key to Sartre's system; it is the "hole of
being," the fall of the In-itself by which the For-itself is constituted. Nothingness is created by a nihilating act on the part
of being, a perpetual act—Sartre calls it an "ontological act"
—wherein the In-itself is put into question by the For-itself.

> It is an absolute event which comes to being by means of being
> and which without having being, is perpetually sustained by

being. Since being-in-itself is isolated in its being by its total
positivity no being can produce being and nothing can happen
to being through being—except for nothingness. Nothingness is
the peculiar possibility of being and its unique possibility. Yet
this original possibility appears only in the absolute act which
realizes it. Since nothingness is nothingness of being, it can come
to being only through being itself. Of course it comes to being
through a particular being, which is human reality. But this
being is constituted as human reality inasmuch as this being is
nothing but the original project of its own nothingness. Human
reality is being in so far as within its being and for its being it
is the unique foundation of nothingness at the heart of being.[20]

Despite the difficulties posed by Sartre's technical language,
it should be apparent that nothingness is the destiny of being,
that nothingness is created by human consciousness, and that
human consciousness, as Sartre later says,[21] neither is being nor
has being. Accordingly, Sartre says in his Conclusion that:
"The For-itself, in fact, is nothing but the pure nihilation of
the In-itself; it is like a hole of being at the heart of Being."[22]

Employing his own language, we could say that Sartre's
ontological nihilism is the consequence of his original choice
of freedom. Freedom is his "project," it is the choice of freedom that necessitates his creation of an ontological system
which identifies consciousness and nothingness; for to identify
man and being is to allow men to be swallowed up by the brute
reality of the world. In choosing freedom, Sartre has chosen
nothingness, for freedom is nothingness, it has no essence,
it is subject to no logical necessity, it is the product of no
causes.

I am condemned to exist forever beyond my essence, beyond
the causes and motives of my act. I am condemned to be free.
This means that no limits to my freedom can be found except
freedom itself or, if you prefer, that we are not free to cease
being free. To the extent that the For-itself wishes to hide its
own nothingness from itself and to incorporate the In-itself as
its true mode of being, it is trying also to hide its freedom from
itself.[23]

Such escape from freedom Sartre calls "bad faith," but ultimately it is illusory, even in an ontological sense, for man *is*
freedom. He is freedom precisely because he is nothingness—
and the realization of freedom produces anguish—freedom is
identical with the nihilation of being, "freedom in its foundation coincides with the nothingness which is at the heart of
man."[24]

Sartre pays a terrible but a necessary price for freedom.
Man's freedom—or his nothingness—both isolates and
estranges him from the world, from the other, from the body,
from sex (surely no other modern writer has so deeply loathed
sex as Sartre). Here, Sartre's thought is genuinely dialectical:
freedom is posited by a dialectic of negation, by a nihilation
of everything that lies outside itself. So likewise his vision is
genuinely tragic: man's project of freedom is doomed to frus-
tration and defeat.[25] Why? Because fundamentally and tragically man is the desire to be God. The For-itself arises as the
nihilation of the In-itself and this nihilation Sartre defines
as the project towards the In-itself. Human reality is the desire
of being-in-itself.

> The fundamental value which presides over this project is ex-
> actly the in-itself-for-itself; that is, the ideal of a consciousness
> which would be the foundation of its own being-in-itself by the
> pure consciousness which it would have of itself. It is this ideal
> which can be called God. Thus the best way to conceive of the
> fundamental project of human reality is to say that man is the
> being whose project is to be God.[26]

With his ultimate goal of engaging in an absolute nihilation
of being, man has the goal of being God. Fundamentally man's
freedom is the choice of being God.[27] Thus Sartre concludes
the analytic portion of his work with these words:

> Every human reality is a passion in that it projects losing itself
> so as to found being and by the same stroke to constitute the
> In-itself which escapes contingency by being its own foundation,
> the *Ens causa sui,* which religions call God. Thus the passion of

man is the reverse of that of Christ, for man loses himself as man in order that God may be born. But the idea of God is contradictory and we lose ourselves in vain. Man is a useless passion.[28]

At first glance it would appear that there is no reason for Sartre to introduce the idea of God (the Being that is the cause of itself) into his system. Yet the idea of God is a logical consequence of the conjunction in his thought of his understanding of being and his idea of nihilation (*neántir* is a word coined by Sartre). In his Introduction, he states:

> Being-in-itself is never either possible or impossible. It is. This is what consciousness expresses in anthropomorphic terms by saying that being is superfluous (*de trop*)—that is that consciousness absolutely cannot derive being from anything, either from another being, or from a possibility, or from a necessary law. Uncreated, without reason for being, without any connection with another being, being-in-itself is *de trop* for eternity.[29]

Underlying this idea of being is, of course, the experience of nausea, the realization of the radical contingency of reality, of the world, of existence. Being simply *is;* nothing more can be said about it. This is the being which must be nihilated if consciousness is to be born, if freedom is *to be*. Moreover, Sartre's idea of nihilation is fully dialectical, it is a genuinely dialectical negation of being, thus it is not to be equated with annihilation, for it is an inversion—a reversal—of being. Only thereby can it be identified with the project of freedom. Freedom is the reversal of being—hence, it is nothingness. But freedom is only a project, it neither is nor has being. Thus freedom is the "project" or the "choice" of the reversal of being, it is directed to the absolute inversion of being: to the absolutely necessary Being, to the Being that is the cause of itself.

Again and again Sartre's position coincides with the dualistic schools of mystical philosophy. This is most deeply true of his idea of being; for example, it largely parallels the idea of *prakriti* in the Samkhya-Yoga school. Nevertheless, at bottom Sartre's idea of being is a reversal of the Christian idea of the creation. It is the sheer, absolute, and autonomous *isness* of *être-en-soi* that inverts the Christian idea of creation. Contrariwise, when the idea of *être-en-soi* is dialectially inverted, it becomes the Christian idea of God. But if this is true, then a dialectical relationship must exist between the idea of nihilation and the idea of God. Why? Because the act of nihilation, in nihilating being, must never be consummated if it is to remain nihilation. Consequently the act of nihilation is not simply a nihilation of being but depends upon a parallel and simultaneous nihilation of God: both God and being must be nihilated by man's project of freedom. When Sartre says, "Everything happens as if the world, man, and man-in-the-world succeeded in realizing only a missing God,"[30] he might more aptly say that man's freedom demands a missing God.

From this point of view, Sartre's system is not dualistic, it contains three ontological categories: being-for-itself (human consciousness), being-in-itself, and God. Or, otherwise stated, nothingness, being, and God. Of course, God does not exist. Nevertheless, he is a necessary dialectical foundation of the system. Only through a dialectical negation of God, does nihilation—the primordial act of human freedom—avoid an otherwise inevitable absorption of its act into the being of God. It is precisely Sartre's idea of nihilation—of human freedom, of the human reality—that prevents his system from becoming fully and positively mystical. For his nihilation is not only a nihilation of being, it is also a nihilation of God; and it is a mystical negation of God: the very act that the mystic directs against the being of the world, Sartre directs against both being and God. This is why Sartre's act of nihilation has so many parallels with the mystical dissolution of being; fundamentally both must identify authentic being with nothingness. Thus Sartre's system may be justly termed atheistic mysticism. Both God and being must be negated in the authentic creation of human freedom; apart from the negation of God, man would no longer be a "useless passion," and hence, most deeply, would no longer *be*. Again,

Sartre's system demonstrates once more that the deepest affirmation of the profane demands a radical negation of the
sacred, which is to say that a dialectical relation exists between
the sacred and the profane, neither can become manifest apart
from a negation of the other. Yet Sartre's thought has not
succeeded in reaching a full dialectical expression, it has not
succeeded in identifying negation and affirmation, despite the
fact that Sartre's idea of nihilation so powerfully witnesses to
the paradoxical presence of the missing God.

Nihilation lies at the heart of Sartre's system, and it should
be identified as an inversion of the traditional mystical act, an
inversion that establishes human freedom, and does so by
transcending being, a transcendence that Sartre defines as "that
inner and realizing negation which reveals the In-itself while
determining the being of the For-itself."[31] Perhaps the point at
which Sartre's understanding of the relation between the human reality and being becomes most fully illuminated is in his
analysis of space. Apart from consciousness, there would be no
space:

> Space cannot be a being. It is a moving relation between beings
> which are unrelated. It is the total independence of the In-itselfs,
> as it is revealed to a being which is presence to "all" the In-itself
> as the independence of each one in relation to the others. It is
> the unique way in which beings can be revealed as having no re-
> lation, can be thus revealed to the being through which relation
> comes into the world; that is, space is pure exteriority. . . . Space
> is not the world, but is the instability of the world apprehended
> as totality, inasmuch as the world can always disintegrate into
> external multiplicity. . . . The existence of space is the proof that
> the For-itself by causing being "to be there" adds nothing to
> being.[32]

Thus, although man creates space, and, indeed, creates the
world—Sartre identifies the world as a total upheaval in the
In-itself caused by the For-itself's nihilation of being[33]—his
'creation' is a carving of a hole in being, a hole that is equivalent to nothingness. This nothingness is not nothingness in

general, but a nothingness created by a particular "privation," a privation of an individual and particular In-itself.[34] Consequently, we find in Sartre—again paralleling the Samkhya-Yoga system—a seemingly unlimited number of absolutely autonomous pure consciousnesses wholly isolated both from one another and from any positive relationship to the brute reality of the world. Sartre can find in the pure exteriority of space—the radical otherness of the world—the foundation of human freedom. Yet Sartre's freedom, like the mystic's, is a freedom to exist in nothingness, the freedom to exist as a "hole" in an absolutely alien being.

III. Teilhard de Chardin

Sartre has candidly remarked that "the world is revealed as this or that (in this or that order) according to the end chosen."[35] In Pierre Teilhard de Chardin one finds that rare if not unique phenomenon, the *homo religiosus* who has chosen to understand and affirm the world revealed by science. Is there another contemporary religious thinker who has dared to embrace what both Kierkegaard and Dostoevsky regarded as the greatest modern enemy of faith? Not only was Teilhard a practicing scientist, but far more significantly, he created a religious way of living with and understanding the truth and reality that is known by science. Immediately we must ask the question of what made it possible for a man of such profound faith to make a religious affirmation of the scientific vision. Reversing Sartre, and virtually the whole body of modern literature, Teilhard believed that: "What is terrible for us is to be cut off from things through some inward and irretrievable diminishment."[36] Strangely enough, it was precisely his faith in Christ that occasioned Teilhard's affirmation of the cosmos. Shortly before his death, he confessed:

> *Throughout* my life, *through* my life, the world has little by little caught fire in my sight until, aflame around me, it has become almost completely luminous from within. . . . Such has been my experience in contact with the earth—the diaphany of

> the divine at the heart of the universe on fire. . . . Christ; His
> heart; a fire: capable of penetrating everywhere and, gradually,
> spreading everywhere.[37]

Teilhard chose to apprehend the world not simply as God's
creation, but as the incarnate Body of Christ.

In his beautiful, and at times overwhelmingly powerful,
treatise on the interior life, *The Divine Milieu,* whose vision he
never abandoned, Teilhard set forth the religious ground of
his yes-saying to the world. Here, he says: "To the full extent
of my power, *because I am a priest,* I wish from now on to be
the first to become conscious of all that the world loves, pursues
and suffers; I want to be the first to seek, to sympathise and to
suffer; the first to unfold and sacrifice myself—to become more
wisely human and more nobly of the earth than any of
the world's servants."[38] Believing that activity and passivity,
growth and diminishment, life and death, are natural phases
of a single effort, he conceives of Christian asceticism, not as
world-detachment in the classical sense, but as an almost
Faustian affirmation of world and self:

> Your essential duty and desire is to be united with God. But
> in order to be united, you must first of all *be*—be yourself as
> completely as possible. And so you must develop yourself and
> take possession of the world *in order to be.* Once this has been
> accomplished, then is the time to accept diminishment for the
> sake of *being in another.* Such is the sole and two-fold precept
> of complete Christian asceticism.[39]

Already Teilhard's position reveals its dialectical ground; thus
he can confess that he looks upon everything as being both God
and dust, as being everything and nothing at once.[40]

Is this true affirmation? Is Teilhard capable of a final yes-
saying to the world? His distinction between the pagan and
the Christian provides considerable room for doubt:

> The pagan loves the earth in order to enjoy it and confine him-
> self within it; the Christian in order to make it purer and draw
> from it the strength to escape from it.

The pagan seeks to espouse sensible things so as to extract delight from them; *he adheres to the world*. The Christian multiplies his contacts with the world only so as to harness, or submit to, the energies which he will take back, or which will take him, to Heaven. He *pre-adheres* to God.

The pagan holds that man divinises himself by closing in upon himself; the final act of human evolution comes when the individual, or the totality, constitutes itself within itself. The Christian sees his divinisation only in the assimilation by an 'Other' of his achievement: the culmination of life, in his eyes, is death in union.[41]

This whole distinction rests upon Teilhard's conviction that the Christian accepts the same world as the pagan (in all its immediacy and multiplicity); but the Christian links the world to God, through God the universe is unified for him, and thereby prepared for its final consummation. Teilhard's formula is: faith consecrates the world, fidelity communicates with it.[42]

It is this conjunction of consecration and communication which must appear paradoxical to the modern mind. The very idea of a divine *milieu* must seem grotesque and blasphemous in the context of the modern situation:

God reveals Himself everywhere, beneath our groping efforts as a *universal milieu*, only because he is the *ultimate point* upon which all realities converge. Each element of the world, whatever it may be, only subsists, *hic et nunc*, in the manner of a cone whose generatrices meet in God who draws them together. . . . It is *precisely because* He is the center that He fills the whole sphere. The omnipresence of the divine is simply the effect of its extreme spirituality and is the exact contrary of the fallacious ubiquity of matter which seems to derive from its extreme dissociation and dispersal.[43]

Moreover, Teilhard's thought culminates in an eschatological hope, a hope indubitably Christian, but a hope that nevertheless casts doubt upon Teilhard's professed fidelity to the earth. He can say: "To desire the Parousia, all we have to do is to let the very heart of the earth, as we Christianise it, beat within us."[44] What can the Christianization of the earth mean if it must culminate in the end of the world? Teilhard believes that Christianization is divinization, an extension of the Incarnation, a "surcreation" leading to a sanctity that is delivered from every temptation:

> The temptations of too large a world, the seductions of too beautiful a world—where are these now?
> They do not exist.
> Now the earth can certainly clasp me in her giant arms. She can swell me with her life, or draw me back into her dust. She can deck herself with every charm, with every horror, with every mystery. She can intoxicate me with her perfume of tangibility and unity. She can cast me to my knees in expectation of what is maturing in her breast.
> But her enchantments can no longer do me harm, since she has become for me, over and above herself, the body of Him who is and of Him who is coming.[45]

The carefully formulated theological positions of this early work are brought to intellectual consummation in Teilhard's great work, *The Phenomenon of Man,* which embodies an even deeper affirmation of the earth. Before we examine this work, however, it would be well to ask certain questions of Teilhard's thought. Admitting that his method is dialectical, that it draws together a positive dialectic of affirming the world with a negative dialectic of negating its ultimate value and reality, does his method culminate in a dialectical synthesis of its positive and negative poles? For that matter, is his positive dialectic genuinely positive, and is his negative dialectic genuinely negative? The assumption of the dialectical method is that the positive and negative movements, if sufficiently radical, will ultimately coincide in a dialectical synthesis: negation becomes affirmation, affirmation becomes negation. That is to say, if Teilhard's method is fully dialectical, it will finally unite its positive and negative poles, collapsing its initial distinction between God and the world, and ultimately allowing God and the world to stand forth in some kind of primordial or eschatological unity. Now Teilhard eschews ontological and theo-

logical language, which is fully consistent with the dialectical
method. He is obviously engaged in attempting a radical transformation of the traditional forms of faith and understanding.
Thus, again and again in *The Divine Milieu* he collapses the
traditional distinctions between the soul and nature, spirit and
flesh, Christ and the world. He refuses to allow the affirmation
of faith to be a negation of the world, thus revealing his deeply
Catholic roots; but does he succeed in creating a vision of the
transformation of the earth that brings God and the world into
an ultimate dialectical synthesis?

The Phenomenon of Man was written as a scientific, not
a metaphysical or theological, treatise, but it is obviously
grounded in Teilhard's Christian vision of the cosmos. Teilhard notes that previously science has always looked at the
world from without, but he chooses to view it from within,
making two basic assumptions that are the foundation of his
work: "The first is the primacy accorded to the psychic and to
thought in the stuff of the universe, and the second is the
'biological' value attributed to the social fact around us."[46] In
other words, he looks upon man as being the preeminent being
in nature and regards human nature as organic. These assumptions lead him to place the highest natural value upon human
consciousness:

> *Seeing.* We might say that the whole of life lies in that verb—
> if not in end, at least in essence. Fuller being is closer union;
> such is the kernel and conclusion of this book. But let us em-
> phasise the point: union can only increase through an increase
> in consciousness, that is to say in vision. And that, doubtless, is
> why the history of the living world can be summarised as the
> elaboration of ever more perfect eyes within a cosmos in which
> there is always something more to be seen. . . . *To see or to
> perish* is the very condition laid upon everything that makes up
> the universe, by reason of the mysterious gift of existence. And
> this, in superior measure, is man's condition.[47]

Teilhard openly embraces an evolutionary vision of the universe, believing it to be the only possible outlook for scientific
thinking, and looks upon man as the axis and leading shoot of

evolution. Indeed, he doubts "whether there is a more decisive moment for a thinking being than when the scales fall from his eyes and he discovers that he is not an isolated unit lost in the cosmic solitudes, and realises that a universal will to live converges and is hominised in him."[48]

These assumptions mean that the traditional Western distinction between subject and object is transformed, no longer are subject and object autonomous epistemological categories, for now: "Object and subject marry and mutually transform each other in the act of knowledge; and from now on man willy-nilly finds his own image stamped on all he looks at."[49] One is reminded of Eliade's conception of archaic man's vision of the cosmos in Teilhard's insistence that there is no chasm between man and nature. What we know as human consciousness, Teilhard finds extended throughout the whole cosmos, beginning with the most elementary cell. Nor does he hesitate to confess that the source of this vision lies within his own consciousness:

> It is impossible to deny that, deep within ourselves, an 'interior' appears at the heart of beings, as it were seen through a rent. This is enough to ensure that, in one degree or another, this 'interior' should obtrude itself as existing everywhere in nature from all time. Since the stuff of the universe has an inner aspect at one point of itself, there is necessarily a *double aspect to its structure,* that is to say in every region of space and time—in the same way, for instance, as it is granular: *coextensive with their Without, there is a Within to things.*[50]

This idea of the within of things, of the cosmos as being both interior and exterior, is the most original and the most crucial idea in *The Phenomenon of Man;* it bridges the gulf between romanticism and realism in Western thought, allowing man to be a wholly natural being, while at the same time granting him the depths of his interior life. By this means, Teilhard can place man at the center of nature, while at the same time understanding "hominisation" as the central and unifying process of the universe, as "the progressive phyletic spiritualisation in human civilisation of all the forces contained in the animal world."[51]

Not only does Teilhard succeed in once more yoking man and nature but he likewise succeeds in reintroducing spirit into the very structure of the cosmos, thus dissolving the chasm between nature and spirit: *"Spiritual perfection (or conscious 'centreity') and material synthesis (or complexity) are but the two aspects or connected parts of one and the same phenomenon."*[52] This conception is embedded in Teilhard's understanding of energy, for although he acknowledges that all energy is physical in nature, he believes that it is composed of two distinct components: a "tangential" energy linking the element with all others of the same order, and a "radial" energy that draws it forward into ever greater complexity and centricity. The process of evolution is both natural and spiritual, moving forward to the greatest cosmic fullness, and moving upward to the highest spiritual goal—thus, fundamentally, evolution is the evolution of consciousness.

> The coalescence of elements and the coalescence of stems, the spherical geometry of the earth and psychical curvature of the mind harmonising to counterbalance the individual and collective forces of dispersion in the world and to impose unification —there at last we find the spring and secret of hominisation.
>
> But why should there be unification in the world and what purpose does it serve?
>
> To see the answer to this ultimate question, we have only to put side by side the two equations which have been gradually formulating themselves from the moment we began trying to situate the phenomenon of man in the world.
>
> Evolution = Rise of consciousness,
> Rise of consciousness = Effect of union.[53]

Now Teilhard can conceive of the transformation of the earth: "If words have any meaning, is this not like some great body which is born—with its limbs, its nervous system, its perceptive organs, its memory—the body of that great Thing which had come to fulfil the ambitions aroused in the reflective being by the newly acquired consciousness that he was at one with and responsible to an evolutionary All?"[54]

Space and time are converging upon a center, or rather, the Center, which Teilhard calls the Omega Point, a center that is neither potential nor ideal, but both present and real. Yet Omega is only discovered at the end of the evolutionary process when it will be revealed as the culmination of the whole process of evolution. It is the last term of the evolutionary series, and yet it is outside all series; for Teilhard bestows upon it the attributes of autonomy, actuality, irreversibility, and transcendence.[55] Indeed, the revelation of the Omega Point coincides with the end of the world:

> Now when sufficient elements have sufficiently agglomerated, this essentially convergent movement will attain such intensity and such quality that mankind, *taken as a whole,* will be obliged —as happened to the individual forces of instinct—to reflect upon itself at a single point; that is to say, in this case, to abandon its organo-planetary foothold so as to pivot itself on the transcendent centre of its increasing concentration. This will be the end and the fulfilment of the spirit of the earth.[56]

In *The Divine Milieu,* Teilhard had spoken of the general drift of matter toward spirit, saying: "This movement must have its term: one day the whole divinisible substance of matter will have passed into the souls of men; all the chosen dynamism will have been recuperated: and then our world will be ready for the Parousia."[57] Now in *The Phenomenon of Man* he has constructed an evolutionary system with an eschatological end.

Finally, in an epilogue, Teilhard casts aside his scientific mantle and reveals the Christian ground of his system. The evolutionary process is now equated with the Kingdom of God, and Christ becomes the primary energy of the cosmos.

> As early as in St. Paul and St. John we read that to create, to fulfil and to purify the world is, for God, to unify it by uniting it organically with himself. How does he unify it? By partially

immersing himself in things, by becoming 'element,' and then, from this point of vantage in the heart of matter, assuming the control and leadership of what we now call evolution.[58]

Moreover, it is Christ, the principle of universal vitality, who became incarnate in consciousness in order to direct and super-animate it.

> By a perennial act of communion and sublimation, he aggregates to himself the total psychism of the earth. And when he has gathered everything together and transformed everything, he will close in upon himself and his conquests, thereby rejoining, in a final gesture, the divine focus he has never left. Then, as St. Paul tells us, *God shall be all in all*.[59]

Teilhard calls his position a superior form of pantheism: "the expectation of perfect unity, steeped in which each element will reach its consummation at the same time as the universe."[60] Or, as Teilhard said in a note written ten years after the writing of the book:

> In the case of a *converging universe* such as I have delineated, far from being born from the fusion and confusion of the elemental centres it assembles, the universal centre of unification (precisely to fulfil its motive, collective and stabilising function) must be conceived as pre-existing and transcendent. A very real 'pantheism' if you like (in the etymological meaning of the word) but an absolutely legitimate pantheism—for if, in the last resort, the reflective centres of the world are effectively no more than 'one with God,' this state is obtained not by identification (God becoming all) but by the differentiating and communicating action of love (God all *in everyone*). And that is essentially orthodox and Christian.[61]

Lying at the core of Teilhard's vision is the idea of evolution as the evolution of consciousness. As he himself notes: "Reduced to its ultimate essence, the substance of these long pages can be summed up in this simple affirmation: that if the universe, regarded sidereally, is in process of spatial expansion (from the infinitesimal to the immense), in the same way and still more clearly it presents itself to us, physico-chemically, as in process of organic *involution* upon itself (from the extremely simple to the extremely complex)—and, moreover, this particular involution 'of complexity' is experimentally bound up with a correlative increase in interiorisation, that is to say in the psyche or consciousness."[62] Furthermore, the evolution of consciousness is a movement toward unity, the course of its involution leads to the convergence of the cosmos, finally leading to the appearance of the Omega Point. With the final manifestation of the Omega Point, the cosmos will be consummated by coming to an end, God will be all in all; or, rather, God will be all in every consciousness, in every person, as finally the fullness of consciousness will reveal itself as being the fullness of God. Consequently, the evolution of consciousness is the evolution of God. But of the real meaning of this primal theme, Teilhard remains silent. Adopting Whiteheadian language, we could say that Teilhard has a doctrine of the consequent nature of God, but no real doctrine of his primordial nature—we are really only told that he is actual and transcendent. Theologically, Teilhard's vision centers in the Incarnation, God enters into matter in order to transform it, the process of evolution is equivalent to the extension of the Kingdom of God; yet Teilhard has no doctrine of creation (except in *The Divine Milieu,* where he identifies creation and Incarnation[63]).

The fact that Teilhard has no doctrine of creation is highly significant, for it means that his doctrine of God is incomplete, with the result that the full meaning of God's relation to the world remains unrealized. Surely a mystical theology is implied by his system, with the doctrine that creation is a fall from God or the Godhead, leading to Teilhard's vision of evolution as the evolution and involution of God. Unfortunately, this analysis has not recorded Teilhard's full employment of the ideas and language of modern science, although one suspects that he has abandoned its principles and methods—thus Teilhard can say: "To think 'the world' (as physics is beginning to realise) is not merely to register it but to confer upon it a form of unity it would otherwise (i.e., without being thought) be without."[64] It is apparent, nevertheless, that Teilhard has transcended science in his vision of the cosmos, for his positive dialectic of evolution is ultimately a negative dialectic, affirmation becomes negation, the yes-saying to the creation is at bottom a celebration of the Body of Christ, and Teilhard hopes for the Day when that Body will be all in all, when the cosmos will have come to an end. Contemporary Christianity has risen to no greater affirmation of the world than that given us by Teilhard de Chardin: if, finally, this affirmation becomes negation, then the question arises as to whether faith is open to an ultimate yes-saying to the world.

7

The Unconscious and the Sacred

I. Eliade and the Unconscious

ELIADE ENVISIONS the history of religions, not simply as a historical discipline, but more deeply as a study of man as a living symbol, in short, as a "metapsychoanalysis."[1] Understood in this sense, the history of religions may be expected to effect an awakening of consciousness, a renewal of the archaic symbols and archetypes of all the world's religions. Humanity will be reborn when man becomes a whole and universal being: yet this transformation will occur only by means of an "opposition to history," which means, at bottom, a reversal of history.

> Still with the aid of the history of religions, man might recover the symbolism of his body, which is an anthropocosmos. What the various techniques of the imagination, and especially the poetic techniques, have realized in this direction is almost nothing beside what the history of religions might promise. All these things still exist even in modern man; it is only necessary to reactivate them and bring them to the level of consciousness. By regaining awareness of his own anthropocosmic symbolism— which is only one variety of the archaic symbolism—modern man will obtain a new existential dimension, totally unknown to present-day existentialism and historicism: this is an authentic and major mode of being, which defends man from nihilism and historical relativism without thereby taking him out of history. For history itself will one day be able to find its true meaning: that of the epiphany of a glorious and absolute human condition.[2]

Deeply moving as this vision may appear, it is nondialectical, and therefore unreal: history cannot give birth to an absolute humanity while remaining history. If religion has become "unconscious" in the man of the desacralized societies,[3] then religion can be reborn only by a radical transformation of these societies; or, as the prophetic traditions of China and the Near East alike have proclaimed, only by a violent reversal of history.

Eliade has learned from Indian philosophy that the unconscious acts in such a way that its activity seems to *prefigure* the mode of being of the Spirit.[4] India knows the unconscious as a cosmic consciousness—for example, the "store-consciousness" (*alayavijnana*) of the Yogacara school of Mahayana Buddhism. In his book on Yoga, while discussing the spontaneous rediscovery of archetypes by the unconscious, Eliade says:

> We may well ask if the "unconscious" is not in this case trying to imitate processes by which "consciousness" (or, in some cases, the "transconscious") seeks to obtain completeness and conquer freedom. For this unconscious discovery of an initiatory schema does not stand alone; it is known that all the great mystical symbolisms are spontaneously rediscovered in dreams, hallucinations, and even in pathological ecstasies. Experiences and symbols of ascent, of the "march toward the center," of the descent into hell, of death and resurrection, of initiatory ordeals, and even the complex symbols of alchemy, have all been recorded in one or another of these states.[5]

Such unconscious imitations of archetypal acts are far from having the value of the acts that they imitate; but nevertheless they indicate the sacred goal of the deeper processes of the unconscious, and therefore Eliade prefers the word 'transconscious' to either 'subconscious' or 'unconscious.'

For this reason, Eliade has long been attracted to Jung, while maintaining a bitter hostility toward Freud. Eliade objects to Freud's ideology, to his positivist understanding of "pure sexuality," for Freud refused to acknowledge the sacred dimension of psychic energy, of libido. Archaic man knows sexuality as a hierophany, and the sexual act as an integral action relating man to the cosmos: thus Eliade believes that the primary and supreme value of sexuality lies in its cosmological function. From this point of view, Eliade brings a new meaning to the Oedipus complex.

> The attraction that the male infant feels towards its mother, and its corollary the Oedipus complex, are only "shocking" insofar as they are analysed *as such;* instead of being presented as they should be, *as so* much imagery. For it is the Image of the Mother that is really in question, and not this or that mother *hic et nunc,* as Freud gives one to understand. It is the Image of the Mother which reveals—and which *alone can reveal* —her reality and her functions, at once cosmological, anthropological, and psychological.[6]

The images of the mother cannot be translated into concrete terms, simply because they are *images,* and not signs or concepts. Such images have no "origin," for what is in question is the archetypal Image of the Mother, and the desire for this image means many things at once, "for it is the desire to re-enter into the bliss of living Matter that is still 'unformed,' with all its possible lines of development, cosmological, anthropological, etc."[7]

Thus Eliade interprets the Image of the Mother as an image of the womb of being, that precosmic and unfallen state when all things were one; in short, as an image of paradise. Accordingly, Eliade discovers this meaning in alchemical texts that speak of a desire to return to the mother's womb.

> The *regressus ad uterum* is sometimes presented in the form of incest with the mother. Michael Maier tells us that "Delphinas, an anonymous philosopher, in his treatise *Secretus Maximus,* speaks very clearly of the mother who must, of natural necessity, unite herself with her son." But it is obvious that the "mother" symbolizes, in these different contexts, nature in her primordial state, the *prima materia* of the alchemists, and that the "return to the mother" translates a spiritual experience corresponding to any other 'projection' outside Time—in other words, to the

reintegration of a primal situation. The dissolution to the *prima materia* is also symbolized by a sexual union which is completed by disappearance into the uterus.[8]

Consequently, the Oedipus complex is at bottom a desire for the primal paradise, and the sexual desire for the mother is fundamentally a desire for union with unfallen being. Unfortunately, Eliade does not carry his analysis further than this, thereby foregoing an opportunity of arriving at a dialectical understanding of Freud. Only if the radically profane form of Freud's understanding of libido and the unconscious is accepted and affirmed, can a genuine coincidence of the opposites be established between the sacred and profane meanings of the unconscious. But this goal demands an exploration of the full meaning of Freud's theory of the Oedipus complex.

II. Freud

Today we know that Freud discovered the Oedipus complex while engaged in a revolutionary quest for his own self-analysis, and that the idea of the Oedipus complex, if not the complex itself, lay at the center of the vision that created what Freud himself regarded as his greatest work, *The Interpretation of Dreams*. Of course, the fact that the doctrine of the Oedipus complex is a confessional truth in no way invalidates its claim to truth itself. As Erich Heller remarks, "All interpretations of the soul must to a high degree be self-interpretations: the sick interpret the sick, dreamers interpret dreams—or, as the Viennese satirist Karl Kraus—with that calculated injustice which is the prerogative of satire—once said of a certain psychological theory: 'Psychoanalysis is the disease of which it pretends to be the cure.' "[9] Ernest Jones' monumental biography of Freud has taught us that Freud was obsessed with death throughout his life,[10] but at the time that he was writing *The Interpretation of Dreams* he was deeply motivated by the death of his father. Almost ten years after publishing that volume, he could say in the preface to its second edition: "It was, I found, a portion of my own self-analysis, my reaction to my father's death— that is to say, to the most important event, the most poignant loss, of a man's life."[11]

Freud considered his most valuable contributions to human knowledge to be the final chapter of *The Interpretation of Dreams* (1900), the final chapter of *Totem and Taboo* (1913), and the essay on "The Unconscious" in his metapsychological series (1915).[12] In the last chapter of *Totem and Taboo,* Freud stated a conviction that he never abandoned:

> In closing this study, which has been carried out in extremely condensed form, I want to state the conclusion that the beginnings of religion, ethics, society, and art meet in the Oedipus complex. This is in entire accord with the findings of psychoanalysis, namely, that the nucleus of all neuroses as far as our present knowledge of them goes is the Oedipus complex.[13]

Strangely enough, and despite his voluminous writing, Freud devoted little actual analysis to the Oedipus complex, and it has brought forth only a limited body of critical commentary from his followers. But there can be no doubt of its vast importance in his thought. Indeed, the central problem of Freud's later writings, the relation between civilized man and primitive man, between the infantile psyche and the infancy of the race, revolves about the Oedipus complex. For the Oedipus complex is the primordial fall, both in the individual psyche and in humanity at large. The symbolic idea of an archaic humanity is every bit as important in Freud's thought as it is in Eliade's; thus Freud concluded *Totem and Taboo* with these words:

> Of course the sharp division between thinking and doing as we draw it does not exist either with savages or with neurotics. But the neurotic is above all inhibited in his actions; with him the thought is a complete substitute for the deed. Primitive man is not inhibited, the thought is directly converted into the deed, the deed is for him, so to speak, rather a substitute for the thought, and for that reason I think we may well assume in the case we are discussing, though without vouching for the absolute certainty of the decision, that "In the beginning was the deed."[14]

The deed to which Freud here refers was the primal murder of
the father, an event which he insisted was both literal and
historical, for apart from that event—the primordial fall—
psychoanalysis, as Freud well knew, would lose its deepest
foundation.

In the *Psychopathology of Everyday Life,* Freud gave expression to a conception of religion that contains deep insight into
the ground of his own thought:

> I believe in fact that a great part of the mythological view of
> the world, which reaches far into the most modern religions,
> *is nothing other than psychological processes projected into the
> outer world.* The obscure apprehending of the psychical factors
> and relationships of the unconscious is mirrored—it is hard to
> put it otherwise; one has to use here the analogy with paranoia
> —in the construction of a *supersensible reality,* which science
> has to retranslate into the *psychology of the unconscious.* One
> could venture in this manner to resolve the myths of Paradise,
> the Fall of Man, of God, of Good and Evil, of Immortality,
> and so on, thus transforming *Metaphysics* into *Metapsychology.*[15]

If Freud transformed 'metaphysics' into 'metapsychology,' he
did so only by creating a profane mythology, for almost in
spite of himself Freud was driven to employ a mythical language in writing of the deeper processes of the unconscious.
Surely nowhere in the world's mythology will one find myths
more bizarre, more fantastic, more absurd, than is the language
of psychoanalysis! The grossness and absurdity of psychoanalytic language is beyond satire; yet Freud—along with
Marx—created one of the two most powerful myths in the
modern world. His mythology reflects our world—if it did not,
in part, create it; and we know that, in some sense, his myths
are true, for to deny their truth would be to deny ourselves.
Freud inverted the language of sacred mythology in creating a
profane mythology, and this dialectical inversion of the sacred
into the profane lies deeply imbedded in his method. Only an
understanding of this Faustian transformation of transcendence into immanence, of the sacred into the profane, can unveil the meaning of the Oedipus complex.

To Norman Brown, who perhaps someday will stand forth as Freud's greatest interpreter, the essence of the Oedipus complex is the project of becoming God.[16] Although Brown does little to substantiate this thesis (his concern is with Freud's later writings, where the Oedipus complex is related to narcissism and the castration complex), he has provided an important clue to the theological meaning of Freud's work, a clue that should be employed in an investigation of Freud's greatest work, *The Interpretation of Dreams*. Here, we find Freud's famous definition of the dream as *"a (disguised) fulfilment of a (suppressed or repressed) wish,"*[17] in the context of a psychological investigation purported to be strictly scientific, where the reflex processes remain the model of every psychical function.[18] Freud views the interpretation of dreams as the royal road to a knowledge of the unconscious, a road fraught with difficulties to be sure, for just as there are no innocent dreams, there are no indifferent dream-interpreters.[19] Since dreams are the expression of repressed wishes, it is natural to expect that the majority of adult dreams will deal with sexual material and express erotic wishes, for no other instinct (*Trieb*) has been so deeply suppressed since childhood as has the sexual instinct (or libido) and its various components.[20] In the last chapter, Freud summarizes the principal findings of his inquiry as follows: "Dreams are psychical acts of as much significance as any others; their motive force is in every instance a wish seeking fulfilment; the fact of their not being recognizable as wishes and their many peculiarities and absurdities are due to the influence of the psychical censorship to which they have been subjected during the process of their formation; apart from the necessity of obeying this censorship, other factors which have contributed to their formation are a necessity for the condensation of their psychical material, a regard for the possibility of its being represented in sensory images and—though not invariably—a demand that the structure of the dream shall have a rational and intellectual exterior."[21] This conclusion, quite obviously, rests upon Freud's demonstration of the distinction between the manifest and the latent content of the dream, as well as upon his assumption of the existence of a dream-censor.

Yet the most important foundation of Freud's interpretation of dreams is his theory of regression. If the direction taken by psychical processes arising from the unconscious during waking life is conceived as progressive, then dreams have a regressive character, a backward movement to the perceptual images (which are deeper than the memory images) underlying the psychical processes. While admitting that he is dealing with an inexplicable phenomenon, Freud nonetheless conceives of dream regression as the turning back of an idea into the sensory image from which it was derived, thereby explaining the fact that all the logical relations belonging to the dream-thoughts disappear during the dream-activity: *"In regression the fabric of the dream-thoughts is resolved into its raw material."*[22] Freud has now arrived at a theoretical justification for his deepest insight, that dreams are a resurrection of infantile experiences.

> If we now bear in mind how great a part is played in the dream-thoughts by infantile experiences or by phantasies based upon them, how frequently portions of them re-emerge in the dream-content and how often the dream-wishes themselves are derived from them, we cannot dismiss the probability that in dreams too the transformation of thoughts into visual images may be in part the result of the attraction which memories couched in visual form and eager for revival bring to bear upon thoughts cut off from consciousness and struggling to find expression. On this view a dream might be described as *a substitute for an infantile scene modified by being transferred on to a recent experience.* The infantile scene is unable to bring about its own revival and has to be content with returning as a dream.[23]

Thus, in dreams we regain the paradise of childhood,[24] and through the dream—as in Proust's pattern—this paradise is made real by being conjoined with events of our daily life.

Dreams reverse consciousness, carrying psychic energy from

words and concepts to the more primordial material of brute sensation; but this regressive action of dreams is not only an individual phenomenon, it is also a reversal of history:

> Dreaming is on the whole an example of regression to the dreamer's earliest condition, a revival of his childhood, of the instinctual wishes which dominated it and of the methods of expression which were then available to him. Behind this childhood of the individual we are promised a picture of a phylogenetic childhood—a picture of the development of the human race, of which the individual's development is in fact an abbreviated recapitulation influenced by the chance circumstances of life. We can guess how much to the point is Nietzsche's assertion that in dreams "some primeval relic of humanity is at work which we can now scarcely reach any longer by a direct path"; and we may expect that the analysis of dreams will lead us to a knowledge of man's archaic heritage, of what is psychically innate in him.[25]

Notice that Freud here identifies the psychically innate with man's "archaic" nature, identifying the first in time with the first in nature, and since infantile desires arise first in the individual, they represent man's innate instincts (*Triebe*), and provide the deepest motivating power of the dream-work: "*a wish which is represented in a dream must be an infantile one.*"[26] Apart from infantile desires, there would be no dreams, for Freud's theory of dreams "regards wishes originating in infancy as the indispensible motive force for the formation of dreams."[27]

Furthermore, Freud insists as an "indispensible and invariable fact" that only sexual wishful impulses from infancy, which have undergone repression, are able to furnish the motive force for the formation of "psychoneurotic symptoms of every kind."[28] Consequently, psychic illness is at bottom the product of the repression of infantile desires; or, differently formulated, neurosis is caused by the repression of man's archaic nature. What is our deepest nature, that nature which we can only truly know in dreams? Is it not, quite simply, the unconscious? In his metapsychological essay "On the Unconscious," Freud set forth four characteristics of the unconscious: (1) there is no law of contradiction in the unconscious, contradictory impulses exist simultaneously; (2) there is no negation in the unconscious, impulses are immediately translated into acts; (3) the processes of the unconscious are timeless; and (4) unconscious processes have no relation to "reality," they are regulated only by pleasure and pain.[29] To this could be added, Freud's well-known philosophical credo from *The Interpretation of Dreams:*

> In Lipp's words, the unconscious must be assumed to be the general basis of psychical life. The unconscious is the larger sphere, which includes within it the smaller sphere of the conscious. Everything conscious has an unconscious preliminary stage; whereas what is unconscious may remain at that stage and nevertheless claim to be regarded as having the full value of a psychical process. The unconscious is the true psychical reality; *in its innermost nature it is as much unknown to us as the reality of the external world, and it is as incompletely presented by the data of consciousness as is the external world by the communication of our sense organs.*[30]

Freud's language in these passages is doubly significant: it reproduces the language of myth—Freud's conception of the unconscious could easily be translated into Eliade's understanding of the sacred—and yet in such a way as to dissolve the reality that lies at the center of the mythical vision.

It has long been known that Nietzsche anticipated Freud in his understanding of the operations of conscience, repression, sublimation, and rationalization; and although Freud did not borrow from Nietzsche—as Jones notes, Freud tried to read him, but found his thought so rich that he renounced the attempt[31]—Freud may nevertheless be considered an authentic descendant of Nietzsche. Thus Freud's psychological category of libido (the primal sexual energy) is the equivalent of Nietzsche's philosophical category of the Will to Power: but nowhere, as will be seen, is Freud's relation to Nietzsche more significant than in the symbol of the Oedipus complex. Note that the Oedipus complex is a primordial event, occurring in the infancy of both the individual and the race, and that it is *the* great originating event: originating both the individual psyche (as we know it) and history itself. Note further (particularly as Freud elucidates the theme in *Totem and Taboo*) that the murder of the father takes place—or the desire for it— as a means of obtaining sexual union with the mother; again, it is the Oedipus complex that alone makes possible the transformation and redirection of libido. Only with the Oedipus complex does repression come into existence, both in the individual and in history; thus the Oedipus complex is the original fall from the unconscious, now man is banished from the paradise of infancy, as a primal rupture is established between the unconscious and consciousness.

Before attempting a theological interpretation of the Oedipus complex, two further points must be made: (1) throughout his mature writings, Freud consistently, with however much naïveté, insisted that the idea of God is a projection of the father image, thus demonstrating that he himself was incapable of dissociating the image of the father from the supreme religious symbol; and (2) Freud always identified libido as the source of all human creativity (he came to identify the sex instinct with the life instinct), believing that it is libido that is repressed or sublimated by the growth of the individual and of culture. What then can be the theological meaning of the Oedipus complex? Surely the Oedipus complex is the project not of becoming God, but rather of murdering God, of murdering the Father, an event that Freud, reversing Nietzsche, identified with the beginning and not with the end of history. The Father must be murdered to make possible the life of the sons—in *Totem and Taboo*, the primal father has banished the sons from sexual contact with the women of the clan, only through his death can they know sex—but the murder of the Father produces an overwhelming sense of guilt; now through "subsequent obedience,"[32] the sons obey the Father, forbid themselves the fruits of their patricide, thus for the first time bringing repression into existence. This fantastic myth, to which Freud clung as the literal truth, can only truly be meaningful if it is interpreted theologically: the Oedipus complex is the primordial project of murdering God, only the death of God can provide an adequate explanation for the origin of repression.

Freud's myth of the fall brings a new and terrible meaning to the profound guilt that Western man has for so long attributed to sex—significantly, sexual energy is the one human energy that the Judeo-Christian tradition (with the exception of the Cabala) has never associated with the sacred. By linking the murder of the father with an original sexual desire for the mother, Freud not only discovered libido in infancy, but conceived of infancy as a false paradise, a paradise marred by the presence of the father. Freud's vision of existence was genuinely tragic, only the death of the father can bring life to the libido of the son, but this libido is doomed to be in perpetual search of its origin in the forbidden mother: existence *is* guilt. So likewise, history is a fall from the father, or, rather, a fall from God; it is grounded in repression, and thus consciousness is alienated from its origin in the unconscious. Through dreams we may reenter the seeming paradise of the unconscious: but it remains a forbidden paradise, a paradise lost. Now the image of God is present only in the unconscious, but there it exercises an awesome but destructive authority, for the father devours the sons who have rebelliously sought for life. As Eliade knows, the fall is a fall into life. We know this life as consciousness; or, as Freud would have it, as libido manifesting itself as consciousness. Yet Freud believed that the unconscious is the true psychical reality, a reality that we can know only by a regression to infancy, and only through the heritage of the Oedipal fall. Thereby we know the unconscious only in its profane form, and can understand consciousness only as the product of the death of God. Is it impossible to move beyond Freud's tragic vision of the unconscious? Granting that we cannot escape Freud's knowledge of the unconscious, is there no way of relating this knowledge to the horizon of the sacred? Is there no hope that the sacred and the profane meanings of the unconscious will finally coincide?

III. Marcuse and Brown

Psychoanalysis presents the paradox to the modern mind of a system that has chosen to ground itself in the language of myth while yet evolving an understanding of the psyche that is at once profane and real, radically profane in the sense that it dissolves the sacred meaning of the unconscious, and indubitably real insofar as its analysis has met with such a profound response from the contemporary sensibility. However, the success of psychoanalysis has been reached by means of a dubious method. The central concepts of psychoanalysis are derived by analogy from the natural sciences and forced to do service in a realm that forcefully resists the naked efforts of empirical methods. Suffice it to recall Freud's dictum that the reflex act remains the model of every psychic activity, or his concepts of libido and regression. Yet the language of psychoanalysis is largely a facade disguising the inverted symbols of myth, which are the real secret of its power: thus libido is in no genuine sense a biological category, for it doesn't simply mean sexual energy, but rather an incestuous sexual energy that becomes meaningful only by means of the Oedipus complex. Only after having intuitively laid the foundations of psychoanalysis upon the myth of this primordial complex, could Freud adopt that reductive method upon which he based his claim to scientific objectivity. Criticisms of the neo-Freudians notwithstanding, it seems probable that Freud's discovery of the far-reaching implications of the Oedipus complex was his most creative act of genius. Without it, psychoanalysis becomes a body of sophisticated insights into human behavior, lacking real depth and causal relatedness (as in Horney and Fromm), or a maze of brilliant but contradictory principles lacking coherent meaning (as in Stekel and Rank). For the mythical truth of the Oedipus complex created the depth and scope of psychoanalysis.

When Jung broke with Freud, he did so because of the pan-sexualism of the Freudian theory of libido, and its foundation in the Oedipus complex; reversing Freud, Jung searched for a "primal libido," prior to the sexual instinct, a libido that could be understood only by teleological and not by mechanistic principles. Gradually Jung was driven to a spiritual under-standing of libido, becoming a prophet and seer, although, in-sisting upon the "scientific" foundation of his psychology.[33] Opening himself to the esoteric traditions of East and West, and adopting the imagery of Gnosticism, Jung recovered the sacred meaning of the unconscious. He formulated the in-dividuation process as the highest form of psychotherapy, a process by which the deeper forces of the unconscious—the collective unconscious—were assumed to manifest themselves in the individual unconsciousness, leading to a numinous wholeness of the psyche, which Jung termed the "self." In Tibetan Tantrism, he found a mandala symbolism that he be-lieved to be the expression of the final phases of the individua-tion process, discovering this symbolism in the dreams of his patients, and in symbols and phantasies of every conceivable kind. Jung's progress—which might perhaps best be conceived as a reversal of Freud—was ever in the direction of a pan-psychism, modeled after the classic pantheistic systems, but sub-stituting the psychological image of the "self" for the mystical symbol of the Godhead. Finally, in his study of alchemy, Jung provided a cosmic setting for his understanding of the collec-tive unconscious—he interpreted the alchemical *opus* as the liberation of the fragments of the "self" that are embedded in matter—by conceiving of a cosmic evolution and involution of the "self." With every step, Jung moved farther and farther away from both the language of science and the world of modern man. His one claim to contemporaneity is his transla-tion of mythical imagery into psychological categories: but finally the mythical world prevails, and Jung's thought loses all semblance of rational meaning.

Jung's work has theological value only insofar as he succeeded in creating a peculiarly modern form of Gnosticism;[34] like all forms of *gnosis,* it is grounded in a nondialectical negation of the world, finally dissolving reason, consciousness, and history in its search for a total consummation and liberation of the "self." Whether or not the Jungian circle has succeeded in creating a genuine epiphany of the sacred, it has certainly succeeded in isolating the unconscious psyche, which it knows as the sacred, from the reality of the profane. Therefore Jung's work is irrelevant to this analysis, for we are in quest of a meaning of the unconscious that will be open to a dialectical coincidence of the sacred and the profane. Precisely because Freud's understanding of the unconscious is so radically profane it is open to a dialectical relation to the sacred. This paradoxical truth is manifest in Freud's two most profound interpreters, Herbert Marcuse and Norman Brown, both of whom have chosen to explore the dialectical implications of Freud's later work, particularly his ideas of narcissism and the death instinct, and their expositions of these themes have much greater power than those of Freud himself.

Herbert Marcuse has achieved a unique mastery of modern Western dialectical thinking, beginning his work with a study of Hegel's ontology, he became a distinguished interpreter of Marxism before embarking upon a study of Freud. Throughout his work, politics has been his deepest passion, and, in *Eros and Civilization,* Marcuse employs psychological categories because they have become political categories in our totalitarian era, believing that in Freud he has found the key to a "non-repressive sublimation." By taking absence from repression as the archetype of freedom, Marcuse conceives of civilization as the struggle against this freedom. He opens his analysis by adopting the Freudian idea that the animal-man becomes a human being only through a fundamental transformation of his nature, the transformation of the *pleasure principle* into the *reality principle:* "The replacement of the pleasure principle by the reality principle is the great traumatic event in the development of man—in the development of the genus (phylogenesis) as well as of the individual (ontogenesis)."[35] Marcuse fails to note that this idea was originated by Nietzsche in *The Genealogy of Morals,* but in Freud it takes on a new form; for the pleasure principle and the reality principle correspond to the spheres of the unconscious and conscious psyches, and *reality* becomes a phenomenon confined to human consciousness. Thereby man—or human consciousness—becomes doomed to a tragic destiny, he is bound to "reality," and therefore can never escape repression. At this point, Marcuse breaks with Freud, and does so on the basis of Freud's own ideas:

> Freud considers the "primordial struggle for existence" as "eternal" and therefore believes that the pleasure principle and the reality principle are "eternally" antagonistic. The notion that a non-repressive civilization is impossible is a cornerstone of Freudian theory. However, his theory contains elements that break through this rationalization; they shatter the predominant tradition of Western thought and even suggest its reversal. His work is characterized by an uncompromising insistence on showing up the repressive content of the highest values and achievements of culture. In so far as he does this, he denies the equation of reason with repression on which the ideology of culture is built. Freud's metapsychology is an ever-renewed attempt to uncover, and to question, the terrible necessity of the inner connection between civilization and barbarism, progress and suffering, freedom and unhappiness—a connection which reveals itself ultimately as that between Eros and Thanatos.[36]

Marcuse hopes for the recovery of the unconscious within history, a recovery reversing the civilization that is founded upon repression, and thus making possible a rebirth of the whole man.

The passage just quoted from Marcuse suggests that his deepest interest lies in the reversal of Western thought, a dialectical negation to be sure, for Western thought in its own way has always striven for a negation of the reality principle:

Western philosophy ends with the idea with which it began. At the beginning and at the end, in Aristotle and in Hegel, the supreme mode of being, the ultimate form of reason and freedom, appear as *nous*, spirit, *Geist*. At the end and at the beginning, the empirical world remains in negativity—the stuff and the tools of the spirit, or of its representatives on earth. In reality, neither remembrance nor absolute knowledge redeems that which was and is. Still, this philosophy testifies not only to the reality principle which governs the empirical world, but also to its negation. The consummation of being is, not the ascending curve, but the closing of the circle: the *re-turn* from alienation. Philosophy could conceive of such a state only as that of pure thought. Between the beginning and the end is the development of reason as the logic of domination—progress through alienation. The repressed liberation is upheld: in the idea and in the ideal.[37]

Western philosophy ended with Hegel because *logos* had exhausted itself, no longer could the essence of being be conceived as *logos:* "And, with this change in the basic experience of being, the logic of domination is challenged."[38] Marcuse believes that Nietzsche surmounted the ontological tradition by exposing the "gigantic fallacy" on which Western philosophy and morality were built—"namely, the transformation of facts into essences, of historical into metaphysical conditions"[39]— and by his call for a new liberation of man by reversing the sense of guilt. Unfortunately, he fails to employ Nietzsche in his own exposition (both Marcuse and Brown are embarrassed by Nietzsche whose thought is obviously so much more important than Freud's); instead he turns to Freud's metapsychological definition of the essence of being as eros, interpreting the death instinct and eros (libido) as metapsychological reformulations of the traditional metaphysical categories of nonbeing and being.

The great problem for Marcuse is the recovery in history of the repressed unconscious, and he attempts to answer this problem by calling for the establishment of memory and fantasy as decisive modes of *cognition*. By this means, the repressed past will be recovered, and regression will assume a progressive function: "The *recherche du temps perdu* becomes the vehicle of future liberation."[40] If reason is an expression of the reality principle, then fantasy—as Freud taught—is essentially connected with the pleasure principle; as a separate mental process, it is born and at the same time left behind by the organization of the pleasure ego into the reality ego.

> However, phantasy (imagination) retains the structure and the tendencies of the psyche prior to its organization by the reality, prior to its becoming an "individual" set off against other individuals. And by the same token, like the id to which it remains committed, imagination preserves the "memory" of the subhistorical past when the life of the individual was the life of the genus, the image of the immediate unity between the universal and the particular under the rule of the pleasure principle.[41]

Because it is bound to the "archaic" past, fantasy expresses the claim of the whole individual, which it directs against a repressive reality. Ultimately fantasy will cancel the established *principium individuationis*.[42] But thus far fantasy has only successfully been expressed in art, and whereas art is the "great refusal" of repression and embodies its own imaginative truth, nevertheless, art cannot transform reality—it can only recall the repressed in order to repress it once more in a "purified" form. Here, Marcuse borrows Nietzsche's aesthetic theory, but without acknowledgment.

The core of Marcuse's hope lies in his adaption of Freud's concept of *primary narcissism*. He believes that Freud's discovery of narcissism—which Marcuse interprets as the notion of an undifferentiated, unified libido prior to the division into ego and external objects—makes possible a new existential relation to reality. For if the primordial ego knew a oneness with the cosmos (Freud speaks of "limitless extension and oneness with the universe"),[43] then narcissism "denotes a fundamental relatedness to reality which may generate a comprehensive existential order."

In other words, narcissism may contain the germ of a different reality principle: the libidinal cathexis of the ego (one's own body) may become the source and reservoir for a new libidinal cathexis of the objective world—transforming this world into a new mode of being. . . . All sublimation would begin with the reactivation of narcissistic libido, which somehow overflows and extends to objects. The hypothesis all but revolutionizes the idea of sublimation; it hints at a non-repressive mode of sublimation which results from an extension rather than from a constraining deflection of the libido.[44]

Employing the aesthetic theory of Kant and Schiller, Marcuse searches for a path to the recovery of primary narcissism, and finds it in "play," a true freedom that is created by fantasy.

Once it has really gained ascendancy as a principle of civilization, the play impulse would literally transform the reality. Nature, the objective world, would then be experienced primarily, neither as dominating man (as in the primitive society), nor as being dominated by man (as in the established civilization), but rather as an object of "contemplation."[45]

Marcuse translates the idealistic language of Schiller ("contemplation") into the contemporary language of Marx and Freud, but thereby he reveals the deeply mythical roots of psychoanalytic language. Like Jung, he seeks a transformation of libido, but unlike Jung he believes that a rebirth of narcissism can transform a genital sexuality into an erotization of the entire personality. This new eros will create a nonrepressive reality principle, thus "re-sexualizing" the body: "The regression involved in this spread of libido would first manifest itself in a reactivation of all erotogenic zones and, consequently, in a resurgence of pre-genital polymorphous sexuality and in a decline of genital supremacy."[46] Now the body in its entirety—and not simply the genital zones—will become an object of libido. The fall into history, created by the victory of the reality principle over the pleasure principle, will be reversed: the opposites will be united, the pleasure principle will become the reality principle, and repression will be abolished. Furthermore, such a transformation of genital libido into universal eros will lead to a disintegration of the institutions in which the "private inter-personal relations" have been organized: alienation will be banished from history. But doesn't this mean that history will come to an end? Thus Marcuse, the stern political realist, becomes a utopian; yet his utopia is nonideological, it demands a reversal of history, a return to primordial humanity, and even an abolition of time.

At all these points, Marcuse's vision of eros coincides with Eliade's vision of the sacred. Both seek cosmic regeneration revolving about a rebirth of archaic man, both employ dualistic categories and a dialectical method (in Marcuse's presentation, the Freudian distinction between the pleasure principle and the reality principle closely parallels Eliade's distinction between the sacred and the profane), and Marcuse's conception of the autonomous faculty of "fantasy" or "imagination," just as his idea of primordial narcissism, can finally bear the weight he gives them only if they are understood in a mystical or eschatological sense. Although Marcuse is consistently indifferent to the realm of the sacred, and is himself a remarkable representative of the profane consciousness, the very passion with which he pursues a final liberation from the alienation of history inevitably impels him in the direction of the sacred. Perhaps most important of all, *Eros and Civilization* demonstrates that the quest for absolute freedom can never be realized in either the pure thought of logos or the pure form of art, but demands a transformation of reality: a transformation promised by the sacred, but understood by the profane, thus witnessing to the possibility of an ultimate reconciliation between the sacred and the profane.

By suspending common sense, and embracing "madness" — both of which were characteristic of the ancient Chinese and Hebrew prophets — Norman Brown has succeeded in arriving at a truly prophetic vision of the birth of a new man. Many of the themes of *Eros and Civilization* are carried forward in Brown's *Life Against Death;* this is particularly true of the dual theme of the demand for a reversal of history and a call for the rebirth of archaic man. Again, the Freudian idea of a primordial narcissism, revolving about a pregenital polymorphous sexuality, lies at the center of Brown's analysis; and Brown, too, has employed a dialectical method, although he has abandoned the political framework of Marcuse's thought. Brown attempts to bring together the dialectical tradition in a new synthesis—by a 'dialectical' method Brown means "an activity of consciousness struggling to circumvent the limitations imposed by the formal-logical law of contradiction"[47]— and, in particular, to effect a living union between left-wing mysticism (e.g., Taoism and Jacob Boehme) and radical Freudianism. Consequently, the unstated goal of *Life Against Death* is a dialectical synthesis of the sacred and the profane, a goal that is in part achieved in Brown's vision of the "magical body."

Brown follows Marcuse in identifying history as the product of repression, and Brown, also, rebels against the pessimistic dualism of Freud's later writings. Nevertheless, his own basic categories of Life and Death are adapted from the late Freudian distinction between the life and death instincts, although he insists upon interpreting this distinction dialectically rather than dualistically: "But if the instinctual duality is Life and Death, our modification of Freud's ontology entails the hypothesis that Life and Death coexist in some undifferentiated unity at the animal level and that they could be reunified in some higher harmony in man."[48] The opposition between Life and Death is not innate, but unknown to nature and to archaic man, for it is created by repression, and therefore is confined to history:

> Regression transforms the timeless instinctual compulsion to repeat into the forward-moving dialectic of neurosis which is history; history is a forward-moving *recherche du temps perdu* with the repetition-compulsion guaranteeing the historical law of the slow return of the repressed. And conversely, life not repressed—organic life below man and human life if repression

were overcome—is not in historical time. If we connect—as Freud did not—the repetition-compulsion with Freud's reiterated theorem that the instinctual processes in the id are timeless, then only repressed life is in time, and unrepressed life would be timeless or in eternity.[49]

Brown's most important principle is that originally Life and Death existed in a "biological" unity; but the advent of history separated Life and Death into conflicting opposites, and then subjected the opposites to repression. Only in historical time, and only through repression, does the unconscious death instinct become that "negativity or nothingness which is extroverted into the action of negating nature and other men."[50]

If aggression is the product of extroverted death, then aggression (or Death) is the product of the repression of libido, which Brown interprets as the repression of the human body. Only if the life instinct can no longer affirm the Life of the body, does anxiety about Death arise; for the horror of death is the horror of dying with what Rilke called unlived lives in our bodies.[51] Repression is always repression of the body, and the advent of the repressed body is the source of that *Angst* which is the condition of man's life in history. However, the repressed body is a fallen body; and Brown's most daring idea is the suggestion that the genital sexual organization is the effect on the body of anxiety in the ego: "Then, since . . . anxiety is the ego's incapacity to accept death, the sexual organizations were perhaps constructed by the ego in its flight from death, and could be abolished by an ego strong enough to die."[52] Let us remember, as Brown does not, that the church fathers believed that the sexual instinct was created by the fall, and note that Brown shares all their horror for what we know as the sexual life of the body: in his vision, genital sexuality will perish with the abolition of repression. If our fallen or genital sexuality is the effect of our refusal of death, then liberation from repression will come with our acceptance of death, with each man's willing his own death. Yet Life and Death are dialectically related; indeed, they were once dialec-

tically *united;* therefore, the affirmation of Life is simultaneously the affirmation of Death—when we can accept our bodies,
then we can will our deaths—and thereby know eternity:
"Psychoanalysis comes to remind us that we are bodies, that
repression is of the body, and that perfection would be the
realm of Absolute Body; eternity is the mode of unrepressed
bodies."[53] Brown believes that we are nothing but body, and
the repression of the body has created everything which we
know as history, reason, and consciousness, all of which were
created by Death when it had lost its primordial unity with
Life, and all of which will be transformed with the rebirth
of unrepressed bodies. But what does Brown mean by 'body'?

The secret of Brown's idea of Life is that he has transposed
Freud's concept of libido into a sacred meaning of the body.
He prefers William Blake's word 'Energy' to 'libido,' although
he believes that Blake's idea of Energy is equivalent to Freud's
idea of libido, and he quotes these words from Blake to substantiate his point: "Energy is the only life, and is from the
Body. . . . Energy is Eternal Delight."[54] Brown links Freud
with a romantic mystical tradition going back to Jacob Boehme
and the Cabala, identifying this tradition as Dionysian or
body mysticism, a mysticism opposed to the dominant Apollonian or sublimation mysticism. While the goal of Apollonian
mysticism is a flight from the body, Dionysian mysticism affirms
Life, and seeks a transformation and perfection of the body.
Historically, Western body mysticism contains three main
strands: the Christian (Pauline) notion of the "spiritual" body,
the Jewish Cabala's notion of Adam's perfect body before the
fall, and the alchemical notion of the subtle body.[55] This is
the body that is celebrated by such modern poets as Hopkins,
Rilke, and Valéry:

> The "magical" body which the poet seeks is the "subtle" or
> "spiritual" or "translucent" body of occidental mysticism, and
> the "diamond" body of oriental mysticism, and, in psycho-
> analysis, the polymorphously perverse body of childhood. Thus,
> for example, psychoanalysis declares the fundamentally bisexual

character of human nature; Boehme insists on the androgynous
character of human perfection; Taoist mysticism invokes fem-
inine passivity to counteract masculine aggressivity; and Rilke's
poetic quest is a quest for a hermaphroditic body.[56]

In such passages, one might well suspect that he were reading
Eliade and not Brown; and Brown's analysis does much to
reveal the nature of the erotic ground of Eliade's quest for
cosmic sacrality.

In his conclusion, Brown calls for an abolition of repression,
going so far as to insist that the abolition of repression is
equivalent to the Christian dogma of the resurrection of the
body: "The speciality of Christian eschatology lies precisely in
its rejection of the Platonic hostility to the human body and
to 'matter,' its refusal to identify the Platonic path of sublimation with ultimate salvation, and its affirmation that
eternal life can only be life in a body."[57] Here, he quotes
Tertullian rather than Paul—"The body will rise again, all
of the body, the identical body, the entire body"—perhaps
because he knows that the Pauline "spiritual" body is in no
sense to be identified with the body of "flesh." Yet neither is
Brown's "magical" body the body which we know; it is an
erotic body, yes, but it is transfigured.

> At the same time—and here again Christian theology and
> psychoanalysis agree—the resurrected body is the transfigured
> body. The abolition of repression would abolish the unnatural
> concentrations of libido in certain particular bodily organs—
> concentrations engineered by the negativity of the morbid death
> instinct, and constituting the bodily base of the neurotic char-
> acter disorders in the human ego. . . . The human body would
> become polymorphously perverse, delighting in that full life of
> all the body which it now fears. The consciousness strong
> enough to endure full life would be no longer Apollonian but
> Dionysian—consciousness which does not observe the limit, but
> overflows; consciousness which *does not negate any more.*[58]

These last words are taken from Nietzsche, and they mark the
limit of Brown's thought. Brown, however, has taken Freud's

thought to its limit, or beyond, and demonstrated that, dialectically conceived, transfigured libido will no longer be 'sexual,' it will pervade the body, and embrace all bodies whatsoever. Finally, true libido is Life and not life. We can imagine that in another age Brown might well have employed the word 'soul' and not 'body'; but neither word will do, for he seeks a 'soul' that is dialectically united with the 'body,' corresponding to the primordial and dialectical union between Life and Death. In psychoanalytic terms, Brown seeks a libido that is unaffected by the Oedipus complex; and this means a libido that has not murdered God, a libido that is unfallen and still in union with the sacred, and, paradoxically, a libido—precisely because it is libido—that is fully profane.

This analysis has left untouched the most exciting section of *Life Against Death,* its portrait of the anal character of Western man, which reaches this conclusion: "The historical series of cultural patterns—the stages in the history of the neurosis—exhibit a dialectic of two seemingly contradictory trends: on the one hand, ever increasing denial of the body, and, on the other hand, the slow return of the repressed in an alienated form."

> Actually these seemingly contradictory trends are two sides of the same coin. The ever increasing denial of the body is, in the form of a negation, an ever increasing affirmation of the denied body. Sublimations are these negations of the body which simultaneously affirm it; and sublimations achieve this dialectical tour de force by the simple but basic mechanism of projecting the repressed body into things. The more the life of the body passes into things, the less life there is in the body, and at the same time the increasing accumulation of things represents an ever fuller articulation of the lost life of the body. Hence increasing sublimation is a general law of history.[59]

Historical "progress" means an increase in the domain of the death instinct at the expense of the life instinct, an increase made possible by the repressive character of sublimation. With the abolition of repression, this process will be reversed, and the death instinct will be reconciled with the life instinct in a fully living body that is willing to die: "And, because the body is satisfied, the death instinct no longer drives it to change itself and make history, and therefore, as Christian theology divined, its activity is in eternity."[60] At the climax of his vision, Brown's language becomes inadequate; to speak of unrepressed bodies as "eternity" is very nearly meaningless, for even if we are told that time is the product of repression, we can only imagine a bodily eternity as the timeless life of the primordial id—and this is not Brown's meaning. When Brown speaks of Absolute Body he is not symbolizing the nature of archaic man, but rather witnessing to an eschatological aeon to come, a Kingdom of God that will draw *all* things into itself. Wedded as he is to the profane language of Freud, he can find no language or symbols that will record his vision of the abolition of repression; yet his loyalty to Freud has given his vision a reality that otherwise it would never have had. If we are to attempt to move beyond Freud and Eliade, and seek a dialectical coincidence of the sacred and the profane, we must open ourselves to the greatest prophet of the modern world, Friedrich Nietzsche.

8

The Sacred and the Profane

I. Yes-Saying and the Body

I N *Ecce Homo,* Nietzsche confessed that he chose the name
of Zarathustra for his prophet of Eternal Recurrence because he believed that the Persian Zarathustra created the most
fateful of all errors—morality: "The translation of morality
into metaphysics, as force, first cause, end-in-itself, is his
work."[1] Now Nietzsche, the first "immoralist," has created the
exact opposite of the historical Zarathustra: "Do you understand? . . . The defeat of morality by itself, through truthful-
ness, the moralist's defeat of himself in his opposite—in me—
that is what the name Zarathustra means in my mouth."[2]
Whereas morality is grounded in no-saying, in *ressentiment,*
the new Zarathustra preaches a gospel of affirmation; accordingly, *Thus Spoke Zarathustra* is an utterly unique work:

> My concept "Dionysian" here became the *highest* deed; mea-
> sured by it all other human deeds seem poor and limited. The
> fact that a Goethe or a Shakespeare would not have been
> able to breathe for a moment in this terrific atmosphere of
> passion and elevation; the fact that compared with Zarathustra,
> Dante is no more than a believer, and not one who *creates* truth
> for the first time—a world-ruling spirit, a *Destiny;* the fact that
> the Vedic poets were priests and not even fit to unfasten Zara-
> thustra's sandal—all this is of no great importance; it gives no
> idea of the distance, of the azure solitude, wherein this work
> dwells. Zarathustra has an eternal right to say: "I draw circles

176

around me and holy boundaries. Ever fewer are they that mount
with me to ever loftier heights. I build me a mountain range
of ever holier mountains."[3]

The new Zarathustra has seen further, willed further, and gone
further than any other man. In this most yes-saying of all
spirits, the highest and the lowest, the sweetest and the most
terrible powers are combined. He contradicts himself in every
word: "Yet in him all oppositions are resolved into a new
unity."[4]

Nietzsche's Zarathustra is a product of the "second innocence" of atheism,[5] the new historical destiny created by the
death of God. Man has been surpassed in Zarathustra, for
Zarathustra has negated all previous history, and this negation
is but the other side of the deepest affirmation.

> The psychological problem the Zarathustra-type presents is this:
> how can he, who to an unprecedented extent says no, and *acts*
> no, in reference to all to which man has hitherto said yes, never-
> theless remain the opposite of a no-saying spirit? How can he
> who bears destiny's heaviest burden, and whose life-task is a
> fatality, yet be the lightest and the most transcendental of
> spirits—for Zarathustra is a dancer? How can he who has the
> hardest and most terrible insight into reality, and who has
> thought the most "abysmal thoughts," nevertheless find in these
> things no objections to existence, or to its eternal recurrence?
> How is it that on the contrary he finds reasons for *being himself*
> the everlasting Yea to all things, "the tremendous and unlimited
> saying of Yea and Amen"? . . . "Into every abyss do I bear the
> benediction of my yea to Life." . . . *But this again is the very*
> *essence of Dionysus.*[6]

Zarathustra calls his hearers to a new Dionysian existence, an
existence of total yes-saying to the sheer horror of a naked
reality, a reality that is first revealed by Zarathustra, and a
reality that can only be known by a reversal of that no-saying
which is Nietzsche's deepest symbol of the meaning of history.
If bad conscience came into existence with the advent of history, as Nietzsche taught, and if bad conscience originated with

an "interiorization" of the instincts thwarted by society,[7] with the birth of a "soul" opposed to the "body," then Dionysian existence demands a baptism of the instincts, a new innocence created by the sanctification of the forbidden; in short, Zarathustra calls for a resurrection of the body.

Nietzsche's ecstatic celebration of the "body" is contained in the first part of *Zarathustra*. Zarathustra has descended alone from the mountains, entered a forest, and encountered a holy anchorite; he is amazed that the old saint has not yet heard that God is dead. Abandoning the saint, he enters a town on the edge of the forest and teaches the doctrine of the Superman, proclaiming that the Superman is the meaning of the earth: "I beseech you, my brothers, *remain faithful to the earth,* and do not believe those who speak to you of other-worldly hopes!"[8] Later he reveals the origin of these false hopes:

> It was suffering and incapacity that created all afterworlds—this and that brief madness of bliss which is experienced only by those who suffer most deeply.
>
> Weariness that wants to reach the ultimate with one leap, with one fatal leap, a poor ignorant weariness that does not want to want any more: this created all gods and afterworlds.
>
> Believe me, my brothers: it was the body that despaired of the body and touched the ultimate walls with the fingers of a deluded spirit. Believe me, my brothers: it was the body that despaired of the earth and heard the belly of being speak to it. It wanted to crash through these ultimate walls with its head, and not only with its head—over there to "that world." But "that world" is well concealed from humans—that dehumanized inhuman world which is a heavenly nothing; and the belly of being does not speak to humans at all, except as a human.[9]

The body despairs of the body when it cannot bear its pain, when it is too weak to accept a naked existence in the flesh; then *ressentiment* arises, rebelling against a power that has overwhelmed a broken self. Such resentment is always a flight from pain, as Nietzsche taught in *The Genealogy of Morals:* "The wish to alleviate pain through strong emotional excitation is, to my mind, the true physiological motive behind all manifestations of resentment."[10] Correspondingly, resentment is the origin of all faith in a Beyond, which means that all such faith is grounded in an inability to accept the full reality of the body. Faith in "that world" is an evasion of suffering, a flight from pain, a refusal of existence in the body, a fatal leap to a heavenly nothing.

Only the sick and decaying who despise the body aspire to a heavenly realm. Having died to the body, they become preachers of the gospel of death: the gospel of eternal life in the "spirit." The healthy body, on the other hand, speaks only of the meaning of the earth: "A new will I teach men: to *will* this way which man has walked blindly, and to affirm it, and no longer to sneak away from it like the sick and decaying."[11] Thus Zarathustra says:

> I want to speak to the despisers of the body. I would not have them learn and teach differently, but merely say farewell to their own bodies—and thus become silent.
>
> "Body am I, and soul"—thus speaks the child. And why should one not speak like children?
>
> But the awakened and knowing say: body am I entirely, and nothing else; and soul is only a word for something about the body.[12]

Again and again, Zarathustra pleads with his hearers to remain faithful to the earth, to return to the body; identifying true existence with existence as body. But what is the meaning of Nietzsche's symbol of the "body"? Zarathustra counsels the "innocence" of the senses,[13] and continually associates the body with the earth. When he says "body am I entirely," he equates the deepest willing of immediate existence in the "here" and "now" with the life of the body; thus accepting but inverting the traditional dichotomy between "body" and "spirit."

If existence in the Spirit may be conceived as transcendent existence, then existence in the body is immanent existence, a total immersion of the self in the immediate moment. Above all, existence in the body means existence in *reality:* in a reality untouched by resentment and free of all illusion.

Nietzsche defined this existence succinctly in the *Twilight of the Idols:*

> Such a spirit who has *become free* stands amid the cosmos with a joyous and trusting fatalism, in the *faith* that only the particular is loathsome, and that all is redeemed and affirmed in the whole—*he does not negate any more.* Such a faith, however, is the highest of all possible faiths: I have baptized it with the name of *Dionysus.*[14]

Freed of all negation, the Dionysian existence of the body is a yes-saying to the cosmos, an affirmation of the deepest reality of the world. Now that God is dead, the great temptation of "that world" is revealed as a nihilistic flight from reality. Consequently, in *The Antichrist,* Nietzsche says: "That we find no God—either in history or in nature or behind nature—is not what differentiates *us,* but that we experience what has been revered as God, not as 'godlike' but as miserable, as absurd, as harmful, not merely as an error but as a *crime against life.*"[15] Pagans are all those who say Yes to life, who will life, and therefore exist as "body." The new Zarathustra has come to resurrect the body, to annul the work of the old Zarathustra by abolishing the Spirit and freeing the "body." Finally the time of true freedom has dawned: God is dead, Dionysus is resurrected!

> Before God! But now this God has died. You higher men, this god was your greatest danger. It is only since he lies in his tomb that you have been resurrected. Only now the great noon comes; only now the higher man becomes—lord.[16]

II. Eternal Recurrence

Erich Heller, in speaking of the impact of the death of God upon the work of Nietzsche and Rilke, asserts that they dedicated their lives to but one task:

> To re-assess and re-define all experience in thought and feeling; to show that the traditional modes of thought and feeling, in so far as they were determined, or decisively modified, by Christian transcendental beliefs—and to which of them does not this apply?—had been rendered invalid by the end of religion;

to replace them; to overcome the great spiritual depression, caused by the death of God, through new and ever greater powers of glory and praise; to adjust, indeed to revolutionize, thought and feeling in accordance with the reality of a world of absolute immanence; and to achieve this without any loss of spiritual grandeur.[17]

Nietzsche met and fulfilled this task in his doctrine of Eternal Recurrence, a doctrine—if such it can be called—which he regarded as his greatest creation, his triumphant hymn of joy in praise of a vast and meaningless cosmos. Yet this hymn of joy was created out of the deepest pain, for Nietzsche regarded the idea of Eternal Recurrence as the nightmare of nightmares. Already in *The Gay Science*—in a passage following the Madman's proclamation of the death of God—he recorded this idea in its most terrible form.

The Heaviest Burden.—What if a demon crept after thee into thy loneliest loneliness some day or night, and said to thee: "This life, as thou livest it at present, and hast lived it, thou must live it once more, and also innumerable times; and there will be nothing new in it, but every pain and every joy and every thought and every sigh, and all the unspeakably small and great in thy life must come to thee again, and all in the same series and sequence—and similarly this spider and this moonlight among the trees, and similarly this moment and I myself. The eternal sand-glass of existence will ever be turned once more, and thou with it, thou speck of dust!"—Wouldst thou not throw thyself down and gnash thy teeth, and curse the demon that so spoke?[18]

Here, is the most horrible reality that man can face; not that there is no God, but that there is no nothingness, no escape from life, no path to extinction. Only the deepest courage can meet this challenge, and Nietzsche asks his reader if he has once experienced a tremendous moment in which he could answer the demon: "Thou art a god, and never did I hear anything so divine!"[19]

No teaching of Nietzsche's has been so consistently misunderstood as his doctrine of Eternal Recurrence, despite the fact that the vision of Eternal Recurrence (*ewigen Wiederkunft*) lies at the center of his mature thought; moreover, it might be said that the symbol of Eternal Recurrence offers the one path to an understanding of absolute immanence, the new reality created by modern man. Perhaps no commentator has realized that the metaphysical form of the doctrine of Eternal Recurrence is no more than the meaning of the reality revealed by Zarathustra when known apart from the deepest affirmation of the new Dionysian faith. Let us first examine the metaphysical form of the doctrine as it is presented in the third part of *Thus Spoke Zarathustra:*

> "Behold," I continued, "this moment! From this gateway Moment, a long, eternal lane leads *backward:* behind us lies an eternity. Must not whatever *can* walk have walked on this lane before? Must not whatever *can* happen have happened, have been done, have passed by before? And if everything has been there before—what do you think, dwarf, of this moment? Must not this gateway too have been there before? And are not all things knotted together so firmly that this moment draws after it *all* that is to come? Therefore—itself too? For whatever *can* walk —in this long lane out *there* too, it *must* walk once more."[20]

In this form, the doctrine coincides with both the ancient Indian idea of *samsara* and the Greek myth of Eternal Return; but it differs profoundly from these sacred visions of a profane reality insofar as it knows only, and reflects only, an absolutely profane being. Now, for the first time, man's profane choice has become fully manifest; and only now has the profane reality become wholly isolated from either the memory or the reflection of the sacred.

Later Zarathustra's animals teach the doctrine to the teacher of the eternal recurrence, and they teach it as his great destiny, and his greatest danger and sickness too. Then, speaking in his name, they declare:

> "I myself belong to the causes of the eternal recurrence. I come again, with this sun, with this earth, with this eagle, with this

serpent—*not* to a new life or a better life or a similar life: I come back eternally to this same, selfsame life, in what is greatest as in what is smallest, to teach again the eternal recurrence of all things, to speak again the word of the great noon of earth and man, to proclaim the overman again to men. I spoke my word, I break of my word: thus my eternal lot wants it; as a proclaimer I perish. The hour has now come when he who goes under should bless himself. Thus *ends* Zarathustra's going under."[21]

Zarathustra is the one who goes under (*der Untergehende*); and he does so by transforming the cosmic terror of the eternal recurrence into the ecstatic joy of Eternal Recurrence, by transforming 'metaphysical' into 'existential' truth. Eternal Recurrence is Zarathustra's cross and his redemption: and his gospel is that cross and redemption are one. Indeed, Zarathustra's cross is an inversion of the cross of Christ and so likewise is his gospel; as can be seen from his initial proclamation of redemption:

" 'Can there be redemption if there is eternal justice? Alas, the stone *It was* cannot be moved: all punishments must be eternal too.' Thus preached madness.

" 'No deed can be annihilated: how could it be undone by punishment? This, this is what is eternal in the punishment called existence, that existence must eternally become deed and guilt again. Unless the will should at least redeem himself, and willing should become not willing.' But, my brothers, you know this fable of madness.

"I led you away from these fables when I taught you, 'The will is a creator.' All 'it was' is a fragment, a riddle, a dreadful accident—until the creative will says to it, 'But thus I willed it.' Until the creative will says to it, 'But thus I will it; thus shall I will it.' "[22]

Thus the metaphysical doctrine of eternal recurrence is a fragment, a riddle, a dreadful accident—until the creative will says to it, "But thus I will it, thus shall I will it"; thereby transforming terror into joy, death into life, fate into a freely chosen destiny: "To redeem what is past in man and to re-create all 'it was' until the will says, 'Thus I willed it! Thus I shall will it!'—this I called redemption and this alone I taught them to call redemption."[23]

Nowhere did Nietzsche succeed more triumphantly in reaching his frequently stated goal of speaking volumes in a few words than he did in the third part of *Zarathustra,* where in thirteen lines he was able to express the full meaning of the symbol of Eternal Recurrence. In Walter Kaufmann's translation, the lines read as follows:

> "O Zarathustra," the animals said, "to those who think as we do, all things themselves are dancing: they come and offer their hands and laugh and flee—and come back. Everything goes, everything comes back; eternally rolls the wheel of being. Everything dies, everything blossoms again; eternally runs the year of being. Everything breaks, everything is joined anew; eternally the same house of being is built. Everything parts, everything greets every other thing again; eternally the ring of being remains faithful to itself. In every Now, being begins; round every Here rolls the sphere There. The center is everywhere. Bent is the path of eternity."[24]

But these lines are so important that they must be given in their original German:

> Oh Zarathustra, sagten darauf die Thiere, Solchen, die denken wie wir, tanzen alle Dinge selber: das kommt und reicht sich die Hand und lacht und flieht—und kommt zurück.
>
> Alles geht, Alles kommt zurück; ewig rollt das Rad des Seins. Alles stirbt, Alles blüht wieder auf, ewig läuft das Jahr des Seins.
>
> Alles bricht, Alles wird neu gefügt; ewig baut sich das gleiche Haus des Seins. Alles scheidet, Alles grüsst sich wieder; ewig bleibt sich treu der Ring des Seins.
>
> In jedem Nu beginnt das Sein; um jedes Hier rollt sich die Kugel Dort. Die Mitte ist überall. Krumm ist der Pfad der Ewigkeit.[25]

The 'wheel' of being is an ancient symbol in both East and West of an eternal round of existence without meaning, purpose, or direction, except insofar as mere existence in such a 'wheel' brings atonement from a primal guilt. Zarathustra's animals—at a moment when Zarathustra himself cannot face the idea of the eternal recurrence of all things—celebrate the wheel of being not as a horrible cycle of perpetual pain but as an eternal dance, evoking the image of the Hindu symbol of the dance of Siva; now pain has become joy, meaninglessness has become order, guilt has become grace. Like the Hindu idea of the world as the divine but meaningless play (lila) of an ultimately impersonal Deity, the idea of eternal recurrence reflects a reality of sheer delight when it knows the world apart from guilt.[26] Only the second innocence created by the death of God is wholly devoid of guilt, but through such innocence the most horrible dimension of a now naked reality assumes the form of a cosmic dance. Note the order of the images that Nietzsche gives the idea of being: Rad ('wheel,' 'cycle'), Jahr ('year'), Haus ('house,' 'home,' 'family,' 'race'), and Ring ('ring,' 'circle,' 'cycle'). The imagery itself is cyclical, moving to and from the idea of the circle, and comprehending first a cyclical image of time (Jahr), and then what can only have been intended as a cyclical image of space (gleiche Haus). Furthermore, all of these images are created by affirmation, by yes-saying; as revealed by the first sentence of the passage ("to those who think as we do, all things themselves are dancing"), and then by the association of the adverb treu ('faithful,' 'loyal,' 'true') with the eternal cycle of being. When known in affirmation, the chaos of the eternal round of birth and death is transformed into the highest order of perfection, as symbolized by the circle.

The culmination of the passage is in the last three sentences, which are surely the most important lines that Nietzsche ever wrote. In jedem Nu beginnt das Sein: when Heidegger declared that Nietzsche's proclamation of the death of God was the nihilistic fulfillment of the historical destiny of the West, he meant that Nietzsche had pronounced the metaphysical question to be meaningless, that there is no Sein of Seiendes.[27]

To Heidegger, Nietzsche is the great enemy of the holy, for Heidegger identifies the holy with the transcendence of *Sein;* but in this line, Nietzsche identifies the "holy" with the immediate moment: "Being begins in every Now." Here, the verb is all important because the verb defines both the subject and the predicate. Like Heraclitus and the early Buddhist philosophers, Nietzsche identifies ultimate reality with the instantaneous moment of the flow of being; but unlike his dialectical predecessors he has isolated this immediate moment from any metaphysical relation with an order or *logos* that transcends it, thus approaching the *Tao* of Chinese mysticism. Thereby he has revealed that the proposition 'Being *is*' is a product of the detachment of the speaker from the immediate moment: to be totally immersed in the Now is to be free of an awareness of a beyond of any kind. When existence is most deeply affirmed, being becomes confined to the Now: the actual moment of existence becomes *Sein.* The act, the affirmation, the willing of the moment—as symbolized by *jedem Nu*—is the eternal creation and re-creation of all reality whatsoever (*das Sein*). Being is created anew in every moment. With the death of God —the collapse of transcendent Being—there can be no meaning or order that transcends the immediate moment. But the collapse of the transcendent makes possible the resurrection of the Now: transcendence has been transformed into immanence, "that world" has become the immediate moment, the eternal has become identical with time.

This transvaluation of the whole traditional order of being is carried forward in the next phrase: *um jedes Hier rollt sich die Kugel Dort,* "the world of There revolves about every Here." If every moment is Being itself, then all moments of being are equivalent because every moment must coincide with every other. So likewise every point of space must be equivalent to every other point, for there is no transcendent order to define either the meaning or the value of point or direction. Any point in space—any fragment of world or self—can be said to have neither direction nor meaning, therefore the traditional distinction between 'here' and 'there' must be collapsed. To exist 'here' is to exist 'there,' to will 'here' is to will 'there.' All things are firmly bound together, or, rather, all things flow into one another with the result that it is no longer possible to say 'here' or 'there,' I or Thou, he or it. The veil of being has been dissolved by the Yes-saying of Dionysian faith, a Yes-saying that has negated the cosmos created by the flight from the "body." Man has been surpassed, and with him has been surpassed every meaning, every order, every value created by his "soul." In *The Genealogy of Morals,* Nietzsche could say: "Ever since Copernicus man has been rolling down an incline, faster and faster, away from the center—whither? Into the void?"[28] Now this void is all, but what the "soul" knows as chaos, the "body" knows as bliss: a Yes-saying faith delights in the resurrection of the brute reality of things. Dionysian faith wants all things, wants all things now, and wants them eternally the same. By dissolving the 'here' and 'there' of things, the 'order' of nature becomes the dance of being, as the deepest affirmation of reality resurrects the sheer immediacy of being. With the dawn of this immediacy, all meaning disappears: the opposites are united, 'here' and 'there' are one.

Die Mitte ist überall, "The Center is everywhere." Again, we encounter the symbol of the sacred "Center"; but whereas the traditional symbol is known only by means of the realization of a chasm between sacred space and profane space, between the "Center" and the void, Zarathustra's *Mitte* is everywhere, throughout all space and time. The higher expressions of mysticism also know such a *coincidentia oppositorum,* as can be seen from a statement attributed to the Taoist thinker, Chuang Chou: "If I renounce the world, I can ride on the bird of unselfconsciousness and go out beyond space, wander in the village of Nowhere and make my home in the open country of Emptiness."[29] However, the Taoist reaches the "village of Nowhere" and the "open country of Emptiness" by inaction (*wu wei*), a mystical passivity that inactivates the will's engagement with space and time. As Chuang Chou says:

Inaction is the real part of fame, the storehouse of all plans,
the responsible head of all business, the master of all knowledge.
Identify yourself completely with infinity-eternity and wander
in the non-self. Carry to the highest what you have received
from Heaven but do not reveal your success in this. Be empty:
that is all. The perfect man's use of his mind is like a mirror.
He does not anticipate (events), nor does he go counter to them.
He responds but he does not retain. Thus it is that he is able
to master things and not be injured by them.[30]

In a parallel manner, the Madhyamika Buddhist knows *samsara* as *nirvana* when his attention is so absorbed by *nirvana*
that all consciousness disappears. Consequently, mysticism effects a *coincidentia oppositorum* by transforming profane
space into sacred space, by effecting a total disengagement of
the will from either an awareness of or a participation in the
profane. Nietzsche reverses this pattern, yet his reversal is dialectical, and it is dialectical precisely because it rests upon a
total inversion of the mystic's realization of a sacred "Center."
Reversing Chuang Chou, we might say for Nietzsche: total
action is the real path to the "Center," identify yourself completely with the here and now and carry to the highest what
you have received from earth. Be full: that is all. Yet paradoxically, Zarathustra's 'action' (his Will to Power) carries
him to a "village of Nowhere" and an "open country of Emptiness"; and this because his Yes-saying has carried him beyond
the history created by man's flight from reality, and into the
very heart of things, where "the Center is everywhere." Unlike
the mystic, Zarathustra responds to all things, and is injured
by all things, but it is just because he is totally immersed in
things that he can know the "Center" to be everywhere.

Krumm ist der Pfad der Ewigkeit, "Curved is the path of
Eternity" (*krumm* also means 'bent' or 'crooked'). Once again
we find a circular image, this time to symbolize eternity.
Obviously the line evokes the metaphysical idea of the
eternal recurrence of all things, and this is clearly Nietzsche's
intention. But what can the eternal recurrence of all things

mean in the context of this passage? Being begins in every Now; the world of There revolves about every Here; and the Center is everywhere. All too clearly the very possibility of a metaphysical idea in the traditional sense has been foreclosed by these affirmations: Yes-saying can know no *logos* of things. Paradoxically, the path of eternity is both 'curved' and 'crooked,' both 'circular' and 'circuitous.' Eternity has no *logos,* nor is there meaning or order in nature or history. Nietzsche's *Ewigkeit* is the very antithesis of the eternity of the philosophers and theologians, and he intends it to bring about a deep revulsion in the man of 'faith.' In the drunken midnight song, Zarathustra sings: "Woe says: Go! But all joy (*Lust*) wants Eternity—wants deep, deep Eternity."[31] As Zarathustra himself interprets these words: "But joy does not want heirs, nor children—joy wants itself, wants Eternity, wants Recurrence, wants everything eternally the same."[32] Finally, Yes-saying and Eternal Recurrence are identical: the deepest affirmation of existence can only mean the willing of the eternal recurrence of all things, the willing of *this* life, of *this* moment, of *this* pain, in such a manner as to will that it recur eternally, and recur eternally the same. We find here no metaphysical cosmology, no Weltanschauung, no *idea* of eternal recurrence; but rather the deepest existence (*Dasein*) in the Now, in the Here and There, in the Center that is everywhere. Eternity is Now; but it is so only when the world of There revolves about every Here, when the Center is everywhere. Only in the deepest willing of Dionysian faith is the true reality of Eternal Recurrence made manifest. And it appears only through the death of God, through the resurrection of the brute reality of the "body": *Krumm ist der Pfad der Ewigkeit.*

III. Christ and Dionysus

Nietzsche concluded his discussion of *Thus Spoke Zarathustra* in *Ecce Homo* by asking: "Have you understood me? *Dionysus versus Christ.*"[33] The new Dionysus, who is by no means to be identified with the Greek Dionysus, is the symbol of Eternal Recurrence, of eternity transformed into time; thus Nietzsche's Dionysus is only born through the death of God, the most important event in history: "There has never been a greater deed; and whoever will be born after us—for the sake of this deed he will be part of a higher history than all history hitherto."[34] Yet Nietzsche's opposition to Christ was directed against the Christ of Christianity, against religion itself, rather than against the actual figure of Jesus. In the same year that he wrote *Ecce Homo* (1888), he could say in *The Antichrist:*

> Using the expression somewhat tolerantly, one could call Jesus a "free spirit"—he does not care for anything solid: the word kills, all that is solid kills. The concept, the *experience* of "life" in the only way he knows it, resists any kind of word, formula, law, faith, dogma. He speaks only of the innermost: "life" or "truth" or "light" is his word for the innermost—all the rest, the whole of reality, the whole of nature, language itself, has for him only the value of a sign, a simile.[35]

Consequently, Jesus stands outside of Christianity, and Nietzsche's portrait of Jesus bears an amazing resemblance to the new Zarathustra:

> Make no mistake at this point, however seductive the Christian, in other words, the *ecclesiastical,* prejudice may be: such a symbolist par excellence stands outside all religion, all cult concepts, all history, all natural science, all experience of the world, all knowledge, all politics, all psychology, all books, all art—his "knowledge" is *pure foolishness* precisely concerning the fact that such things exist. *Culture* is not known to him even by hearsay, he does not need to fight it—he does not negate it. The same applies to the state, to the whole civic order and society, to work, to war—he never had any reason to negate "the world"; the ecclesiastical concept of "world" never occurred to him. To negate is the very thing that is impossible for him."[36]

Again and again, in *The Antichrist,* Nietzsche portrays Jesus as a kind of naïve forerunner of Zarathustra; he is incapable of resentment, is free of history, and is himself the exact opposite of Christianity.

> If one were to look for signs that an ironical divinity has its fingers in the great play of the world, one would find no small support in the *tremendous question mark* called Christianity. Mankind lies on its knees before the opposite of that which was the origin, the meaning, the *right* of the evangel; in the concept of "church" it has pronounced holy precisely what the "bringer of the glad tidings" felt to be *beneath* and *behind* himself— one would look in vain for a greater example of *world-historical irony*.[37]

The very word 'Christianity' is a misunderstanding; there was only one Christian, and he died on the cross. And his gospel *died* on the cross: "What has been called 'evangel' from that moment was actually the opposite of that which *he* had lived: *'ill* tidings,' a *dysangel*."[38] True Christianity is not 'faith' in redemption through Christ, nor is it repentance or prayer; only Christian *practice* is Christian: "True life, eternal life, has been found—it is not promised, it is here, it is *in you:* as a living in love, in love without subtraction and exclusion, without regard for station."[39]

> "Sin"—any distance separating God and man—is abolished: *precisely this is the "glad tidings."* Blessedness is not promised, it is not tied to conditions: it is the only reality—the rest is a sign with which to speak of it.[40]

Only the practice, the immediate living, of the "glad tidings" leads to God; indeed, says Nietzsche, "it *is* God."[41] What God? Surely not the "Christian" God, the God of "eternity." What, then; can Jesus' God be Dionysus? Is "Being begins in every Now" the dialectical equivalent of "eternal life is *in you*," "blessedness is the only reality"? Was Nietzsche on the threshold of an ultimate dialectical coincidence of the opposites? Will the death of God make possible a true resurrection of Jesus? Is Zarathustra the resurrected Jesus? Surely it cannot be an accident that less than a year after writing *The Antichrist*, when insanity was bursting upon him, Nietzsche could alternately sign his notes "Dionysus" and "The Crucified."

Northrop Frye, in writing of William Blake's mystical vision, says: "This effort of vision, so called, is to be conceived neither as a human attempt to reach God nor a divine attempt to reach man, but as the realization in total experience of the identity of God and Man in which both the human creature and the superhuman Creator disappear."[42] How tempting to take these words as a precise formula for Nietzsche's vision of Eternal Recurrence! After all, a Christian literary critic, G. Wilson Knight, has described *Thus Spoke Zarathustra* as being both the fulfillment of European poetry and a return to the New Testament;[43] and a distinguished student of Zen Buddhism, R. H. Blyth, has said that Nietzsche's doctrine of Eternal Recurrence is a definition of the man who lives by Zen.[44] Yet it should clearly be realized that to adopt this approach to Nietzsche is to set oneself deeply against the Christian tradition, the Christian Church, Christian theology, and Christendom itself: no one can rejoice in Nietzsche who is unwilling to celebrate the death of the Christian God. Precisely because Christian theology—even in its most radical expressions—has been unwilling to negate itself, it has been closed to Nietzsche's vision. The one contemporary religious thinker who is open to Nietzsche's vision of Eternal Recurrence is Mircea Eliade, a thinker who stands outside of Western Christendom, who ignores 'theology,' and whose own understanding of the sacred has for the most part been drawn from beyond the Christian world. By directing his vision away from the 'Christian God,' Eliade has arrived at a dialectical understanding of the sacred, a 'non-theological' understanding of the dialectical relationship between the sacred and the profane, and therefore he has fully understood the radical nature of the sacred, and is open—as is no theologian—to the radical nature of the profane.

Any candid interpretation of the symbol of Eternal Recurrence must acknowledge that it embodies a vision of the radical profane; indeed, it resurrects a profane reality, which means a reality stripped of all "idealization," a reality—the "body"—having neither meaning nor order, neither direction nor goal, whose sheer immediacy is overwhelming. Nietzsche confessed that love of fate, *amor fati,* was his inmost nature;[45] for a yes-saying to the earth does not mean simply a Stoic bearing of necessity, but rather a love of fate, a rejoicing in the very pain of existence. To re-create all "it was" until the will says, "Thus I willed it! Thus I shall will it"—is to baptize the pure contingency of existence, to hallow—to make holy—the deepest horror of fate. What Eliade calls the "irreversibility" of time is transformed by the Dionysian symbol of Eternal Recurrence into the presence of eternity: *In jedem Nu beginnt das Sein.* If the death of God brings about a resurrection of the "body," then only the inversion of the sacred can resurrect the profane. Thus the profane myth of Eternal Recurrence presents an exact dialectical parallel to the sacred myth of Eternal Return. Let us recall Eliade's analysis of the myth of Eternal Return:

> The primitive, by conferring a cyclic direction upon time, annuls its irreversibility. Everything begins over again at its commencement every instant. The past is but a prefiguration of the future. No event is irreversible and no transformation is final. In a certain sense, it is even possible to say that nothing new happens in the world, for everything is but the repetition of the same primordial archetypes; this repetition, by actualizing the mythical moment when the archetypal gesture was revealed, constantly maintains the world in the same auroral instant of the beginnings. Time but makes possible the appearance and existence of things. It has no final influence upon their existence, since it is itself constantly regenerated.[46]

Or, as Eliade conceives the Christian *redemption* of time: "Time itself is ontologised: Time is made to *be,* which means that it ceases to become, it transforms itself into eternity."[47] Briefly stated, Eternal Return transforms time into eternity, Eternal Recurrence transforms eternity into time; yet the forms of the myth are exactly parallel. What Eternal Return knows as "Everything begins over again at its commencement every instant," Eternal Recurrence knows as "Being begins in every Now." What the sacred myth knows as a repetition continually regenerating the "irreversibility" of profane time into the presence of a transcendent eternity, the profane myth knows as a repetition continually transforming the transcendence of eternity into the absolute immanence of the radical profane. Both myths revolve about a dialectical movement of repetition: the one annulling the profane in its repetition of the sacred, the other annulling the sacred in its repetition of the profane.

Therefore, the one dialectical movement of repetition is the innermost reality of the two myths; furthermore, since a dialectical movement reaches affirmation by negation, the repetition of the sacred can occur only by a continual negation of the profane, just as the repetition of the profane demands a perpetual negation of the sacred. Dialectically, only the negative 'presence' of an absolutely immanent moment can make possible the repetition of a transcendent eternity, just as only the negative 'presence' of a transcendent eternity can make possible the repetition of Zarathustra's Now. When repetition is 'eternal,' the negative moment is continually negated; but the negative moment must be dialectically present to make possible the act of repetition. Thus it is inevitable that Eliade, who has arrived at a dialectical understanding of the sacred, should be so fully open to the power of the profane, whereas Nietzsche should be so fully cognizant of the power of the sacred. However, of the two, Nietzsche is by far the more radical—more dialectical—thinker, if only because Eliade refuses to open himself to the *creative* power of the profane. Nietzsche's vision of Eternal Recurrence promises an ultimate coincidence of the opposites—in Zarathustra, "all oppositions are resolved into a new unity." As Heller noted, Nietzsche dedicated himself to the task of investing the reality of a world of absolute immanence with the power of the sacred. So successfully did Nietzsche fulfill his task that even as responsible a scholar as Karl Löwith can say: "The new eternity which

Nietzsche rediscovered by his being an Antichrist is the old eternity of the cosmic cycle of the pagans."[48] Are the "new eternity" and the "old eternity" the same? Does the birth of the radical profane give witness to a new and final presence of the radical sacred? Must an ultimate concidence of the opposites *unite* the sacred and the profane?

Eliade has confessed that, in the purer expressions of the sacred, the sacred is both inside and outside of "time"; here, the sacred and the profane are no longer in simple opposition.[49] But thus far Eliade has been unable to create a positive dialectic of the sacred, although he has frequently revealed his conviction as to which direction such a positive dialectic must take. That direction is *backwards,* backwards to the archaic sacred: like the Oriental mystic, Eliade conceives of the way to the ultimate sacred as a *return* to the "nontime" of the primordial beginning. The following statement of Eliade's is particularly interesting insofar as it borders upon the Dionysian language of Nietzsche:

> The repetition of archetypes shows the paradoxical wish to achieve an ideal form (the archetype) in the very framework of human existence, to be in time without reaping its disadvantages, without the inability to "put back the clock." Let me point out that this desire is no "spiritual" attitude, which depreciates life on earth and all that goes with it in favour of a "spirituality" of detachment from the world. On the contrary, what may be called the "nostalgia for eternity" proves that man longs for a concrete paradise, and believes that such a paradise can be won *here,* on earth, and *now,* in the present moment. In this sense, it would seem that the ancient myths and rites connected with sacred time and space may be traceable back to so many nostalgic memories of an "earthly paradise," and some sort of "realizable" eternity to which man still thinks he may have access.[50]

As always, Eliade, in such statements, reveals his non-Christian ground; he is unable to say Yes to the future, to envision a truly New Creation, to look *forward* to the Kingdom of God.

Consequently, he remains closed to the *religious* power of the profane, whether it be present in Dostoevsky, Proust, or Nietzsche, and rebels against the historical destiny of his own time. For the religious man of our time, only a positive response to the *sacred* power of the radical profane can make possible a Yes-saying to our destiny, an openness to a Kingdom of God which lies not *behind* but *beyond*.

Can it be, that seen in this perspective, Nietzsche must be judged to be a Christian prophet? Not Christian, in the ecclesiastical sense, of course; but Christian in the sense that he was able—despite, indeed, because, of the profound chaos that he knew to be our destiny—to pronounce a final Yes upon the future. One of his last notes—signed "The Crucified"—reads: "Sing me a new song: the world is transfigured and all the heavens are full of joy."[51] Nor was Nietzsche without an understanding of the dialectical nature of the borderline that separated his vision of Eternal Recurrence from the reality of the sacred; thus, in the fourth part of *Thus Spoke Zarathustra,* the last pope seeks a resting place in Zarathustra's cave with these words:

> "O Zarathustra, with such disbelief you are more pious than you believe. Some god in you must have converted you to your godlessness. Is it not your piety itself that no longer lets you believe in a god? And your overgreat honesty will yet lead you beyond good and evil too. Behold, what remains to you? You have eyes and hands and mouth, predestined for blessing from all eternity. One does not bless with the hand alone. Near you, although you want to be the most godless, I scent a secret, sacred, pleasant scent of long blessings: it gives me gladness and grief."[52]

If Zarathustra's blessing is not with the "hand," is it with the "body," the earth, the Will to Power? Does not Zarathustra, like Jesus, bring a "life" in which guilt has been abolished, in which blessedness is the only reality, in which resentment and negation are no longer possible? Does not the New Creation—Eternal Recurrence—of Zarathustra parallel the New Creation of Jesus—the Kingdom of God—insofar as it shatters history, dissolves all rational meaning, and brings to an end the rule of Law? Both Eternal Recurrence and the Kingdom of God free their believers from the power of history, but it was precisely this power which was resurrected in Christendom, and whose resurrection created the *idea* of the "Christian God"—Nietzsche says somewhere that Christianity is the stone upon the grave of Jesus. Does not the true resurrection of Jesus demand the death of "God"?

In *Beyond Good and Evil,* while discussing a great ladder of religious cruelty, Nietzsche says that it has many rungs, but three of them are of the greatest importance. The first is the sacrifice of men to one's god, the second rung, attained in the "moral period" of mankind, is the sacrifice of one's strongest instincts, one's "natural man."

> And finally—what remains that could be sacrificed? Don't we in the end have to sacrifice everything consolatory, holy, and healing: all hope, all belief in invisible harmony, in future blessedness and justice? Don't we have to sacrifice God himself and idolize a rock, the forces of stupidity, of gravity, fate, nothingness —all in order to be sufficiently cruel to ourselves? To sacrifice God for nothingness—this is the paradoxical mystery of ultimate cruelty that remained in store for the generation now growing up. All of us know something about it already.[53]

The sacrifice of God to God? Is this ultimate act of "religious cruelty" the path to Eternal Recurrence? Nietzsche understood cruelty as have few men, and cruelty plays a crucial role in his understanding of history; for the advent of history, of society, brings about a cooping up of man's animal nature, the natural outlet of his instincts (*Triebe*) is blocked, repression comes into existence, and with it guilt in response to these unreleased but now forbidden instincts. Now the "body" becomes guilty, the instincts need to be punished, and man, with his need for self-torture, invents bad conscience and religion as a means of appeasing his primal guilt. Thus, in *The Genealogy of Morals,* Nietzche says that man focused upon God the last of the opposites he could find to his true and animal instincts:

"He projected all his denials of self, nature, naturalness out of himself as affirmations, as true being, embodiment, reality, as God (the divine Judge and Executioner), as transcendence, as eternity, as endless torture, as hell, as the infinitude of guilt and punishment."[54] Man's will to find himself guilty has created "God," his will to believe that he might be punished to all eternity without ever erasing his guilt. Such psychological cruelty is an insanity of the will that is without parallel: "Man harbors too much horror; the earth has been a lunatic asylum for too long."[55]

If religious cruelty is now to sacrifice God, then the wheel has come full circle. In one passage, even while calling his readers to atheism, Nietzsche acknowledged that the religious "instinct" is growing powerfully, but it is rejecting theistic gratification with a deep distrust.[56] Is Nietzsche's "atheism" a *religious* atheism? Did Nietzsche regard Jesus as such an atheist? We know that Nietzsche believed that Jesus' proclamation of the Kingdom of God abolishes guilt, stands outside of "religion," and offers a present blessedness as the *only* reality. When Nietzsche said that, for Jesus, only the *practice* of the gospel *is* "God," did he not mean that Jesus' God is an absolutely immanent reality, a God whose very reality dissolves the false transcendence of the "religious" God? If the true gospel frees man from history, does it not thereby free him from the God created by religious cruelty? Does not Nietzsche's Jesus demand the death of God, the death of the God of 'history,' the God of 'being'? Dare we believe that Nietzsche's Jesus is the true Jesus, or as true an image of Jesus as our time has known? If so, then Zarathustra is the resurrected Jesus, and Dionysus and Christ are one! Just as Jesus came to bring an end to "religion," so Zarathustra comes to bring an end to a false transcendence, a transcendence having its origin in No-saying and resentment. Zarathustra says Yes: and his Yes resurrects the "body," transforms a transcendent eternity into an immanent Now, and baptizes the contingency—the sheer, naked, *present* reality—of existence. If Zarathustra's Yes makes incarnate the new reality of Eternal Recurrence, does his dialectical negation of the sacred promise a new epiphany of a Kingdom of God beyond "God"? Does his dialectical affirmation of the radical profane promise an ultimate abolition of the old order of 'history' and 'being' that will resurrect the radical sacred? Does Eternal Recurrence promise an ultimate *coincidentia oppositorum* of the sacred and the profane, not in 'being' and 'history,' but in the immediate moment, in the Now? Does a Yes-saying to *all* reality offer a way to the Christ who is not "beyond," but "here" and "now"? Must we say Christ *versus* Dionysus? Or dare we confess a Christ who *is* Dionysus?

Finally, may we imagine that Eliade's longing for a "cosmic sacrality" is fulfilled in Zarathustra's gospel of Eternal Recurrence? Eternal Recurrence abolishes the 'time' and 'space' that we know, no longer is there a forwards or backwards, here or there, or past and future. Indeed, the old 'cosmos' has been abolished by the death of God. As the Madman declares:

> "Whither is God" he cried. "I shall tell you. *We have killed him* —you and I. All of us are his murderers. But how have we done this? How were we able to drink up the sea? Who gave us the sponge to wipe away the entire horizon? What did we do when we unchained this earth from its sun? Whither is it moving now? Whither are we moving now? Away from all suns? Are we not plunging continually? Backward, sideward, forward, in all directions? Is there any up or down left? Are we not straying as through an infinite nothing? Do we not feel the breath of empty space? Has it not become colder? Is not night and more night coming on all the while?[57]

This terrible "night" created by the death of God has made incarnate the most awesome nothingness imaginable; now begins the deepest *Angst* that man has ever known; but Zarathustra calls his hearers to affirm this nothing, and to affirm it joyfully, to say Yes to this nightmare of nightmares, this most dreadful of all horrors. Zarathustra calls us to sacrifice God to this ultimate Nothing: for this sacrifice, this final act of

religious cruelty, is the path to Eternal Recurrence. As Kierkegaard knew, in relation to the absolute there is only one tense:
the present. No longer can we dream that the path to the
sacred is *backwards,* nor can we live in the vain hope that the
true path is only *forwards:* the Center is everywhere, eternity
begins in every Now.

Notes

Chapter One

1. *BR*, p. 9.
2. Martin Heidegger, *Being and Time*, tr. by John Macquirrie and Edward Robinson (SCM Press, Ltd., London, 1962), p. 92.
3. Roger Caillois, *Man and the Sacred*, tr. by Meyer Barash (The Free Press of Glencoe, 1959), p. 13.
4. *PCR*, p. 1.
5. Rudolf Otto, *The Idea of the Holy*, tr. by John W. Harvey (Oxford University Press, London, 1946), pp. 25–30.
6. *SP*, p. 14.
7. *FC*, p. 143.
8. *Y*, p. 48.
9. *Y*, p. xvi.
10. *MER*, p. ix.
11. *SP*, p. 203.
12. This theme is taken up in the second half of the book.
13. *Y*, p. xviii.
14. *IS*, p. 67.
15. *SP*, p. 213.
16. *PCR*, p. xi.
17. *MER*, p. 142.
18. *IS*, p. 120.
19. *IS*, pp. 35 ff. The fullest statement of Eliade's methodology is contained in Mircea Eliade, "Methodological Remarks on the Study of Religious Symbolism," *The History of Religions: Essays in Methodology*, ed. by Mircea Eliade and Joseph Kitagawa (The University of Chicago Press, 1959), pp. 86–107. The original French of this essay may be found in *MA*, pp. 238–268.
20. Cf. Max Scheler, *On the Eternal in Man*, tr. by Bernard Noble (SCM Press, Ltd., London 1960), pp. 159–172; G. van der Leeuw, *Religion in Essence and Manifestation*, tr. by J. E. Turner (George Allen & Unwin, Ltd., London, 1938), pp. 671–695; Joachim Wach, *The Comparative Study of*

Religions, ed. by Joseph Kitagawa (Columbia University Press, 1958), pp. 24 f. For a history of phenomenology, cf. Herbert Spiegelberg, *The Phenomenological Movement* (Martinus Nijhoff, The Hague, 1960), esp. Vol. I, pp. 1–7, 73–163, 228–353; Vol. II. pp. 653–701.

21. Edmund Husserl, *Ideas: General Introduction to Pure Phenomenology,* tr. by W. R. Boyce Gibson (George Allen & Unwin, Ltd., London, 1952), p. 242.

22. *Ibid.,* pp. 110 f.

23. *Ibid.,* p. 111.

24. *Ibid.,* pp. 189, 233.

25. *Ibid.,* pp. 110 f.

26. *Ibid.,* p. 176.

27. *Ibid.,* pp. 176 f.

28. *Ibid.,* p. 223.

29. *Ibid.,* p. 221.

30. *Ibid.,* p. 386.

31. Heidegger, *Being and Time,* p. 58.

32. *Ibid.,* p. 88. Twenty years later, in his "Letter on Humanism," Heidegger denied that "Being-in-the-World" means secular in the Christian sense or turned away from God. But he nevertheless confesses—in this his later and 'mystical' period of thought—that "world" is in a way transcendence within and for existence.

33. *PCR,* p. xii.

34. Scheler, *op. cit.,* p. 171.

35. *Ibid.,* p. 170.

36. *Ibid.,* p. 173.

37. For the meaning of negative dialectic, cf. Herbert Marcuse, *Reason and Revolution* (Beacon Press, Inc., 1960), pp. vii–xiv.

38. Raffaele Pettazzoni, "The Supreme Being: Phenomenological Structure and Historical Development," *The History of Religions,* ed. by Eliade and Kitagawa, p. 66; quoted by Eliade in "History of Religions and a New Humanism," *History of Religions* (Summer, 1961), p. 8.

39. *SP,* p. 14; *C,* p. 14.

40. *IS,* p. 173.

41. *MDM,* pp. 234 f.

42. Mircea Eliade, "La vertu creatrice du mythe," *Eranos-Jahrbuch,* XXV (Rhein-Verlag, Zurich, 1957), p. 82.

43. *MDM,* p. 242.

44. *MDM,* pp. 55 f.

45. For a penetrating essay relating historicism to modern theology, cf. Hans Frei, "Niebuhr's Theological Background," *Faith and Ethics,* ed. by Paul Ramsey (Harper & Row, Publishers, Inc., 1957), pp. 9–64.

46. *MER,* pp. 147 ff; *SP,* p. 112.

47. Friedrich Nietzsche, *The Use and Abuse of History,* tr. by Adrian Collins (The Liberal Arts Press, Inc., 1949), esp. pp. 20, 36, 71 ff.

48. Eliade, "History of Religions and a New Humanism," p. 6.

49. *C,* p. 12.

50. *C,* pp. 436 f.

51. *C*, p. 14.

52. Martin Heidegger, *Existence and Being,* ed. by Werner Brock (Vision Press, Ltd., London, 1949), p. 300.

53. Martin Heidegger, *An Introduction to Metaphysics,* tr. by Ralph Manheim (Yale University Press, 1959), p. 117.

54. *Y*, pp. 81 f.

55. Nicolas Berdyaev, *The Meaning of History,* tr. by George Reavey (Geoffrey Bles, Ltd., London, 1945), p. 16.

56. Nicolas Berdyaev, *The Beginning and the End,* tr. by R. M. French (Harper & Row, Publishers, Inc., 1952), p. 211.

57. *PCR*, p. 430.

58. Eliade, "La vertu creatrice du mythe," p. 60; *MDM*, p. 15.

59. *C*, pp. 8, 25.

60. Eliade, "Methodological Remarks on the Study of Religious Symbolism."

61. *MDM*, pp. 14 f.

62. Heidegger, *Existence and Being,* p. 313.

63. *Ibid.*, p. 285.

64. Heidegger, *Being and Time,* p. 30.

65. Martin Heidegger, "The Way Back Into the Ground of Metaphysics," *Existentialism: From Dostoevsky to Sartre,* ed. and tr. by Walter Kaufmann (Meridian Books, Inc., 1956), p. 218.

66. Heidegger, *Introduction to Metaphysics,* p. 7.

67. Cf. Thomas Langan, *The Meaning of Heidegger* (Columbia University Press, 1959), pp. 161–165.

68. Heidegger, *An Introduction to Metaphysics,* pp. 193 f.

69. *Ibid.*

70. Cf. Thomas J. J. Altizer, *Oriental Mysticism and Biblical Eschatology* (The Westminster Press, 1961), pp. 109 ff.

71. Cf. *ibid.*, pp. 194 f.

Chapter Two

1. *MER*, pp. 3 f.

2. *MER*, p. 75.

3. *MER*, pp. 27 f.

4. Eliade, "Methodological Remarks," p. 99. Cf. *SP*, p. 12.

5. *BR*, pp. x f.

6. *BR*, p. xi.

7. *MER*, p. 95.

8. *Ibid.*

9. *MER*, p. 34.

10. *Ibid.* For a related, yet differing, interpretation of Plato's relation to the archaic ontology, cf. Altizer, *Oriental Mysticism and Biblical Eschatology,* pp. 36–50.

11. *MER*, p. 91.

12. *MER*, p. 155.

13. *MER*, pp. 155 f.

14. In addition to his major work on shamanism, published in 1951, Eliade has published several articles that summarize and reinterpret this work, and he has recently published an article reviewing the literature published on shamanism since 1950. Cf. "Recent Works on Shamanism," *History of Religions* (Summer, 1961), pp. 152–186.

15. Cf. *PCR*, pp. 1–33.

16. *C*, pp. 436 f.

17. *C*, p. 434.

18. *C*, pp. 35–44; *MDM*, pp. 75–78.

19. *C*, p. 429.

20. *C*, p. 428.

21. *MDM*, pp. 79 f. Cf. *C*, pp. 45–53.

22. *MDM*, p. 80.

23. *MDM*, p. 60.

24. *MDM*, p. 98. Cf. *C*, p. 240.

25. *C*, p. 235.

26. *C*, pp. 235–244, 428; *IS*, pp. 27–56.

27. *C*, p. 24.

28. *PCR*, p. 463.

29. *MDM*, pp. 65 f. Cf. *C*, p. 140.

30. Eliade, "Recent Works on Shamanism," p. 186.

31. *PCR*, p. 394.

32. *MER*, p. 35.

33. *MER*, pp. 35, 20. Cf. *PCR*, pp. 32 f., 392 f.

34. Dom Gregory Dix, *The Shape of the Liturgy* (The Dacre Press, London, 1949), p. 245.

35. *PCR*, p. 392.

36. *PCR*, pp. 393 f. Cf. *MER*, pp. 29 ff.

37. Søren Kierkegaard, *Repetition: An Essay in Experimental Psychology*, tr. by Walter Lowrie (Princeton University Press, 1946), p. xxii.

38. *Ibid.*, p. 34.

39. *Ibid.*, pp. 3 f. For a contemporary existential and nontheological adaption of Kierkegaard's category of repetition, cf. Heidegger, *Being and Time*, pp. 388, 437 f., 442 f., 447.

40. *PCR*, p. 188.

41. *MER*, p. 81. Cf. *PCR*, p. 398.

42. *SP*, p. 64.

43. *SP*, p. 12.

44. *SP*, p. 64. Cf. *BR*, p. 59.

45. *MER*, p. 86.

46. *MER*, pp. 89 f.

47. Eliade's exposition of the meaning of the Greek myth of the eternal return is illuminated by a passage that he cites (*MER*, p. 89n) from Henri-Charles Puech's article, "La Gnose et le tempts," *Eranos-Jahrbuch*, XX (1951), pp. 60 f.: "Dominated by an ideal of intelligibility that assimilates authentic and complete being to that which exists in itself and remains identical with itself, to the eternal and immutable, the Greek

holds that motion and becoming are inferior degrees of reality, in which identity is no longer apprehended—at best—save in the form of permanence and perpetuity, hence of recurrence. The circular movement that ensures the maintenance of the same things by repeating them, by continually bringing back their return, is the most immediate, the most perfect (and hence the most nearly divine) expression of that which, at the pinnacle of the hierarchy, is absolute immobility. According to the celebrated Platonic definition, time, which determines and measures the revolutions of the celestial spheres, is the moving image of eternity, which it imitates by revolving in a circle. Consequently all cosmic becoming, and, in the same manner, the duration of this world of generation and corruption in which we live, will progress in a circle or in accordance with an indefinite succession of cycles in the course of which the same reality is made, unmade, and remade in conformity with an immutable law and immutable alternations. Not only is the same sum of existence conserved in it, with nothing being lost and nothing created, but in addition certain thinkers of declining antiquity—Pythagoreans, Stoics, Platonists—reached the point of admitting that within each of these cycles of duration, of these *aiones,* of these *aeva,* the same situations are reproduced that have already been produced in previous cycles and will be reproduced in subsequent cycles—*ad infinitum.* No event is unique, occurs once and for all (for example, the condemnation and death of Socrates), but it has occurred, occurs, and will occur, perpetually; the same individuals have appeared, appear, and reappear at every return of the cycle upon itself. Cosmic duration is repetition and *anakuklosis,* eternal return." For a Christian appraisal of the classical myth of eternal return and its relation to both modern man and Christianity, cf. Karl Löwith, *Meaning in History* (The University of Chicago Press, 1949), pp. 1–11, 204–207.

48. *MER,* p. 123.
49. *Ibid.*
50. *MER,* p. 92.

Chapter Three

1. *MDM,* pp. 125 f. Cf. *PCR,* pp. 29 f.
2. *MER,* p. 104.
3. *Ibid.*
4. *MA,* p. 67.
5. *MER,* p. 110.
6. *MER,* pp. 160 f. For a related, yet more radical, interpretation of the relation between faith and being, cf. Altizer, *Oriental Mysticism and Biblical Eschatology,* pp. 189–199.
7. *MER,* p. 162.
8. *SP,* p. 111.
9. *SP,* pp. 111 f.
10. *MER,* pp. 129 f.

11. *MER*, pp. 111 f. In an essay entitled "Cosmic Reversal and Eschatology" (*MA*, pp. 155–199), Eliade traces the continuity between Old Testament eschatology and archaic myths of cosmic regeneration.

12. *IS*, p. 163.

13. *IS*, p. 169. Theological readers who are persuaded that there is no Biblical idea of eternity are referred to James Barr, *Biblical Words for Time* (SCM Press, Ltd., London, 1962), esp. pp. 63–78, 82–97, 145–152.

14. *IS*, p. 170.

15. *IS*, p. 171.

16. *IS*, p. 172.

17. *Ibid.*

18. William Temple, *Nature, Man and God* (Macmillan & Co., Ltd., London, 1951), p. 478.

19. Cf. Altizer, *Oriental Mysticism and Biblical Eschatology*, pp. 101–112, 177, 188.

20. Rudolf Bultmann, *Jesus and the Word*, tr. by Louise Pettibone Smith and Erminie Lantero (Charles Scribner's Sons, 1934), pp. 215 f.

21. Even an Anglo-Catholic scholar, Dom Gregory Dix, can say: "It is even true to say that though the increasingly gentile churches of the second, third and fourth centuries tried hard to retain the original eschatological emphasis in the eucharist, they did in the end find it something which in its original form the gentile mind proved unable to assimilate" (*The Shape of the Liturgy*, p. 263). One of the great virtues of Dix's book is his demonstration of the deeply ethical foundations of the early practice of the eucharist—an emphasis that has been recovered by the modern liturgical movement of the Roman Catholic Church.

22. Albert Schweitzer, *The Mysticism of Paul the Apostle*, tr. by William Montgomery (Adam & Charles Black, Ltd., London, 1953), p. 3.

23. *Ibid.*, p. 23.

24. *Ibid.*, p. 296.

25. *Ibid.*, p. 343.

26. Martin Werner, *The Foundation of Christian Dogma*, tr. by S. G. F. Brandon (Adam & Charles Black, Ltd., London, 1957), p. 166.

27. *Ibid.*, p. 114.

28. Published for private circulation (Zurich, 1952); quoted by Jacob Taubes, "On the Nature of the Theological Method: Some Reflections on the Methodological Principles of Tillich's Theology," *Journal of Religion* (Jan., 1954), p. 20.

29. Quoted by Walter Lowrie, *A Short Life of Kierkegaard* (Princeton University Press, 1958), p. 234.

30. Cf. Paul Tillich, *The Protestant Era* (The University of Chicago Press, 1948), pp. 72–74.

31. Lowrie, *A Short Life of Kierkegaard*, p. 87.

32. Søren Kierkegaard, *The Sickness Unto Death*, tr. by Walter Lowrie (A Doubleday Anchor Book, Doubleday & Company, Inc., 1954), p. 224.

33. Søren Kierkegaard, *Fear and Trembling*, tr. by Walter Lowrie (A Doubleday Anchor Book, Doubleday & Company, Inc., 1954), p. 62.

34. *Ibid.*, p. 121.

35. Søren Kierkegaard, *The Concept of Dread,* tr. by Walter Lowrie (Princeton University Press, 1946), p. 134.

36. Søren Kierkegaard, *Concluding Unscientific Postscript,* tr. by David F. Swenson and Walter Lowrie (Princeton University Press, 1944), p. 18.

37. *Ibid.,* p. 55.

38. *Ibid.,* pp. 68, 175.

39. *Ibid.,* p. 176.

40. *Ibid.,* pp. 177 f.

41. *Ibid.,* p. 182.

42. *Ibid.*

43. *Ibid.,* p. 189.

44. *Ibid.,* p. 188.

45. *Ibid.,* p. 296.

46. *The Journals of Søren Kierkegaard,* ed. and tr. by Alexander Dru (Oxford University Press, 1951), p. 173.

47. Kierkegaard, *Postscript,* p. 178.

48. *Ibid.,* p. 201.

49. Søren Kierkegaard, *Philosophical Fragments,* tr. by David F. Swenson (Princeton University Press, 1946), p. 62.

50. *Ibid.,* p. 49.

51. *Ibid.*

52. Kierkegaard, *The Concept of Dread,* p. 75n.

53. *Ibid.,* p. 81.

54. Norman Brown, *Life Against Death* (A Vintage Book, Random House, Inc., 1957), p. 109.

55. Kierkegaard, *The Concept of Dread,* pp. 82 f.

56. Kierkegaard, *The Sickness Unto Death,* pp. 153 f., 179, 208.

57. Kierkegaard, *Fragments,* p. 49.

58. James Brown, *Kierkegaard, Heidegger, Buber and Barth* (originally published as *Subject and Object in Modern Theology*), (Collier Books, 1962), p. 66.

59. *A Kierkegaard Anthology,* ed. by Robert Bretall (Modern Library, 1960), p. 409.

60. Søren Kierkegaard, *Attack Upon "Christendom,"* tr. by Walter Lowrie (Beacon Press, Inc., 1956), pp. 32 f.

61. Walter Lowrie, Introduction to *Attack Upon "Christendom,"* p. xiii.

62. Kierkegaard, *Postscript,* p. 218.

63. *Ibid.,* p. 219.

Chapter Four

1. Ernst Cassirer, *The Philosophy of Symbolic Forms,* Vol. II, *Mythical Thinking,* tr. by Ralph Manheim (Yale University Press, 1955), pp. 129 ff.

2. Cf. Altizer, *Oriental Mysticism and Biblical Eschatology,* pp. 132–151.

3. Eliade, "Methodological Remarks on the Study of Religious Symbolism," p. 102.

4. *MA,* p. 87.

5. *PCR*, p. 29.

6. *MA*, pp. 152 f.

7. *MA*, p. 116.

8. *MA*, p. 152.

9. Paul Tillich, *Systematic Theology* (The University of Chicago Press, 1951), Vol. I, p. 255.

10. *Ibid.*, Vol. I, p. 256.

11. Paul Tillich, *Systematic Theology* (The University of Chicago Press, 1957), Vol. II, p. 44.

12. *Ibid.*

13. Mircea Eliade, "Le Createur et son 'Ombre,'" *Eranos-Jahrbuch*, XXX (1962), pp. 238 f. For a similar analysis of Mephistopheles, cf. *MA*, pp. 95–99.

14. *PCR*, pp. 46–58.

15. *PCR*, p. 52.

16. *IS*, p. 173.

17. *PCR*, p. 127.

18. *MDM*, p. 137.

19. Eric Voegelin, *Order and History*, Vol. I, *Israel and Revelation* (Louisiana State University Press, 1956), pp. 428–515.

20. Arthur Waley, *The Way and Its Power* (George Allen & Unwin, Ltd., London, 1956), p. 165.

21. *Ibid.*, p. 55.

22. *PCR*, p. 419.

23. *PCR*, pp. 358 f.

24. Friedrich Nietzsche, *The Birth of Tragedy*, i, tr. by Francis Golffing (A Doubleday Anchor Book, Doubleday & Company, Inc., 1956), p. 23.

25. Euripides, *The Bacchae*, tr. by Philip Vellacott (Penguin Books, Inc., 1954), pp. 185.

26. Nietzsche, *The Birth of Tragedy*, vii, p. 51.

27. *PCR*, pp. 419 f.

28. *PCR*, p. 420.

29. *IS*, p. 90.

30. Cf. *MA*, p. 148.

31. *Letters of Rainer Maria Rilke*, tr. by Jane Bannard Greene and M. D. Herter Norton (W. W. Norton & Company, Inc., 1948), Vol. II, pp. 373 f.

32. Cf. Erich Heller, "Nietzsche and Rilke," *The Disinherited Mind* (Dufour Editions, 1953), pp. 97–140.

33. Heidegger, *Being and Time*, p. 311.

34. *Ibid.*, p. 303.

35. Karl Rahner, *On the Theology of Death*, tr. by Charles H. Henkey (Herder & Herder, Inc., 1961), p. 71.

36. *Ibid.*

37. *BR*, p. 136.

38. *Y*, p. 361.

39. *Y*, p. 362.

40. *Y*, p. 364.

41. *Y*, p. 340.
42. *Y*, p. 10.
43. *Y*, p. 9.
44. *Y*, p. 10.
45. *Y*, p. 93.
46. *Y*, pp. 98 f.
47. *Y*, p. 100.
48. *Y*, p. 185.
49. *Y*, p. 206.
50. *Y*, p. 271.
51. *MA*, p. 137.
52. *PCR*, pp. 420 f.
53. Cf. *MA*, pp. 95–154.
54. *The Gospel According to Thomas* (Harper & Row, Publishers, Inc., 1959), pp. 17, 53.
55. *MA*, pp. 126 f.
56. Nicolas Berdyaev, *The Destiny of Man* (Charles Scribner's Sons, 1937), p. 64. Cf. Nicolas Berdyaev, *Solitude and Society* (Geoffrey Bles, Ltd., London, 1947), pp. 86–93.
57. G. Wilson Knight, *Christ and Nietzsche* (Staples Press, Ltd., London, 1948), p. 127.
58. *FC*, p. 34.
59. *FC*, p. 52.
60. *FC*, p. 78.
61. *FC*, p. 151.
62. *FC*, pp. 149 f.
63. *FC*, p. 160.
64. *FC*, p. 166.
65. *FC*, p. 173.
66. *FC*, p. 175.
67. *FC*, p. 178.
68. In a final footnote to his lecture on "Mephistopheles and Androgyne" (1958), Eliade stresses the paradoxical nature of the symbol of the *coincidentia oppositorum:* "On the one hand, man is haunted by the desire to escape from his particular situation and to reintegrate himself as a transpersonal modality; on the other hand, he is paralyzed by the fear of losing his 'identity' and of 'forgetting' himself." *MA*, p. 154.

Chapter Five

1. James Joyce, *Ulysses* (Modern Library, Inc., 1942), p. 35.
2. Heidegger, *Being and Time*, p. 464.
3. Martin Heidegger, *Kant and the Problem of Metaphysics,* tr. by James S. Churchill (Indiana University Press, 1962), p. 237.
4. *Ibid.*, p. 252.
5. *Ibid.*, p. 236.
6. *Ibid.*, p. 241.

7. Albert Camus, *The Myth of Sisyphus,* tr. by Justin O'Brien (Vintage Books, Inc., 1959), pp. 77–83.

8. Quoted by Henri de Lubac, *The Drama of Atheist Humanism,* tr. by Edith M. Riley (Sheed & Ward, Inc., 1950), p. 183.

9. Quoted by de Lubac, *ibid.,* p. 173.

10. Paul Evdokimoff, *Dostoevsky et le probleme du mal,* p. 33. Quoted by de Lubac, *ibid.,* p. 173n.

11. Fyodor Dostoevsky, *The Possessed,* tr. by Constance Garnett (Modern Library, Inc., 1936), p. 115.

12. *Ibid.,* p. 626.

13. *Ibid.,* p. 114.

14. *Ibid.,* p. 115.

15. *Ibid.,* p. 629. This idea of Christ's being conquered by the laws of nature was inspired in Dostoevsky by a portrait of Holbein's depicting the descent from the cross. Cf. Fyodor Dostoevsky, *The Idiot,* tr. by Constance Garnett (Modern Library, Inc., 1942), p. 389: "Looking at such a picture, one conceives of nature in the shape of an immense, merciless, dumb beast, or more correctly, much more correctly, speaking, though it sounds strange, in the form of a huge machine of the most modern construction which, dull and insensible, has aimlessly clutched, crushed and swallowed up a great priceless Being, a Being worth all nature and its laws, worth the whole earth, which was created perhaps solely for the sake of that Being."

16. *Ibid.,* p. 628.

17. *Ibid.,* p. 601. Cf. *The Idiot,* pp. 213 f.

18. *Ibid.,* p. 239.

19. Albert Schweitzer, *The Quest for the Historical Jesus,* tr. by W. Montgomery (Adam & Charles Black, Ltd., London, 1954), pp. 368 f.

20. Dostoevsky, *The Possessed,* p. 630.

21. *Ibid.,* p. 114.

22. *Ibid.,* p. 627.

23. *Ibid.,* p. 241.

24. Northrop Frye, *Anatomy of Criticism* (Princeton University Press, 1957), pp. 40 f.

25. *Ibid.,* pp. 60 f.

26. Marcel Proust, *Remembrance of Things Past,* Vol. II, p. 997. All citations from this novel are taken from the translation of C. K. Scott Moncrieff and Frederick A. Blossom (who translated *The Past Recaptured*), published by Random House in 1932.

27. R. C. Zaehner, *Mysticism: Sacred and Profane* (Oxford at the Clarendon Press, 1957), pp. 50–61.

28. Proust, *op. cit.,* Vol. II, p. 1024.

29. Samuel Beckett, *Proust* (Grove Press, no date), p. 49.

30. Proust, *op. cit.,* Vol. I, p. 479.

31. *Ibid.,* Vol. II, p. 1021.

32. *Ibid.,* Vol. II, pp. 1025 f.

33. *Ibid.,* Vol. II, pp. 1001 f.

34. *Ibid.,* Vol. II, p. 1001.

35. *Ibid.*, Vol. II, p. 1013.

36. Georges Poulet, *Studies in Human Time,* tr. by Elliott Coleman (The Johns Hopkins Press, 1956), pp. 297, 295.

37. *Ibid.*, p. 297.

38. *Ibid.*, p. 308.

39. *Ibid.*, p. 305.

40. Proust, *op. cit.*, Vol. II, p. 994.

41. René Girard, "Introduction," *Proust,* ed. by René Girard (Prentice-Hall, Inc., 1962), p. 10.

42. Proust, *op. cit.*, Vol. II, p. 992.

43. *Ibid.*, Vol. II, p. 993.

44. *Ibid.*, Vol. II, p. 996.

45. *Ibid.*

46. *Ibid.*, Vol. II, p. 995.

47. *Ibid.*

48. *Ibid.*, Vol. II, p. 994.

49. A preliminary and premature attempt of mine to effect this correlation is contained in "Nirvana and Kingdom of God," *Journal of Religion* (April, 1963), pp. 105–117.

Chapter Six

1. Heller, *The Disinherited Mind,* p. 178.

2. *Ibid.*, p. 180.

3. Martin Buber, *Two Types of Faith,* tr. by Norman P. Goldhawk (Routledge & Kegan Paul, Ltd., London, 1951), p. 168.

4. Martin Buber, *I and Thou,* tr. by Ronald Gregor Smith (Charles Scribner's Sons, 1958), p. 120.

5. Franz Kafka, *Wedding Preparations and Other Posthumous Prose Writings,* tr. by Ernst Kaiser and Eithne Wilkins (Martin Secker & Warburg, Ltd., London, 1954), pp. 38 ff., 45.

6. *Ibid.*, p. 103.

7. *IS,* pp. 37 ff.

8. *IS,* p. 55.

9. Heller, *op. cit.*, p. 178.

10. Buber, *Two Types of Faith,* p. 169.

11. Susan Anima Taubes, "The Absent God," *Journal of Religion* (Jan., 1955), p. 6.

12. Jean-Paul Sartre, *Nausea,* tr. by Lloyd Alexander (New Directions, 1959), pp. 19 f.

13. *Ibid.*, p. 31.

14. *Ibid.*, p. 164.

15. *Ibid.*, p. 173.

16. *Ibid.*

17. *Ibid.*, p. 176.

18. Jean-Paul Sartre, *Being and Nothingness,* tr. by Hazel E. Barnes (Philosophical Library, Inc., 1956), p. lviii.

19. *Ibid.*, p. 47.
20. *Ibid.*, p. 79.
21. *Ibid.*, p. 123.
22. *Ibid.*, p. 617.
23. *Ibid.*, pp. 439 f.
24. *Ibid.*, p. 440.
25. *Ibid.*, pp. 90, 202, 365, 376 f., 481, 495, 615, 620, 623.
26. *Ibid.*, p. 566.
27. *Ibid.*, p. 599.
28. *Ibid.*, p. 615.
29. *Ibid.*, p. lxviii.
30. *Ibid.*, p. 623.
31. *Ibid.*, p. 180.
32. *Ibid.*, p. 184.
33. *Ibid.*, pp. 617 f.
34. *Ibid.*, p. 618.
35. *Ibid.*, p. 477.
36. Pierre Teilhard de Chardin, *The Divine Milieu*, tr. by Bernard Wall (Harper & Row, Publishers, Inc., 1960), p. 53.
37. Quoted by Bernard Wall, *ibid.*, p. 14n.
38. *Ibid.*, p. 80.
39. *Ibid.*, p. 70.
40. *Ibid.*, p. 98.
41. *Ibid.*, pp. 96 f.
42. *Ibid.*, p. 118.
43. *Ibid.*, p. 91.
44. *Ibid.*, p. 137.
45. *Ibid.*, p. 138.
46. Pierre Teilhard de Chardin, *The Phenomenon of Man*, tr. by Bernard Wall (Harper & Row, Publishers, Inc., 1959), p. 30.
47. *Ibid.*, p. 31.
48. *Ibid.*, p. 36.
49. *Ibid.*, p. 32.
50. *Ibid.*, p. 56.
51. *Ibid.*, p. 180.
52. *Ibid.*, pp. 60 f.
53. *Ibid.*, p. 243.
54. *Ibid.*, pp. 245 f.
55. *Ibid.*, p. 270.
56. *Ibid.*, p. 287.
57. Teilhard de Chardin, *The Divine Milieu*, p. 86.
58. Teilhard de Chardin, *The Phenomenon of Man*, pp. 293 f.
59. *Ibid.*, p. 294.
60. *Ibid.*
61. *Ibid.*, p. 308.
62. *Ibid.*, p. 300.
63. Teilhard de Chardin, *The Divine Milieu*, pp. 31, 79.
64. Teilhard de Chardin, *The Phenomenon of Man*, p. 249n.

Chapter Seven

1. *IS*, p. 35.
2. *IS*, p. 36.
3. *BR*, p. 128.
4. *MDM*, p. 122.
5. *Y*, pp. 226 f.
6. *IS*, pp. 14 f.
7. *IS*, p. 15.
8. *FC*, p. 155.
9. Erich Heller, "The Modern German Mind: The Legacy of Nietzsche." *French and German Letters Today* (The Library of Congress, 1960), p. 31.
10. Ernest Jones, *The Life and Work of Sigmund Freud* (Basic Books, Inc., 1953–1957), Vol. III, pp. 278 ff.
11. Sigmund Freud, *The Interpretation of Dreams*, tr. and ed. by James Strachey (Basic Books, Inc., 1958), p. xxvi.
12. Jones, *op. cit.*, Vol. III, pp. 38 f.
13. Sigmund Freud, *The Basic Writings of Sigmund Freud*, tr. and ed. by A. A. Brill (Modern Library, Inc., 1938), p. 927.
14. *Ibid.*, p. 930.
15. Quoted and translated by Jones, *Freud*, Vol. III, pp. 352 f.
16. Norman Brown, *Life Against Death* (A Vintage Book, Random House, Inc., 1957), pp. 118, 127 f.
17. Freud, *The Interpretation of Dreams*, p. 160.
18. *Ibid.*, p. 538.
19. *Ibid.*, p. 182.
20. *Ibid.*, p. 396.
21. *Ibid.*, p. 533.
22. *Ibid.*, p. 543.
23. *Ibid.*, p. 546.
24. *Ibid.*, p. 245.
25. *Ibid.*, pp. 548 f.
26. *Ibid.*, p. 553.
27. *Ibid.*, p. 589.
28. *Ibid.*, pp. 605 f.
29. Sigmund Freud, *Collected Papers*, tr. by Joan Riviere (The Hogarth Press, Ltd., London, 1953), Vol. IV, pp. 118–122.
30. Freud, *The Interpretation of Dreams*, pp. 612 f.
31. Jones, *Freud*, Vol. II, p. 344.
32. Freud, *The Basic Writings of Sigmund Freud*, p. 917.
33. Cf. Thomas J. J. Altizer, "Science and Gnosis in Jung's Psychology," *The Centennial Review* (Summer, 1959), pp. 304–320.
34. Cf. Thomas J. J. Altizer, "The Challenge of Modern Gnosticism," *The Journal of Bible and Religion* (Jan., 1962), pp. 18–25.
35. Herbert Marcuse, *Eros and Civilization* (A Vintage Book, Random House, Inc., 1962), p. 14.
36. *Ibid.*, pp. 16 f.

37. *Ibid.*, p. 107.
38. *Ibid.*, p. 108.
39. *Ibid.*, p. 109.
40. *Ibid.*, p. 18.
41. *Ibid.*, p. 129.
42. *Ibid.*, p. 132.
43. Sigmund Freud, *Civilization and Its Discontents,* tr. by Joan Riviere (The Hogarth Press, Ltd., London, 1949), p. 14.
44. Marcuse, *Eros and Civilization,* pp. 153 f.
45. *Ibid.*, p. 173.
46. *Ibid.*, p. 184.
47. Brown, *Life Against Death,* pp. 318 f.
48. *Ibid.*, p. 87.
49. *Ibid.*, p. 93.
50. *Ibid.*, p. 102.
51. *Ibid.*, pp. 108 ff.
52. *Ibid.*, pp. 112 f.
53. *Ibid.*, p. 93.
54. *Ibid.*, p. 31.
55. *Ibid.*, p. 310.
56. *Ibid.*, p. 313.
57. *Ibid.*, p. 309.
58. *Ibid.*, p. 308.
59. *Ibid.*, p. 297.
60. *Ibid.*, p. 308.

Chapter Eight

1. Friedrich Nietzsche, *Ecce Homo,* tr. by Clifton P. Fadiman, *The Philosophy of Nietzsche* (Modern Library, Inc., no date), p. 135.
2. *Ibid.*, p. 136.
3. *Ibid.*, pp. 104 f.
4. *Ibid.*, p. 105.
5. Friedrich Nietzsche, *The Genealogy of Morals,* XXI, tr. by Francis Golffing (An Anchor Book, Doubleday & Company, Inc., 1956), p. 224.
6. Nietzsche, *Ecce Homo,* p. 107.
7. Nietzsche, *The Genealogy of Morals,* XVI.
8. Friedrich Nietzsche, *Thus Spoke Zarathustra,* tr. by Walter Kaufmann, *The Portable Nietzsche* (The Viking Press, Inc., 1954), p. 125.
9. *Ibid.*, pp. 143 f.
10. Nietzsche, *The Genealogy of Morals,* XV, p. 263.
11. Nietzsche, *Thus Spoke Zarathustra,* p. 144.
12. *Ibid.*, p. 146.
13. *Ibid.*, p. 166.
14. Friedrich Nietzsche, *Twilight of the Idols,* 49, *The Portable Nietzsche,* p. 554.
15. Friedrich Nietzsche, *The Antichrist,* 47, *The Portable Nietzsche,* p. 627.

16. Nietzsche, *Thus Spoke Zarathustra*, p. 398. Cf. *Twilight of the Idols*, pp. 500 f.

17. Heller, *The Disinherited Mind*, p. 127.

18. Friedrich Nietzsche, *Joyful Wisdom*, 341, tr. by Thomas Common (Frederick Ungar Publishing Company, 1960), pp. 270 f.

19. *Ibid.*, p. 271.

20. Nietzsche, *Thus Spoke Zarathustra*, p. 270.

21. *Ibid.*, p. 333.

22. *Ibid.*, pp. 252 f.

23. *Ibid.*, p. 310.

24. *Ibid.*, pp. 329 f.

25. Nietzsche's *Werke* (Leipzig, 1923), Band VI, p. 317.

26. Cf. Eliade's interpretation of the Hindu symbols of *lila* and *maya* as reflections of the divine body of "joy" underlying the illusion of the cosmos. *MA*, pp. 40 f.

27. Martin Heidegger, *Holzwege* (Frankfurt, 1957), pp. 201, 193. Heidegger laments the oblivion of the transcendence of Being. Yet the late Heidegger can say: " 'Being' is neither God nor the basis of the world. Being is further from all that is being and yet closer to man than every being, be it a rock, an animal, a work of art, a machine, be it an angel or God. Being is the closest. Yet its closeness remains farthest from man." ("Letter on Humanism," tr. by Edgar Lohner, in *Philosophy in the Twentieth Century*, ed. by William Barrett and Henry D. Aiken, Random House, Inc., 1962, Vol. III, p. 282.) Perhaps nowhere else does Heidegger so clearly reveal how his attachment to a traditional mystical form of the holy so deeply sets him against the historical destiny of our time, and so likewise does it set him against Nietzsche.

28. Nietzsche, *The Genealogy of Morals*, XXV, p. 291.

29. E. R. Hughes, *Chinese Philosophy in Classical Times* (Everyman's Library, 1942), p. 198.

30. *Ibid.*, p. 199.

31. Nietzsche's *Werke*, Band VI, p. 333. Cf. *Thus Spoke Zarathustra*, pp. 339 f.

32. *Ibid.*, VI, p. 469. Cf. *Thus Spoke Zarathustra*, p. 434.

33. Nietzsche, *Ecce Homo*, p. 145.

34. Nietzsche, *Joyful Wisdom*, 125, *The Portable Nietzsche*, p. 96.

35. Nietzsche, *The Antichrist*, 32, *The Portable Nietzsche*, p. 605.

36. *Ibid.*, 32, pp. 605 f.

37. *Ibid.*, 36, p. 609.

38. *Ibid.*, 39, p. 612.

39. *Ibid.*, 33, p. 606.

40. *Ibid.*

41. *Ibid.*, 33, p. 607.

42. Northrop Frye, *Fearful Symmetry* (Princeton University Press, 1958), p. 431.

43. Knight, *Christ and Nietzsche*, pp. 158–218.

44. R. H. Blyth, *Zen in English Literature and Oriental Classics* (E. P. Dutton & Company, Inc., 1960), pp. 23, 35 f.

45. Friedrich Nietzsche, *Nietzsche Contra Wagner, The Portable Nietzsche*, p. 680.

46. *MER*, pp. 89 f.

47. *IS*, p. 169.

48. Karl Löwith, *Meaning in History* (The University of Chicago Press, 1949), p. 219.

49. *MA*, p. 87.

50. *PCR*, p. 408.

51. *The Portable Nietzsche*, p. 685.

52. Nietzsche, *Thus Spoke Zarathustra*, p. 374.

53. Friedrich Nietzsche, *Beyond Good and Evil*, 55, tr. by Marianne Cowan (Henry Regnery Company, 1955), pp. 61 f.

54. Nietzsche, *The Genealogy of Morals*, XXII, p. 226.

55. *Ibid.*, p. 227.

56. Nietzsche, *Beyond Good and Evil*, 53, p. 60.

57. Nietzsche, *Joyful Wisdom*, 125, *The Portable Nietzsche*, p. 95.

Index

NOTE: Only those references to Mircea Eliade which occur in the second half of the book have been indexed.

Abraham, 60, 129
Altizer, Thomas J. J., 203, 205 f., 211, 213
Aristotle, 166
Augustine, 74, 82

Barr, James, 206
Barth, Karl, 13 f.
Baudelaire, Charles, 130
Beckett, Samuel, 117, 130
Benz, Ernst, 100
Berdyaev, Nicolas, 34, 100
Bhagavad Gita, 26
Blake, William, 172, 192
Blyth, R. H., 192
Boehme, Jacob, 100, 170, 172 f.
Brown, James, 78
Brown, Norman, 156, 164, 166, 169 ff.
Buber, Martin, 127, 130
Bultmann, Rudolf, 14, 16, 67

Cabala, 161, 172
Caillois, Roger, 24
Camus, Albert, 107, 130

Cassirer, Ernst, 81
Chuang Chou, 187 f.
Copernicus, 187
Cusanus, 82

Dilthey, Wilhelm, 32, 44
Dix, Gregory, 53 f., 206
Dostoevsky, Fyodor, 37, 39, 61, 107 ff., 139, 196, 210

Eliade, Mircea, 105, 113, 128 f., 144, 150 ff., 159, 161, 169, 173, 175, 192 ff., 199, 209, 215
Euripides, 90
Evdokimoff, Paul, 108

Frazer, J. G., 41
Frei, Hans, 202
Freud, Sigmund, 47, 82, 151 ff., 153 ff., 162 ff.
Frye, Northrop, 115, 192

Gnosticism, 14, 56, 126 f., 163 f., 213
Gospel of John, 39, 66, 69 f., 146

Gospel of Thomas, 99 f.

Hegel, Georg, 46, 74, 82, 164, 166
Heidegger, Martin, 23, 25, 27, 29, 32 f., 37 ff., 72, 81 f., 92 f., 106 f., 185 f., 202, 204, 215
Heller, Erich, 126 f., 129 f., 153, 180, 194
Heraclitus, 82, 186
Hölderlin, Friedrich, 37
Husserl, Edmund, 28 f.

Ignatius, 70

Jesus Christ, 64, 66 ff., 71 f., 109 ff., 190 ff., 196 ff.
Jones, Ernest, 153, 159
Joyce, James, 105, 107, 115
Jung, Carl Gustav, 16, 151, 163 f., 168
Junger, Ernst, 16

Kafka, Franz, 61, 107, 126 ff.
Kant, Immanuel, 168
Kaufmann, Walter, 184
Kierkegaard, Søren, 13 f., 25, 33, 39, 54 f., 60, 65, 73 ff., 82, 139, 200
Knight, G. Wilson, 100, 192
Kraus, Karl, 153

van der Leeuw, Gerardus, 28
Lipps, Theodore, 159
Löwith, Karl, 194 f., 205
Lowrie, Walter, 79
Luther, Martin, 38, 79

Madhyamika Buddhism, 82, 98, 188
Marcuse, Herbert, 164 ff., 170, 202
Marx, Karl, 82, 155, 164, 168

Newman, J. H., 68
Nietzsche, Friedrich, 20, 23 f., 32 f., 47, 89 ff., 103, 106 f., 113, 158 ff., 165 ff., 173, 175, 176 ff.

Otto, Rudolf, 24, 116, 128

Parmenides, 81
Paul, 38, 60, 68 ff., 99, 146, 172 ff.
Pettazzoni, Raffaele, 31
Plato, 46, 53, 58, 82, 173
Poulet, Georges, 118 f.
Prophets, 14, 60, 63, 88, 169
Proust, Marcel, 41, 107, 115 ff., 157, 196
Puech, Henri-Charles, 204 f.

Rahner, Karl, 93 f.
Rilke, Rainer Maria, 92 f., 115, 131, 171 ff., 180
Rimbaud, Arthur, 115 f., 130

Samkhya School, 95, 136, 139
Sartre, Jean-Paul, 24, 27, 130 ff., 139
Scheler, Max, 28, 30
Schiller, Johann Christoph Friedrich von, 168
Schopenhauer, Arthur, 89
Schweitzer, Albert, 67 ff., 82, 111
Soloviëv, Sergei, 112
Spiegelberg, Herbert, 202

Tantrism, 17, 97 ff., 163
Taoism, 82, 88 f., 98, 170, 173, 186 ff.
Tao Te Ching, 88
Taubes, Susan Anima, 130
Teilhard de Chardin, Pierre, 139 ff.
Temple, William, 66
Tertullian, 76, 173
Tillich, Paul, 74, 84 ff., 92

Troeltsch, Ernst, 32

Vedānta, 95, 97
Voegelin, Eric, 208

Wach, Joachim, 28
Waley, Arthur, 88
Weil, Simone, 130

Werner, Martin, 71
Whitehead, Alfred North, 148

Yogacara Buddhism, 151

Zaehner, R. C., 116
Zarathustra, 176
Zen Buddhism, 82, 98, 121, 192